THEORIES OF RAPE
Inquiries into the Causes of Sexual Aggression

Lee Ellis, Ph.D.

Department of Sociology, Minot State University, Minot, North Dakota

⬤HEMISPHERE PUBLISHING CORPORATION

A member of the Taylor & Francis Group

New York   Washington   Philadelphia   London

To the memory of my father

THEORIES OF RAPE: Inquiries into the Causes of Sexual Aggression

Copyright © 1989 by Hemisphere Publishing Corporation. All rights reserved. Printed in the United States of America. Except as permitted under the United States Copyright Act of 1976, no part of this publication may be reproduced or distributed in any form or by any means, or stored in a data base or retrieval system, without the prior written permission of the publisher.

3 4 5 6 7 8 9 0   B R B R   9 8 7 6 5 4 3 2 1

This book was set in Times Roman by Hemisphere Publishing Corporation. The editors were Carolyn Ormes and Karla Philip; the production supervisor was Peggy M. Rote; and the typesetters were Wayne Hutchins, Linda Andros, and Sharon L. Kohne. Cover design by Renée E. Winfield.

Library of Congress Cataloging-in-Publication Data

Ellis, Lee, 1942–
    Theories of rape: inquiries into the causes of sexual aggression
/ Lee Ellis.
        p. cm.
    Bibliography: p.
    Includes indexes.

    1. Rape. 2. Rape—Psychological aspects. I. Title.
    HV6558.E45   1989
    364.1′532′019—dc19   89-1997
    ISBN 0-89116-172-4 (case)   CIP

Contents

Foreword

Rape is one of those deeply emotional terms denoting a criminal act that is particularly abhorrent to the vast majority of human beings. Effective action to combat this offense calls for a better understanding of who commits rape and why. Such an understanding can almost certainly be attained by arranging what we know into a unified theoretical scheme.

This book shows that rape (excluding statutory rape) includes a wide variety of acts, ranging from those in which a male known to, and often liked by, a female uses force to go beyond the sexual limits she sets to highly predatory acts in which strangers threaten grievous bodily harm, often with a lethal weapon, and violate every sense of personal privacy that we recognize and normally respect. The research reviewed pertaining to incidence rates shows that the problem is all too pervasive in most human societies, including all those rooted in the traditions of Western civilization.

As Professor Ellis' review suggests, these different forms of rape may not be committed by exactly the same types of individuals. Supporting this view, my own research on personality suggests that acquaintance rapists are more likely to be extroverts, whereas the more violent rapists are mostly introverts. Both types do appear to have personalities characterized by lack of empathy, strong aggressive impulses, and other psychopathic tendencies.

Professor Ellis has brought to bear many modern research and theoretical developments from a wide diversity of disciplines and perspectives to better understand rape. His book has succeeded in combining a great deal of evidence to indicate that, while we are fundamentally biological creatures, our biological nature in no way diminishes either our social nature or our capacity and propensity to learn. Instead, his analysis and synthesis of diverse ideas suggest how utterly inseparable biological variables and social learning variables really are and how so much of what we learn about biology helps us to better understand social influences and vice versa. Whether or not each of his specific proposals, on how rape is learned and on why some people are more disposed to the requisite learning than others, is correct will take many years to determine. Nevertheless, this book has almost certainly helped advance our understanding of rape simply because it draws together and organizes our current knowledge so well.

Many social scientists may question Professor Ellis' decision to deal forthrightly and in considerable depth with several controversial issues relevant to rape, such as race, social class, pornography, and even social reactions to rape victimization. I, personally, think that although he climbs out on several precarious limbs, he does not do so recklessly or for no reason. The controversial issues he confronts are simply too important not to receive the scrutiny of the scientific method, no matter what the eventual outcome.

By clearly outlining the different theories presently available, by looking at the evidence supporting and faulting these theories, and by trying to combine the most positive features of each one into a more broadly ranging theory, this book makes a very important contribution to our understanding of rape, and perhaps even significantly expands our more general comprehension of human behavior. At the very least, this book provides a basis for furthering scientific research into the causes of rape and, ultimately, hastens the day when rape risks are substantially lower than they are now.

H. J. Eysenck, Ph.D., D.Sc.
Professor Emeritus of Psychology, University of London, England

Preface

Reducing and eventually eliminating the threat of rape is an objective toward which social science knowledge may someday make significant progress. The theoretical and research work required to accomplish this goal is formidable, however, and only within the last 12 years or so have large numbers of social scientists committed themselves to the task. Much of the impetus seems to have come from the publication of a book by Susan Brownmiller, entitled *Against Our Will* (1975), although arguments similar to hers were made a few years earlier (e.g., Betries, 1972; Mehrhof & Kearson, 1972). Brownmiller essentially formulated what has come to be called the *feminist theory of rape,* which has since emerged as probably the leading theory of rape. In any case, since the mid 1970s hundreds of social science articles and books have appeared to help identify the causes of rape and to propose remedies for rape.

In the same year that Brownmiller's book was published, Edward O. Wilson (1975) published *Sociobiology: The New Synthesis,* a book that provided important groundwork for the development of a second contemporary theory of rape called the *evolutionary* (or *sociobiology*) *theory.* I began this book in 1985 with the expectation that it would be a 30-page article providing a condensed review of the empirical evidence for and against the two existing theories of rape. By 1986, when I presented a verbal summary of a 50-page version of the manuscript at the American Society of Criminology's meeting in Atlanta, not only had its length already exceeded what I had intended, but considerable evidence regarding a third recognizable theory had been brought to my attention—a theory of rape largely working out of Albert Bandura's (1977) social learning perspective (although it also contained some elements of feminist theory) (see Malamuth, 1984).

Although I knew that the paper exceeded the maximum length for a journal article, in early 1987 I submitted a 90-page version of the manuscript to *Deviant Behavior*. This resulted in contacts with representatives of the journal's publisher, Hemisphere Publishing Corporation, who suggested that I expand the manuscript into a book. Given the rapid pace at which research on rape was still being published, and the opportunity a book gave to synthesize all that had been learned into a new unified theory of rape, I took the suggestion.

A major goal throughout this project was to provide a picture of the progress being made in identifying the causes of rape that was as current, comprehensive, and objective as possible. The second major goal was to make the coverage as easy to read as possible—not always a simple task given the complexity of some of the research designs that a number of researchers have employed to resolve some of the hypotheses and questions posed. Basically, to accomplish these two major goals, the research studies (except those dealing strictly with the prevalence of rape) have all been organized around the theories of rape to which they seem most relevant. Thus, this book offers a "bird's-eye view" of where the scientific research now stands regarding knowledge of what causes rape. Because this, and any other aerial view, will obscure many important details, however, readers wishing to contribute to the future developments in this field of study should not rely on this text as a substitute for the original articles and books cited.

Also, despite attempts to be objective, some of the interpretations and proposed conclusions are bound to strike many readers as not justified by the evidence. In anticipating these reactions, let me simply say that all of the proposals have been made in the spirit of free inquiry and with the understanding that every error in fact and in logic is fair game for criticism. Those who take issue with my interpretations and conclusions are invited to identify the errors and are challenged to propose alternative ideas and provide additional evidence. Doing so should facilitate accumulation of the knowledge required to reduce rape.

To help readers quickly locate evidence and arguments that are cited in the text references, specific pages are often indicated. These page references should direct attention to where the most pertinent passages can be found (or, if the passages are lengthy, the page on which they begin). Doing this has become the exception rather than the rule in behavioral and social science publications in recent years, even when documenting very specific points in a lengthy book. I have sometimes spent over an hour trying in vain to verify the relevance of a citation. While citing page numbers is still no guarantee against citation errors, it at least should save readers considerable time in verifying the relevance of a reference.

Over the course of writing this book, I sought advice from many people to whom I am most grateful for reading and commenting on various drafts. They are John Briere, Jim Check, Edward Donnerstein, Hans J. Eysenck, William Fisher, John Gray, David Huff, Rhonda Kostenko, Daniel Linz, Neil Malamuth, Lori Olson, J. Philippe Rushton, Joseph Scott, and Dolf Zillmann. While the importance of their collective advice and criticisms would be hard to exaggerate, they bear no responsibility for the final product, or for any errors the book may contain. I also thank Heather Ellis, Penny Hamilton, and Lori Monger for their help in assembling and verifying the references.

L. Ellis

1

THE NATURE AND EXTENT OF RAPE

RAPE AS A SOCIAL PHENOMENON

Even though rape is widely recognized as a significant social problem in many human societies, only the past 15 years or so have witnessed a serious scientific effort to understand and, ultimately, help curb the prevalence of this crime (Gibbons, 1987:266). This book will review and attempt to synthesize those efforts, especially as they help to formulate a basic theoretical understanding of rape. However, before such a review, it is important to delineate the nature and extent of this crime.

Rape refers to a physically forceful attempt at sexual intimacy when one of the individuals involved chooses not to become sexually intimate (no attention will be given to *statutory rape* in this book) (Amir, 1971; Media & Thompson, 1974:12; Russell, 1982). While rapes by women and male rape victimization have been documented (Groth, 1979; Sarrel & Masters, 1982; Quinsey, 1984:90; Russell, 1984:67; Struckman-Johnson, 1986), by and large, the victims of rape are female, and the offenders are male (Kagan, 1964:143; Murstein, 1970:475; Smith, 1974:188; Metzger, 1976; Marcus, 1977:44).

Since the word *rape* is usually considered a legal term, one can argue that it should only be used to refer to whatever criminal behavior happens to be legally

1

defined as *rape* in a given society at a given point in time. However, because of variations in the inclusiveness of rape statutes from one society to another, and within them over time (see Tobach & Sunday, 1985:136), such an approach would severely hamper attempts to study rape as a cross-cultural phenomenon. Examples of how legal definitions substantially alter what is objectively considered rape are these:

1. While rape, however it has been defined, has always been found to be predominantly a male offense against women, in some political jurisdictions rape has been defined so that it can *only* involve male offenders and female victims (Holmstrom & Burgess, 1975:33; Cann, Calhoun, Selby, & King, 1981; Shaalan, El-Akabaoui, & El-Kott, 1983:277; Carter, 1986:83; Conklin, 1986:43).
2. In most states, one cannot technically commit the crime of rape if under the age of 18 because such persons are exempt from criminal statutes.
3. In many states, forced sex between spouses remains exempt from rape statutes (Finkelhor & Yllo, 1982:477; Russell, 1982).
4. In many states, the definition of rape requires some degree of vaginal penetration, thus technically excluding a variety of other forced sex acts from constituting rape, no matter how much force may have been involved (Carrow, 1980:17; Koss, Gidycz, & Wisniewski, 1987:168).
5. Finally, since *rape* is technically a legal term, one could even argue that rape is impossible among persons living in preliterate societies where no formal (i.e., written) laws are in force (see Goldschmidt, 1976:210).

    In light of the above points, one can understand why some have suggested that, at least for scientific purposes, it might be better to substitute the terms *forced sex* or *sexual assault* for *rape* (Finkelhor & Yllo, 1982:462; Crawford & Galdikas, 1986). For the purposes of this book, the term rape will be essentially stripped of its "legal baggage," and thus used to refer to a collection of behavior patterns involving forceful attempts at sexual intimacy, regardless of whether those behavior patterns happen to conform to all of the legal statutes in the jurisdiction where the act took place or not. Therefore, regardless of nuances in legal issues surrounding what is and is not considered rape, the term will be used throughout this book to refer to all forms of physical sexual intimacies in which significant physical force is used or threatened by one of the parties involved contrary to the will of the other. Such factors as the age and sex of the offender and the victim, and whether or not the act happened to violate a particular criminal statute in a particular society at a given point in time will not be at issue. Such terms as *forced sex* and *sexual assault,* thus, may be considered synonymous with the concept of *rape* as the terms will be used in the text (see also Malamuth & Check, 1985:300).

THE PREVALENCE OF RAPE

In recent years, the *Uniform Crime Reports (UCR),* which derives its statistics from citizen reports to police in the United States, has estimated the annual rate of rape (including attempted rape) to be about 70 per 100,000 women per year (U. S. Bureau of Justice, Statistics, 1985), up substantially from about 25 per 100,000 women reported in the 1950s (U. S. Department of Justice, 1975:55), and almost four times the rate reported in the 1940s (Bowker, 1979; Nelson, 1982:211; see also Russell, 1984:53 for evidence that U. S. rape statistics are increasing). In contrast, crime victimization surveys in the United States (conducted annually since 1973 among representative sample of households) have found the prevalence of completed or attempted rape to be 3 to 4 times higher than the *UCR* estimates—that is, about 200 per 100,000 women (over the age of 12) each year (Ennis, 1967:8; Bowker, 1979; U.S. Bureau of Justice, Statistics, 1982). But, unlike the official statistics, these estimates of the rape rate in the United States have risen much less dramatically over the past 12 years (U.S. Bureau of Justice Statistics, 1986). While there are certainly other possibilities, this suggests that much of the increase in *UCR* rape rate estimates is due to increases in the probability of reporting rape to the police.

More in-depth surveys specific to rape victimization have concluded that even the federally sponsored crime victimization surveys underestimate the risk of rape by more than half. For example, a survey conducted by Russell (1984:35) in San Francisco found that, over a lifetime, approximately 24% of women will be raped, and another 20% will experience an attempted rape. While it is impossible to precisely compare total lifetime risks with annual risks, Russell's (1982:43) survey indicates that the real risk of rape was at least 13 times greater than *UCR* estimates. Thus, it appears that only about 1 out of 12 of the women who indicated (on the Russell survey) having experienced rape or a rape attempt said they reported the incident to police (Russell, 1984:35). Added to these estimates, Russell (1982) found that 14% of ever-married women said they had been sexually assaulted by their husbands (defined as sex via the use of force, or at least without consent, as when drunk or under the influence of other drugs). Overall, Russell (1984:51) concluded that approximately 46% of women in San Francisco will experience rape or an attempted rape in their lifetime, and that about half of them will experience more than one rape incident. Russell's definition of *rape*, however, should be understood to have been somewhat broader than most criminal statutes at the present time. She defined *rape* as vaginal, anal, and oral sexual contact involving force or threat of injury, or when the victim was asleep, unconscious, severely drugged, or otherwise physically helpless. According to a recent survey, such a definition also may be broader than what most persons in the general population would define as *rape* (Howard, 1988:112).

Among college women, Koss (1985) found that 38% reported sexual victimization that met most state definitions of *rape* or *attempted rape*. In a more extensive nationwide college survey—and using a somewhat stricter legal definition of *rape*—Koss, Gidycz and Wisniewski (1987) found that 28% of women reported having experienced a rape or rape attempt since age 14, and that 8% of college males admitted to having committed rape at least once. A study by Muehlenhard and Linton (1987:193) found that 15% of females had experienced at least one date rape and 7% of males had committed this offense in their lifetime. However, with regard to sexual aggression in a much broader sense (tantamount to any unwelcomed sexual initiatives in a dating situation), the figures were 78% for females and 57% for males. Yegidis (1986) reported that 22% of college females reported date rape victimization and 11% of college males admitted date rape on at least one occasion. Overall, such evidence supports the view of Reynolds (1984:149) that rape is probably the most frequently committed serious violent crime in the United States.

While the overwhelming majority of rape victims are females, especially in regard to predatory rapes by strangers, when one considers sexual assault in broad terms, significant percentages of males report being victimized. Lott, Reilly, and Howard (1982) found that 6% of college males reported having been sexually assaulted (most often by female offenders) at least once (see also Sarrel & Masters, 1982). More will be said about sex differences in rape victimization probabilities in Chapter 7.

Before considering any explanations for rape, it is important to understand why estimates of its prevalence vary so greatly. Obviously, the estimates are far too varied to be dismissed as resulting from sampling error. Instead, they appear to reflect major differences in the criteria used to identify rape (see Williams, 1984; Koss, Gidycz & Wisniewski, 1987). Figure 1 illustrates the wide spectrum of intimate sexual acts involving a significant degree of force. As the degree of force and threat of injury increase, the perceived seriousness of an act of rape increases, and so too does its probability of being reported to police (Lawson & Hillix, 1985). However, of all rapes reported to police, 10% to 15% fail to meet one or more of the legal criteria for rape in the particular political jurisdiction in which the incident occurred (McCahill, Meyer, & Fischman, 1979; Feldman-Summers & Palmer, 1980:36; Gove, Hughes, & Geerken, 1985:487).

From the evidence thus far reviewed, one may say that rape exists along a continuum in terms of the amount of force, risk of injury, and degree of nonconsent involved (Eysenck, 1984:315; Malamuth, 1986:960). Because the majority of rapes and rape attempts occur among persons who are acquainted and romantically involved to some degree and are not highly predatory or violent in nature (Rabkin, 1979; Ageton, 1982:130; Koss, 1985), they have a low probability of being reported to police (Gove, Hughes, & Geerken, 1985:487). While the degree of force in rapes involving acquaintances is often substantial, these rapes (herein called *date rapes*) do not usually involve the degree of risk of

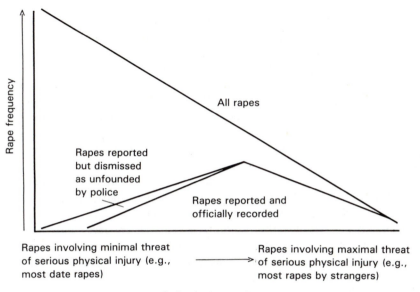

Rapes involving minimal threat of serious physical injury (e.g., most date rapes)

Rapes involving maximal threat of serious physical injury (e.g., most rapes by strangers)

Seriousness continuum

FIGURE 1

serious physical injury as rapes by strangers (President's Commission, 1967:40; Curtis, 1974; McDermott, 1979; Katz & Mazur, 1979; E. M. Ellis, Atkeson, & Calhoun, 1981; Yegidis, 1986). Rapes with the greatest probability of being reported to police are those which involve attacks by strangers (Smith & Bennett, 1985) —those termed *classic* or *predatory rape* (Williams, 1984). Rapes by strangers are also more likely to be taken seriously by police, courts, and jurors than rapes by acquaintances (Russell, 1982:247).

Overall, most victimization studies have indicated that between 20% and 30% of women in the United States will experience at least one rape or rape attempt, (Kirkpatrick & Kanin, 1957; Russell & Miller, 1979; Johnson, 1980; Korman & Lester, 1982; Koss & Oros, 1982; Story, 1982; Wilson & Durenberger, 1982; Bernard & Bernard, 1983; Brickman & Briere, 1984; Di Vasto, et al., 1984; Hall & Flannery, 1984; Meyer, 1984; Yegidis, 1986; Muehlenhard & Linton, 1987:193), but that only about one-fourth of these incidences will involve the infliction of substantial pain or serious threat of injury (Kirkpatrick & Kanin, 1957). Thus, as indicated in Figure 1, the majority of rapes are among persons who are romantically involved (Seligmann, et al., 1984), and have the lowest probability of being reported to police (Russell, 1984:96). The percentage of women who report being victimized by acquaintances (or date rape) is fairly comparable to survey results from men regarding their committing such rapes. On anonymous questionnaires, 20% to 25% admit to having used some degree of physical force at least once to make some kinds of sexual advances beyond their dates' wishes (Kanin, 1967b; Kanin & Parcell, 1977; Koss & Oros, 1982). More specific to rape, 10% to 15% of college males have reported having actually forced a date to have sex against her will (Guinzburg, 1983; Rapaport & Burkhart, 1984; Koss & Leonard, 1984:216). In the Koss and Leonard study, an additional 22% of males said they had used verbal coercion and deception (e.g., threats to end a relationship or false pledges of love) in order to pressure dates into sexual intercourse. To account for why greater percentages of females report having been victimized by rape than males report having committed the offense, obviously some males may be denying or downplaying the degree of force that they used, and a few females may have exaggerated the degree of force involved. However, a far more important consideration appears to be the fact that many rapists victimize fairly large numbers of women (Muehlenhard, Friedman & Thomas, 1985:297).

Possibly the most disturbing of all recent surveys are ones conducted in the United States which have posed some hypothetical questions to male respondents. Results indicated that close to half of the males sampled said that, under some circumstances, they would have at least "some likelihood" of committing rape if somehow assured of never being caught or punished for doing so (Malamuth, Haber, & Feshback, 1980; Check & Malamuth, 1983). Similarly, an unpublished study (see Deisher, Wenet, Paperny, Clark, and Fehrenbach, 1982:285) and one reported by Check and Malamuth (1985:416) found that between 40% and 50% of all high school boys in Los Angeles expressed the view that it would be acceptable to force a girl to have sex if she repeatedly sexually teased her date, or if she agreed to have sex but changed her mind at the last minute (also see Giarrusso, Johnson, Goodchilds, & Zellman, 1979).

Rape is, of course, far from being a uniquely American phenomenon. Accounts of rape have appeared throughout recorded history (Zillmann, 1984:3). Extensive ethnographic studies of preliterate societies indicate that only about 10% to 30% of these societies appear to be rape free, or virtually so (Brown, 1952; Minturn, Grosse, & Haider, 1969; Broude & Greene, 1976:417; Sanday, 1981). In stating this, it should be added that many of these societies are inadequate in size and in reporting procedures for making reliable statistical estimates. In West Sumatra, one of the reputed "rape-free" societies that was large enough for making accurate estimates, Sanday (1986:84) found the actual rape rate was about 19 per 1 million females, low by most Western standards, but not entirely "rape-free." Also, Samoa, a society reported by Margaret Mead in the 1930s to be essentially rape free, has since been shown to have an official rape rate twice as high as that for the United States (Marshall, 1983:1044), suggesting the need for careful verification of individual ethnographic accounts for a particular society. Furthermore, ethnographers have reported (in about 10% of the preliterate societies) that it was common for women to desire that men make physically aggressive sexual overtures (Broude & Greene, 1976:417; also see LeVine, 1977). This point will be addressed in greater detail later in discussing rape fantasies, but such reports indicate that separating rape from all forms of voluntary sexual experiences is not always easy. Another complication in making cross-cultural comparisons of rape rates is highlighted by Chagnon's (1988:986) report that while rapes, per se, appear to be rare amongst the Yanomamo (a South American tribal group he has studied extensively), many men abduct women from neighboring camps and force them to become permanent mates of the abductor. Whether the Yanomamo should thus be considered a largely rape-free society or not is obviously debatable. Even after taking these and other definitional and measurement difficulties into account, there is almost certainly a great deal of variability in the extent to which rape is prevalent from one society to another, and there indeed may be societies in which even acquaintance rapes are virtually nonexistent (see Malinowski, 1929; Turnbull, 1972; Findlay, 1974; Benderly, 1982).

Other evidence of considerable cross-societal variability in the risk of rape comes from comparing official statistics from industrial societies that have fairly similar legal statutes pertaining to rape. Such studies have confirmed a general impression that rape rates in the United States are unusually high for industrialized nations, especially in recent years. Confining attention to offenses reported to police (thus, focusing upon predatory rapes), United States rape rates appear to be over three times higher than in England, West Germany, Sweden, and Denmark (Abramson & Hayashi, 1984:181; Kutchinski, 1988:5), five to ten times higher than in France, Holland, Belgium, and Japan (Schiff, 1971; Abramson & Hayashi, 1984:181; Russell, 1984:30), and at least twice as high as in Canada (Quinsey, 1984:90).

Unfortunately, self-report victimization surveys in countries other than the United States are quite limited. The only one located was conducted in Winnipeg, Canada. It found that 27% of women reported having been the victim of at least one sexual assault (excluding forced kissing) (Brickman & Briere, 1984). The definitions and procedures used in this study appeared most comparable to Russell's survey (1984; Russell & Miller, 1979) (reviewed earlier in this chapter) in which 46% of San Francisco's women reported having experienced at least one rape attempt in their lifetime.

SUMMARY

There are many complex methodological issues to be dealt with in attempting to define *rape*, and estimate its prevalence. The most difficult issue surrounds the degree of force used or threatened. In the case of predatory rapes, there is essentially no doubt about the criminal, assaultive nature of the offense. However, the much more common forms of rape are those perpetuated by acquaintances who have begun to establish a courtship relationship. The types of rapes that occur within a courtship relationship usually involve no weapon and little, if any, threat of physical harm. These rapes sometimes also entail some ambiguity in the willingness of the victim to have sexual intercourse (see Muehlenhard & Hollabaugh, 1988:874), a topic to be elaborated in later chapters.

Regardless of how restrictive or inclusive one's definitions are, however, all relevant studies suggest that rape is more of a risk in the United States than in other industrialized societies. While data from nonindustrialized societies tend to be harder to compare than those among industrialized societies, they seem to suggest that rape rates in the United States are among the highest in the world, especially for the past two decades. If so, it is both appropriate and understandable that most of the theoretical work on the causes of rape should come from the United States (although individuals from several other countries, especially Canada, have also contributed substantial material).

2

THREE CONTEMPORARY THEORIES OF RAPE

Since the mid 1970s three new theoretical proposals for explaining rape have been advanced, and an unprecedented flurry of scientific research activity has followed. The theories will be referred to as the *feminist theory,* the *social learning theory,* and the *evolutionary theory.* All three may be contrasted with past proposals that have largely attempted to explain rape as due to chronic unemployment and difficulty in finding sex or marriage partners (Bonger, 1916; von Hentig, 1951), to inadequate socialization and/or mental illness (Guttmacher, 1951; Guttmacher & Weihofen, 1952; Rada, 1978), or to being raised in a sexually violent subculture (Amir, 1971). (For criticisms of these proposals see Gage & Schurr, 1976:280; Marolla & Scully, 1979; Sanday, 1981; Schwendinger & Schwendinger, 1983:71.) To be fair to the proponents of these earlier proposals, however, it should be said that they were largely formulated on the basis of studies of violent rapes by strangers (predatory rapes), whereas the three theories proposed recently have all been formulated in light of a growing body of research that has also examined the more prevalent, but far less violent, forms of rape committed by acquaintances (date rape). As will be pointed out later, several theorists have suggested that the causes of predatory rape may be somewhat different than the causes of rape by acquaintances.

The three theories will be individually outlined before specific research evidence for and against each theory is presented (in Chapters 3, 4, and 5).

THE FEMINIST THEORY OF RAPE

Among the major proponents of the feminist theory of rape are Mehrhof and
Kearon (1972), LeGrande (1973), Brownmiller (1975), Davis (1975), Clark
and Lewis (1977), Rose (1977), Groth (1979), Dworkin (1981), Riger and
Gordon (1981), and Schwendinger and Schwendinger (1983). According to
Smith and Bennett (1985), the feminist theory has quickly become the dominant
social science explanation for rape.

Basically, the feminist theory considers rape to be the result of long and
deep-rooted social traditions in which males have dominated nearly all important political and economic activities. Reflecting and reinforcing this male domination and exploitation of women is the existence of prostitution (Brownmiller,
1975) and especially pornography (Dworkin, 1979, 1981, 1984, 1985; MacK-
innon, 1984, 1985). In both cases, women tend to be treated (or portrayed) in
subservient and degrading ways.

According to most versions of the feminist theory, one result of male domination over women is that women are excluded from political decision-making
processes which affect them, including those matters dealing with rape and its
control. With women excluded from positions of political and economic power,
the feminist theory of rape maintains that women are considered unequal partic-
ipants in interpersonal interactions. At the extreme, women come to be viewed
by men (and often by themselves, as well) as little more than property over
which men compete (Clark & Lewis, 1977; Dworkin, 1981). Thus, many feminist writers view the prospects of rape as more or less a direct function of the
degree to which females are politically and economically powerless relative to
men (Davis, 1975; Herschberger, 1970; Metzger, 1976), and/or are viewed as
property (Betries, 1972; Griffin, 1971; Klein & Kress, 1976; LeGrande, 1973;
Rafter & Natalizia, 1981).

From an interpersonal standpoint, feminist theory essentially regards rape
as a male response to the social inequality between the sexes and the tendency
of this inequality to affect the way men and women interact sexually. Some
feminist theorists have postulated that a "feedback process" serves to perpetuate social inequality by making the prospects of rape so intimidating as to
restrict the life-styles of many women. Because of the fear of rape (and other
forms of sexual harassment), women tend to restrict themselves to relatively
"safe" activities in which contact with males (especially unfamiliar ones) is
minimized and/or confined to "protective conditions" (Riger & Gordon,
1981). These restrictions prevent women from succeeding occupationally, economically, and politically, and thus the cycle—in which rape is an integral
element—tends to be perpetuated (Saint Louis Feminist Research Project,
1976:7).

Even though it clearly identifies political and economic factors as the underlying cause of rape, unfortunately the feminist theory is vague about the "direc-

tion" of this relationship in regard to reducing rape risks in the future (Ellis & Beattie, 1983:88). That is, the theory can be taken as implying that reductions in sex disparities in matters of political and economic power will either reduce rape, or will increase it by frustrating males into using rape to reestablish their supremacy (Baron & Straus, 1984; Gibbon, 1987:279). Reflecting this ambiguity, feminists have been somewhat divided on questions of how to diminish rape risks. One faction has concentrated upon the need for increased arrests and imposing harsher penalties for rape offenders, and even for persons who exploit women through pornography and prostitution (e.g., Brownmiller, 1975; Chappell, Geis, Schafer, & Siegel, 1977). The other faction had advocated that efforts to reduce rape should be focused upon equalizing the sexes' overall socioeconomic power (e.g., Feldman-Summers & Palmer, 1980; Schwendinger & Schwendinger, 1983).

In summary, the feminist explanation for rape focuses upon the male domination of sociopolitical and economic affairs as the ultimate determinant of a society's risk of rape. Working backwards in the causal order, the feminist explanation purports that rape is, most immediately, the result of a male's decision to behave toward women in a possessive, dominating, and demeaning manner. Thus, sexual gratification is not considered a prime motive by feminist theory, but rather, rape is seen as the use of sexuality to establish or maintain dominance and control of women by men (Burt, 1980:229; Thompson & Buttell, 1984; Groth, Burgess, & Holmstrom, 1977). Some feminist writers have even declared that rape is a "pseudosexual act," motivated largely out of desires for power and a hatred of women rather than by any sexual passion (Groth, 1979:2; Groth & Burgess, 1978). Through aggressive sexual attacks, males attempt to establish (or reconfirm) a tradition of supremacy over females (Smith & Bennett, 1985:296).

Before leaving this theory, it should be mentioned that support for the feminist theory of rape and support for the so-called feminist movement, while possibly related, should not be equated. To help ensure that a distinction is made between an individual's beliefs about the merits of a scientific theory and one's support for a social movement (involving equal political participation, employment opportunities, and legal protection for women), Hans Eysenck (personal correspondence, May 26, 1988) recommended calling the feminist theory of rape the *sociological theory of rape*. While appreciative of Eysenck's reasoning, his terminology was not used here for three reasons. First, at least in the United States, the term *feminist theory of rape* has come to be commonly used for at least the past 10 years to describe the theory that has just been outlined. Second, calling a theory of rape a sociological theory would imply that all (or at least most) sociologists subscribe to this particular theory, and that other behavioral scientists do not, which are possibilities for which no evidence (either for or against) has been found. Third, identifying theories (as well as variables) according to names of various social science disciplines tends to be divisive and misleading (since it implies a particular discipline is somehow "responsible" for its own theories and variables, and that individuals in other disciplines should propose their own theories and variables).

THE SOCIAL LEARNING THEORY OF RAPE

Proponents of the social learning theory of rape include Donnerstein (1985), Malamuth (1981, 1983, 1984), Zillmann (1984), Check (1985) and Linz (1985). A major impetus for this theory came from the 1973 Presidential Commission on Pornography and Obscenity. The Commission effectively concluded that exposure to pornography seemed to have no significant tendencies to increase aggression or other forms of antisocial behavior, a conclusion that has since been challenged (Cline, 1974; Dienstbier, 1979; Liebert & Schwartzberg, 1977). Much of the research which has challenged this "no effects" conclusion of the 1973 Commission is based upon studies of forms of pornography that were rare prior to the mid 1970s—violent pornography (either in the form of explicit depiction of rape, or in terms of interweaving themes of sex with themes of horror and mutilation) (Smith, 1976; Malamuth & Spinner, 1980; Court, 1984:149; Sapolsky, 1984:95).

In general terms, social learning theory of rape has roots in research begun about two decades ago which determined that repeated exposure to almost any type of stimulus tends to promote positive feelings toward it (Wilson & Nakajo, 1965; Zajonc, 1968; Harrison, 1969; Zajonc & Rajecki, 1969; Moreland & Zajonc, 1976). Treatment for various types of phobias often involves implementing this principle by repeatedly exposing patients to the feared object for increasingly longer periods of time and in increasingly more salient forms (Bandura, 1967).

Subsequent theorizing by Bandura (1973, 1978:16, 1986) suggests that aggression is learned primarily through imitation (modeling), and thereafter sustained largely through various forms of intermittent reinforcement. Bandura (1978:15) argued that models for aggression mainly came from three sources: (a) primary associations with family members and peers, (b) one's culture (and subculture), and, (c) in recent times, the mass media. He saw television and other visual mass media as especially influential in that they (a) taught actual methods of aggression, (b) often showed little of the normal social restraints in expressing aggression, (c) desensitized viewers to violence through repeated exposure, and (d) taught methods of rationalizing, and excusing personal responsibility for, aggression (1978:25). The social learning theory of rape basically portrays rape as part of aggressive behavior toward women learned through four interrelated processes: (a) by imitating rape scenes and other acts of violence toward women, as one may see in real life or as depicted in the mass media (Nelson, 1982:200; Huesmann & Malamuth, 1986), (b) by associating sexuality and violence, as when viewing sex and violence repeatedly depicted in the same context (as in many violent pornographic and slasher/horror films) (Malamuth, 1983, 1984; Check & Malamuth, 1986:185; Malamuth, Check, & Briere, 1986:338), (c) by perpetuating various "rape myths," such as "No means Yes," and "Women secretly desire to be raped" (Burt, 1980), and, (d) by desensitizing viewers to the pain, fear, and humiliation of sexual aggression (Linz, 1985; Donnerstein, Linz, & Penrod, 1987:126). These four hypothesized effects may be called the *modeling effect,* the *sex-violence linkage effect,* the *"rape myth" effect,* and the *desensitization effect,* respectively.

Social learning theory is similar to feminist theory in several respects; in fact, at times they have been virtually equated (e.g., Malamuth, 1984; Malamuth, Check, & Briere, 1986), and some proponents of what is being called the social learning theory here have written on behalf of the feminist theory (Check & Malamuth, 1985). First, both theories see social and cultural learning as largely responsible for rape. Second, they both identify features of modern Western culture that encourage men to exploit women sexually as contributing to the rape crisis (Burt, 1980:229). Third, both theories largely repudiate any suggestions that nonlearning, extracultural variables are responsible for variations in male propensities to commit rape, although proponents of the feminist theory tend to be more emphatic than proponents of the social learning theory in this regard (see especially Schwendinger & Schwendinger, 1983).

Regarding differences between the two theories, whereas feminist theory concentrates upon socioeconomic (and even political) exploitation as the underlying cause of rape, social learning theory sees cultural traditions more directly linked with interpersonal aggression and sexuality as responsible for sexual assault. Also, social learning theorists seem less insistent upon viewing rape as an essentially nonsexual act than feminist writers. Following Bandura's (1978) assumption that most aggression is instrumental, rather than an end in itself, social learning theorists appear more receptive than feminist theorists to the view that rape may often reflect a genuine desire by rapists to have sex with their victims (especially regarding date rape). Nevertheless, there are social learning theorists who agree with feminist theorists that rape, by and large, is not at all sexually motivated (e.g., Briere & Malamuth, 1983). Finally, while both feminist and social learning theorists consider exposure to pornography as promoting male tendencies to rape, feminist theory explains this almost entirely in terms of pornography's tendencies to degrade women and divest them of socioeconomic power (Brownmiller, 1957; Dworkin, 1981), while social learning theory explains the hypothesized connection primarily in terms of modeling, sex-violence linkage, "rape myth," and desensitization effects.

Overall, the social learning theory may be best considered a rather complex blend of Bandura's influential theory of instrumental aggression and the feminist theory of rape (see Malamuth, 1986; Check & Malamuth, 1986; Malamuth & Briere, 1986). Proponents of the social learning theory see both longstanding cultural traditions and individual experiences combining to propel males toward widely varying degrees of aggressive behavior directed toward women (both sexually and nonsexually). Social learning theorists see rape as resulting from the joint influences of cultural and experiential factors mediated by attitudes, sex role scripts, and other thought processes that link physical aggression and sexuality in the minds of males.

THE EVOLUTIONARY THEORY
OF RAPE

Deutsch (1944:227) was probably the first to suggest that male propensities to rape could have an evolutionary basis. She argued that the loss of a distinct period of sexual receptivity (estrus) by women marked the beginning of their subjugation to the sexual wills of men, and implied that rape could be one of the consequences. Recent advocates of an evolutionary (or sociobiological) theory of rape include Barash (1979:55), Symons (1979), Gibson, Linden, and Johnson (1980), Rhodes (1981), Konner (1982:290), Shields and Shields (1983), Thornhill and Thornhill (1983, 1987), Quinsey (1984), Marshall (1984), Crawford and Galdikas (1986), and Thiessen (1986). The following arguments are more or less common to their writings.

Males and females, especially among mammals, seem to have evolved tendencies to emphasize different things with respect to allocating their time and energy to the tasks of reproduction. In particular, among nearly all mammalian species, whereas females emphasize care of offspring (Chamove, Harlow & Mitchell, 1967; Williams, 1975; Smith, 1978; Leshner, 1978:214; Daly & Wilson, 1980:280), males tend to emphasize securing as many sex partners as possible (Bateman, 1948; Trivers, 1972; Hagen, 1979:88; Symons, 1979; Daly & Wilson, 1978:81).

To determine why such sex differences have evolved, one may note that females must commit a great deal of reproductive time and energy gestating offspring that males do not (in fact, cannot) commit (Hrdy, 1981; Daly & Wilson, 1983). Assuming (a) that variation in reproduction is a crucial feature of all life (Darwin, 1859), (b) that transmitting one's genes to future generations can be accomplished primarily only through reproduction (Dawkins, 1976), and (c) that each sex has a more or less equal total amount of time and energy to commit to reproduction, one can deduce that the time and energy males do not devote to gestation can be diverted to other reproductive activities. Given the relative speed with which males can make new offspring (gene carriers), there is no more productive activity that males can commit themselves to than that of copulating with many sex partners (Quinsey, 1984).

Another consequence of their not gestating offspring is that males are at a decisive *dis*advantage, relative to females, in being able to identify their offspring once the offspring have been born (Dawkins, 1976:114; Daly & Wilson, 1978; Durden-Smith & deSimone, 1983:270). Thus, for two reasons—their lower initial "investment" in each offspring, and their lower parental certainty—evolutionary theorists believe that males have a stronger tendency for evolving traits (behavioral and otherwise) that increase their chances of inseminating large numbers of females, rather than fastidiously taking care of a few offspring. If so, forceful copulatory tactics (or *rape,* in human terms) may have been naturally selected (Hagen, 1979; Symons, 1979:284; Gibson, Linden, & Johnson, 1980; Quinsey, 1984:89).

Some additional arguments advanced to support the evolutionary theory of rape include the following. Because of the minimal time and energy males devote to producing new offspring compared to females, mating with numerous sex partners would be much more advantageous to males than it would be for females (Hagen, 1979; Jones, 1986). As a simple illustration, the world record for the number of offspring fathered by a human male is 888, whereas 69 offspring is the most ever borne by one human female (Daly & Wilson, 1978:59). Basically, these sex disparities in reproductive potential mean that there is a tremendous potential "payoff" (in terms of genes transmitted to future generations) for males who can inseminate large numbers of females, using whatever methods necessary (including force).

While natural selection may have favored males who were prone to use forceful tactics to inseminate females, natural selection would have also favored females who resisted such tactics. Being forced to copulate prevents a female from exercising a choice as to who will father her offspring, and her choice can be used to reduce the sex disparities in parental investment (Thornhill, 1980:57). In other words, to the degree a female can avoid mating with males who are unlikely to remain with her beyond the point of insemination, she can effectively enhance her overall reproductive potential (Wilder, 1982).

Presumably, natural selection pressure upon females to discriminate against males who show little inclination to remain committed beyond the first few copulations would be especially strong in species, such as humans, who have extremely long periods of offspring dependency following birth (Symons, 1979; Richard & Schulman, 1982). In many species, the female appears to exercise at least some degree of discrimination by not sexually responding to a male's overtures until he has exhibited evidence of being able and willing to make a long-term commitment to her and any offspring she may bear (Symons, 1979; Mellen, 1981).

Basically, evolutionary theorists consider aggressive copulatory tactics as an extreme response to natural selection pressure for males generally to be more assertive than females in their attempts to copulate. However, because forced copulations reduce the ability of females to confine coitus primarily to males who will help care for offspring that they produce, females should have evolved strong tendencies to avoid and/or resist forced copulation. According to evolutionary theorists, the resulting tension between the different optimal approach to reproduction for males and females is responsible for much of the fr

tion, compromise, and deception both sexes exhibit during courtship (and, to a lesser degree, throughout life) (Trivers, 1972; Dawkins, 1976:163).

In summary, the evolutionary theory of rape considers sexual assault as resulting from natural selection for males who are eager to copulate with numerous sex partners, and females who are strongly committed to retaining major control over who will mate with them. The natural selection pressure for this sex difference largely emanates from the fact that males can produce offspring (in potentially large numbers) without gestating them, whereas females cannot. Any genes that happen to incline males to rape, therefore, could become quite prevalent in a mammalian population, except to the degree that fairly effective "counterstrategies" (from females or their relatives) were to also evolve.

SUMMARY

Three contemporary theories of rape have been outlined in this chapter. The feminist theory considers rape to be primarily an act of aggression without genuine sexual motivation used by males to "keep women in their place" in socioeconomic and political terms. The social learning theory regards rape as behavior that males learn through the acquisition of social attitudes favorable to rape, and through the imitation of depictions of sexuality interlinked with aggression. And, the evolutionary theory of rape considers rape to be an act emanating from natural selection pressure for males to be more eager than females for copulatory experiences with a wide variety of sex partners, and their use of forceful tactics to satiate their sexual desires.

Before bringing this discussion to a close, it should be mentioned that two colleagues (J. P. Rushton and H. J. Eysenck) suggested that a fourth contemporary theory of rape should be identified. Both had in mind a theory positing genetically based and neurologically mediated variations in personality patterns such that some males are more prone to commit rape than other males. While such a theory has been advocated in the case of criminality in general (Eysenck, 1977), thus far the theory has not been specifically applied to rape, although it certainly could be.

The best example of such a genetically based, neurologically mediated theory has come to be called *arousal* (or *optimal arousal*) *theory* (Ellis, 1987a; Goma, Perez, & Torrubia, 1988). Various versions of this theory have appeared over the past 15 years to help explain genetic susceptibility to a number of behavior patterns, including:

1. Delinquency, criminality, and psychopathy (Mednick, 1977; Goma, Perez, & Torrubia, 1988; Magnusson, 1988),
2. Childhood hyperactivity (Bell, Alexander, & Schwartzman, 1983; Zeltall, Gohs, & Culatta, 1983),

3. Sensation-seeking and risk-taking (Zuckerman & Neeb, 1980; Lykken, 1982; Farley, 1986),
4. Alcoholism (Tarter, Alterman, & Edwards, 1984),
5. Social gregariousness and extroversion (McEwan & Devins, 1983),
6. Gambling (Blaszczynski, 1985:44; Blaszczynski, Winter, & McConaghy, 1986), and
7. Religiosity (Ellis, 1987c).

According to arousal theory, genetic factors help to organize each individual's brain to be responsive, at widely varying degrees, to the aversive aspects of his or her environment (Hare, 1982; Lykken, 1982; Goma, Perez, & Torrubia, 1988). Some individuals—those with suboptimal levels of arousal under "normal" environmental conditions—appear to be unusually difficult to condition through punishment (although not necessarily through reward) (Mednick, 1977; Ellis, 1986, 1987a; Goma, Perez, & Torrubia, 1988). The reason, according to the theory, is that punishment tends to raise such an individual's level of arousal to a preferred range, thus not really punishing the behavior, and actually, to some extent, even reinforcing it (Ellis, 1987a:503). Since most people are theoretically already near an optimal level of arousal under "normal" environmental conditions, aversive stimulations for them will raise their levels of arousal to superoptimal levels, and thus punish the behavior exhibited at the time it is experienced.

The theory contends that much of how animals (including humans) learn to behave in ways that are tolerated by conspecifics (i.e., other species members) depends on their ability to anticipate, and be sensitive to, any pain that will result from their actions. Some people appear to be so incapable of anticipating, and/or so insensitive to, pain (either physical or emotional) that any ill consequences associated with their hurting others fails to deter them from such behavior. Theoretically, these suboptimally aroused individuals would have a high probability of committing rape and most other serious crimes. They would also exhibit personality traits such as sensation-seeking and risk-taking.

The decision not to give specific attention to arousal theory or other genetically based, neurologically mediated theories of rape was made for two reasons. First, no article or book has yet been published specifically applying this type of theory to rape (except as rape is a type of serious criminality). Second, elements of arousal theory are contained in a fourth theory of rape that will be proposed in chapters 6 and 7 after the review of evidence directly pertaining to the scientific merits of each of the three theories outlined in this chapter.

3

THE FEMINIST THEORY:
HYPOTHESES AND EVIDENCE

Theories cannot be confirmed by direct observation. Therefore, when two or more theories purport to explain the same phenomenon, the relative merit of each theory is judged primarily on the basis of how well hypotheses derived from each theory match empirical reality (Zetterberg, 1965; Park, 1969; McCain & Segal, 1982:76). Basically, the theory that most accurately predicts the greatest number of empirical observations is deemed the better (or more elegant) theory. By merely declaring one theory "better" than another according to current evidence (rather than "true" in any final or absolute sense), one leaves open the possibility that new theories eventually will be proposed that are even better than those currently available (Carneiro, 1977:219).

With these general criteria in mind, hypotheses were derived from the three contemporary theories of rape, and empirical evidence for and against each hypothesis was amassed. The results of this literature survey are presented in this and subsequent chapters.

While efforts were made to locate and impartially summarize all of the pertinent research, omissions were made in the case of a number of studies that seemed only marginally relevant, and in the case of many qualifications to a number of the studies that were included. The reader, therefore, is advised to use these chapters, not as complete and definitive surveys of all the evidence for or against the various hypotheses, but as tentative summaries of those studies that seemed most relevant to each theory. The following hypotheses are among those that may be derived from the feminist theory of rape.

HYPOTHESIS 1:

Rape Should Be Associated With Sex Disparities In Social Status and Power

As indicated earlier, the feminist theory is ambiguous about the direction of the relationships between rape and social dominance variables, except in maintaining that if all status disparities between the sexes were eliminated, so too would rape be eliminated (e.g., Griffin, 1971; Findlay, 1974; Clark & Lewis, 1977). While this would tend to imply that even small gains in equalizing the sexes in social status and power will be linked to reductions in rape rates (as discussed in Chapter 2), some feminist theorists have asserted that initial reductions in sexual inequality might cause increases in rape (because it would frustrate males into intensifying their use of rape to reassert their lost supremacy).

The evidence bearing on this issue is available at two levels of analysis: (a) the interpersonal level, and (b) the community/societal level. At the interpersonal level, Griffin (1978) found rape victimization to be more common among women with low income—especially those outside the work force (e.g., homemakers, the unemployed, students)—than among working women with high incomes (see Cohen & Felson, 1979:596; McDermott, 1979:10). Also, Svalastoga (1962) reported that rape victims generally exceeded their assailants in social status despite the fact that, in the United States as a whole, males exceeded females in status. Similarly, Garrett and Wright (1975) found that women married to rapists (the rape victims were not the rapists' wives) surpassed their husbands in average education level by approximately one year. In contrast, in the United States since the early 1970s, men and women have been essentially equal in average educational attainment (Burstein, 1979:374). Thus, somewhat contrary to the general societal pattern, both victims and spouses of rapists tend to be superior to the rapists in status. In a related vein, spouse abuse generally has been found to be more common in marriages where the interpersonal power and/or occupational status of the wife seemed to be greater than that of the husband (Allen & Straus, 1979; Hornung, McCullough, & Sugimoto, 1981). Overall, at the interpersonal level, evidence appears consistent with the feminist explanation for rape in suggesting that rapists are using sexual aggression to compensate for low status relative to females they encounter.

At the community/societal level, two studies have been conducted. One compared 26 United States cities regarding their rape rates (based both on reports to police and on reports to interviewers in victimization surveys) and their sex disparities in social and economic status (Ellis & Beattie, 1983). While most of the evidence indicated that there was no significant association between a city's rape rates and the degree to which average sex differences existed in social status, wherever differences were found, they supported the hypothesis that gains in sexual equality were frustrating males to the point of increasing their raping tendencies. In other words, there was a slight tendency for cities with the highest rape rates to have fewer sex disparities in the social status measures than the cities with the lowest rape rates, even after controlling for several demographic factors.

The second study compared official rape rates in all 50 states with various indicators of social status disparities between the sexes (Baron & Straus, 1984). This study concluded that while there appeared to be a slight tendency for states with the greatest degree of sexual inequality to have the lowest rape rates, overall few differences were significant, thus also weakly supporting what might be called the *frustration version* of the feminist theory of rape.

Together, these two studies indicate that, if a significant association exists between rape rates and sex disparities in social status at the community/societal level, it is such that reducing the disparities will cause a slight increase in the risk of rape. At the interpersonal level, both rape victims and rape offenders appear to be of low social status, but especially the offenders (a point that will be discussed later). Overall, these studies support the frustration version of the feminist theory of rape.

HYPOTHESIS 2:

Rape is Primarily Motivated by a Desire for Power and Dominance Rather than a Desire for Sex

Most proponents of feminist theory—and some proponents of social learning theory—have maintained that the underlying motivation for rape is that of domination rather than sexuality (e.g., Mehrhof & Kearon, 1972; Brownmiller, 1975; Scarpitti & Scarpitti, 1977; Groth, 1979; Holdstrom & Burgess, 1980:427; Rodabaugh & Austin, 1981). Inasmuch as domination often is achieved through physical force, according to feminist theory, rape is a form of aggression used not to satiate sexual urges, but to ensure that women are sufficiently frightened and intimidated so that men are able to maintain socioeconomic and political supremacy (Groth, 1979:2; Thio, 1983:156; Persell, 1984:586; Thompson & Buttell, 1984).

Studies that have correlated rape and violence probabilities bear upon this hypothesis, and, as the feminist theory would lead one to expect, societies (or states within the United States) which have high rates of violence in general also tend to have high rates of rape (Sanday, 1981; Benderly, 1982; Baron & Straus, 1984; Schwendinger & Schwendinger, 1985:98). Similarly, the increases in rape rates and in assault rates in the United States have almost perfectly paralleled one another over the past half century (Kutchinski, 1988:6). In addition, at the individual level of analysis, males who were violent in general also were found to be unusually aggressive in their efforts to gain sexual access during dating situations (Sigelman, Berry, & Wiles, 1984).

While the above studies certainly support the feminist theory, their main weakness is that they made no attempt to measure motivation per se. Studies that have tried to do so have generally not supported the feminist theory. Since this is probably a controversial conclusion (given how central this hypothesis has been to the feminist theory of rape), the evidence will be summarized in some detail.

First, self-reports from rapists have given little indication that they were mainly attempting to dominate their victims, except as it might help the rapists to copulate (Field, 1978:169). Scully and Marolla (1984) reported that few men convicted of rape mentioned a desire to dominate as their main objective. Instead, survey results suggest that rape may be motivated as much by desires for excitement and risk-taking as by a desire for either sex *or* domination (see also Scully & Marolla, 1985). A study of date rapists also found the male offenders rarely mentioning aggression or domination as what they were trying to accomplish by their behavior, while "getting extremely sexually aroused" was often mentioned in the context of trying to explain (or excuse) their actions (Yegidis, 1986:53).

Second, from evidence that predatory rapists report unusually high proportions of "deviant sexual fantasies" (Walker & Meyer, 1981), it was suggested by Quinsey (1984:105) that sex was probably the main motivation for most rapists, even though the expression of their desires often assumed extremely sadistic and violent forms.

Third, studies in which date rapists reported often trying a number of tactics other than rape suggest that domination is not their main objective since these other tactics include such things as falsely pledging love, threatening to break off the relationship, trying to get their date drunk, and simply ignoring the female's protests as they fondle or disrobe her (Rapaport & Bukhart, 1984). Only when these nonraping tactics fail (or seem likely to fail) do most date rapists resort to physical constraint, and eventually even injury (Koss & Leonard, 1984; Mosher & Anderson, 1986; also see Yegidis, 1986:52). From this evidence, Mosher and Anderson (1986:78) reasoned that it would be more parsimonious to consider all of these male behavior patterns, including rape, as reflecting the same basic goal (i.e., to have sex) than to contend that when they rape, their goal is power and domination, but when they lie or try to get their dates intoxicated, their goal is sex.

Fourth, in an article directly challenging the hypothesis that domination, rather than sex, was the major motivation behind most rapes, Kanin (1985) hypothesized that rapists (at least date rapists) have been socialized into desiring and expecting more in the way of sexual activity during courtship than nonrapists (thus explaining why rapists tend to be more sexually active than other males, as will be discussed later). Even though Kanin found rapists to be more sexually active than nonrapists, he also found that the sexual exploits of rapists, on the average, fell short of their aspirations to a greater degree than for most nonrapists. Furthermore, Kanin (1985:223) offered detailed evidence that rapists use many kinds of deceptive and devious tactics in addition to physical force in attempting to satiate their abnormally high sexual aspirations. Similar to studies cited in the preceding paragraph, recent investigations by Kanin have found rapists were over three times more likely to report trying to get their dates intoxicated, and to lie in order to have sex, than were males who said they had never used force during courtship. Kanin (1984:104) also proposed that, while sex appears to be the *main* motivation in the case of most date rapes, it is possible that domination and power still motivate most predatory rapes (see also Check & Malamuth, 1985:420).

Fifth, in a study of people's judgments about sexual harassment, Thomann and Wiener (1987) found the criteria people used to determine whether a case was or was not a bonafide sexual harassment case to be extremely similar to the criteria used to determine if a rape had indeed occurred (see also Jensen & Gutek, 1982). Unless one wishes to argue that most instances of sexual harassment (and possibly even nonharassing sexual overtures) also are largely acts of domination and aggression, one should seriously consider that sexuality is the main motivation for most rapes as well.

Finally, as already reported, Kutchinski (1988:6) found that fluctuations in rape rates and in nonsexual assault rates in the United States have closely paralleled one another for many years (thus supporting the feminist theory). However, for Denmark, Sweden, and West Germany (where data were also available for sex offenses other than rape), Kutchinsky (1988:9) found that rape rate fluctuations tended to be intermediate to fluctuations in general assault rates and fluctuations in nonviolent sex offense rates (e.g., pedophilia and incest). Unless these nonviolent sex offenses also are considered nonsexual acts, the most reasonable interpretation would be that rape is at least "half-way" sexually motivated.

Overall, while the motivation behind rape is inherently difficult to determine (especially if it is assumed that rapists themselves may not know what their motives are) (Malamuth, in press), most of the evidence bearing on the matter seems to contradict the hypothesis that domination and aggression, rather than sex, are of paramount importance. This is certainly not to argue that domination and aggression have nothing to do with rape, but that they seem to reflect more of the tactical aspects of rape, rather than the objective of the act. Nevertheless, because this hypothesis is central to what appears to be the leading theory of rape at the present time (Smith & Bennett, 1985), and, according to Hagan, this hypothesis is currently accepted as true by "most authorities on rape" (Hagan, 1988:187), more research is necessary. More will be theorized in regard to rape motivation in Chapters 6 and 7.

HYPOTHESIS 3:

Increased Exposure to Pornography and Prostitution Should Increase Male Tendencies to Rape (or to Generally Behave More Aggressively Toward Women)

According to the feminist theory of rape, both pornography and prostitution tend to depict women as being property over which men attempt to gain and retain control and domination (Brownmiller, 1975; Morgan, 1980; Dworkin, 1981). In this way, pornography and prostitution tend to perpetuate male attitudes toward women that are conducive to rape. Only two studies were found relevant to the effects of prostitution, and their results were contradictory. A study by Kinsie (1950) related rates of rape (and other assaults) in various United States cities with brothel closures and vice squad arrests of prostitutes. He concluded that modest declines in rape rates generally resulted when enforcement of laws against prostitution was increased. Barber (1969), however, reported that rape rates rose substantially following the closure of brothels in Australia.

Regarding pornography, feminist writers have maintained that it has served to institutionalize the social inferiority and servitude of women, and thus has prompted many men to treat women as persons (or even "things") simply to be exploited and dominated (sexually and otherwise) (Morgan, 1980; Diamond, 1980; Wheeler, 1985). Within such an atmosphere, the potential for women to achieve social equality is extremely low, and, therefore, rape will persist. Many studies have attempted to assess the merits of this view. At this point, however, only studies pertaining primarily to *nonviolent* forms of pornography will be reviewed under the feminist theory. The reason for excluding violent pornography is that, even though feminist theory would predict that violent pornography also causes rape, most of its proponents have argued that essentially all forms of pornography cause rape (e.g., Brownmiller, 1975; Barry, 1979; MacKinnon, 1986). The effects of exposure to *violent* pornography will be extensively considered when hypotheses derived from the social learning theory of rape are discussed.

Before considering any evidence that pornography affects male behavior as the feminist theory (and, later, the social learn theory) hypothesizes, one should keep in mind that definitions of *pornography* (and related concepts, such as erotica and obscenity) vary. Steinem (1980:37), for example, argued that while both erotica and pornography depicted explicit sexual behavior, only the latter was likely to cause rape and violence against women. For her, the line between erotica and pornography was crossed whenever male domination or control was at least implied in depictions of explicit sexual activity. Unfortunately, what was meant by "male domination and control" was not made very clear. Some might see magazines containing photographs of only females in sexually provocative poses as reflecting male domination and control unless these magazines contain an equal number of photographs of males in similarly provocative poses. Also, movies that show males more actively pursuing females than vice versa, or that show males in the "superior" (i.e., on-top) position more than females in that position, may tip the balance between pornography and erotica, according to Steinem's criterion. The point here is not to suggest any solutions to the difficult questions surrounding exactly what constitutes pornography and what does not, but to forewarn readers that many operational definitions have been used, and apparent inconsistencies between research findings may sometimes be the result of differences in those definitions.

One line of evidence bearing on the hypothesis that exposure to pornography causes rape involves comparing rape rates in countries over periods of time during which the availability of pornography underwent dramatic change. Studies in Denmark during the 1960s, when the country's obscenity laws were repealed, found that rape rates seemed unaffected by the decriminalization of pornography (BenVeniste, 1971; Kutchinski, 1971, 1973). However, the studies by Kutchinski were sharply criticized on methodological grounds (Check & Malamuth, 1984:191). Data from several countries, not just Denmark, brought Court (1976, 1980, 1984) to conclude that increases in the availability of all forms of pornography were associated with substantial increases in societywide rape rates.

Some recent cross-sectional studies in the United States—which involved comparing over-the-counter sales of "men's magazines" in the various states—also found evidence that these largely nonviolent and relatively "soft" forms of pornography have rape-promoting effects. First, Malamuth and Check (1981) found a substantial positive correlation between the frequency that college men reported reading magazines such as *Playboy* and *Penthouse* and their self-reported likelihood of ever trying to force a female to have sex. Second, in a study by Baron and Straus (1984), rape rates in the 50 states were correlated with over-the-counter sales of *Playboy* and similar men's magazines. Baron and Straus found a strong positive relationship, even after controlling for several demographic differences among the states between rape rates and the per capita sale of the magazines.

As a major replication and extension of the Baron and Straus study, Scott and Schwalm (1988a) included more men's magazines, additional demographic control variables, and even controlled for the circulation of general readership magazines such as *Newsweek* and *Time*, and for outdoor sports magazines such as *Field and Stream, Guns and Ammo,* and the *American Rifleman.* Their analysis suggested that fairly substantial positive correlations remained between a state's rape rates and its per capita sale of men's magazines even when controls for these variables were imposed. And, quit consistent with the feminist theory of rape, Scott and Schwalm (1988a) reported that the correlations were as strong, if not stronger, in the case of fairly "soft" and nonviolent magazines, such as *Playboy*, as in the case of more hard-core and sometimes more violent erotic magazines, such as *Hustler*.

So far, what has been discussed are all correlative studies, and should be interpreted with extreme caution with respect to suggesting any causal effects of exposing males to erotic magazines (see Scott & Schwalm, 1988a:248). While experimental studies would come closer to answering questions about the causal nature of any such relationship, for ethical reasons, experimental studies have never been conducted in which rape, per se, has been used as a dependent variable. However, some studies have systematically exposed male subjects to various forms of nonviolent pornography in order to determine if their *attitudes* were affected in ways suggestive of a greater propensity to commit sexual assault. Such experiments basically found no evidence that short-term (less than 2 hours) exposure to nonviolent pornography increased male expressions of callousness and insensitivity to the feelings of women (Mosher, 1971; Jaffe, Malamuth, Feingold, & Fesbach, 1974). However, experimental research by Zillmann and Bryant (1982, 1984) involving several hours of exposure to extremely explicit, but still nonviolent, pornography did reveal that the exposure reduced the length of sentences both men and women recommended imposing upon rape offenders, and increased male tendencies to "trivialize" rape (see also Donnerstein, 1984). Check and Malamuth (1986:205) have suggested that even though the Zillmann and Bryant studies did not use violent pornography, the films they used still contained many "dehumanizing elements"—meaning pornography in which the female was treated more as a temptress and sex object rather than a mutually participating sex partner. Therefore, Check and Malamuth contend that pornography that is devoid of both violent *and* dehumanizing content should have no effects upon male tendencies to rape.

As far as behavior (rather than attitudes) is concerned, some experimental studies have used fairly general violence toward women (usually a female lab assistant) as the dependent variable. These experiments found little to no evidence that male tendencies to behave aggressively toward women were enhanced by the exposure to nonviolent pornography (Mosher, 1971; Baron & Bell, 1973; Donnerstein, Donnerstein, & Evans, 1975; Donnerstein & Barrett, 1978; Donnerstein & Berkowitz, 1981; Sapolsky & Zillmann, 1981; Ramirez, Bryant, & Zillmann, 1982; Malamuth, Check, & Briere, 1986:338). In fact, some studies using mildly explicit erotic female nude photographs (as opposed to motion pictures, or highly explicit verbal descriptions of sexual behavior) found that viewing this material actually seemed to reduce hostile feelings and actions in most males (Baron, 1974; Baron & Bell, 1977; Donnerstein, Donnerstein, & Evans, 1975; White, 1979). Nevertheless, several other studies found that various forms of aggression by male subjects (albeit often directed toward other males) were significantly enhanced by viewing largely nonviolent forms of pornography, especially after the male subjects have been insulted by the female (Schmidt & Sigusch, 1970; Tannenbaum, 1971; Schmidt, et al., 1973; Jaffe, Malamuth, Feingold, & Feshback, 1974; Malamuth, Feshback, & Jaffe, 1977; Donnerstein & Barrett, 1978a, 1978b; Donnerstein & Hallam, 1978). Likewise, exposure to explicit nonviolent pornography has been shown to increase many male viewer's subjective feelings of hostility and aggressiveness (Jaffe, 1974; Zillmann, Hoyt, & Day, 1974; Fisher & Harris, 1976; Sapolsky, 1977; Zillmann, Bryant, & Carveth, 1981). And, Check (1985) found that men's willingness to force their regular sex partners to try forms of sexuality that were not to the partner's liking was increased by exposure to both violent and nonviolent pornography, except possibly in the case of extremely "soft" forms of pornography.

Several major efforts have been made in recent years to untangle these complicated and seemingly contradictory findings (e.g., Zillmann, 1986; Donnerstein, Linz, & Penrod, 1987; Linz, Donnerstein, & Penrod, 1987). Confining attention at this point only to the effects of exposure to nonviolent (though often quite explicit) forms of pornography, the following generalizations seem to coincide with most of the research conducted thus far. First, short-term (less than 1 hour) exposure to nonviolent erotica (e.g., nude female pin-up photographs) appears not to increase male aggression or feelings of hostility, and may actually reduce it. Second, short-term exposure to nonviolent, moderately explicit pornography (e.g., scenes of females in seductive poses, couples copulating but without focusing on their genitals while doing so) seems to minimally increase male aggression and feelings of hostility, unless a male is provoked (e.g., by insults) within the first hour or so following exposure (Linz, Donnerstein, & Penrod, 1987:101). If provoked and the male has an opportunity to aggress against the female who provoked him, he is more likely to do so after nonviolent pornography exposure than under control conditions (Donnerstein & Barnett, 1978b; Donnerstein & Hallam, 1978). (In trying to account for this in social learning terms, rather than feminist terms, Zillmann (1982) and Donnerstein (1983) have proposed that arousal levels are raised by exposure to pornography and tend to be maintained over short periods of time under conditions in which opportunities to aggress are presented to the subjects.) Third, exposure to very explicit nonviolent pornography (e.g., movie scenes focused upon the genitals while copulating), at least when it is extended over several hour-long exposures, has only recently received significant research attention. At this point, the evidence suggests that such exposure may heighten male tendencies to aggress toward women, and to assign less severe sentences to hypothetical rape offenders (Zillmann, Bryant & Carveth, 1981; Zillmann, 1986), however, not all of the researchers on this subject have agreed with this interpretation (e.g., Donnerstein, 1985a, 1985b; Linz, 1985; Donnerstein & Linz, 1986).

To summarize in regard to this hypothesis, research is still helping to clarify the effects of exposing males to pornography, and only recently has it begun to consider long-term exposure to extremely explicit (XXX-rated) pornography.

The fact that pornography has continued to become increasingly available in most Western societies over the past two decades (Smith, 1976; Malamuth & Spinner, 1980: Dietz & Evans, 1982) underscores the importance of the investigations surrounding its possible effects on rape. Finally, it should be emphasized that the feminist theory also leads to the hypothesis that exposure to *violent* forms of pornography should increase a male's likelihood of committing rape. Since the hypothesis addressing the effects of violent pornography can be more explicitly derived from the social learning theory, evidence pertaining to it will be reviewed in Chapter 4.

HYPOTHESIS 4:

Societal Trends Toward Sexual Eqalitarianism Should Be Associated with a Lessening of Rape Victimization

A number of studies have found that people's attitudes in the United States (and possibly other Western countries) have become increasingly egalitarian in recent years with respect to appropriate sex roles (Mason, et al., 1976; Thornton & Freedman, 1979; Cherlin & Walters, 1981; Helmreich, et al., 1982; Thornton, et al., 1983). The feminist theory of rape would predict that these trends should be accompanied by a decrease in rape, all else being equal.

As noted in Chapter 1 (p. 3), while official statistics in the United States indicate that rape victimization has substantially increased over the past quarter of a century, victimization and self-report data (which tend to concentrate upon somewhat less violent forms of rape) indicate essentially no change or only very slight increases. Neither of these trends supports the hypothesis. However, the inconsistency can be explained in two ways without doing harm to the feminist theory. One is to note that trends toward sexual equality have been accompanied by legal extensions of the definition of rape and by an increased willingness of women to report rape offenses (Finkelhor & Yllo, 1982:477). Second, it is possible that gains in sexual equality have been more than offset by the increased availability of pornography and prostitution, which feminist theorists regard as promoting rape (Ellis & Beattie, 1983:89).

Finally, in a comparative analysis, Abramson and Hayashi (1984) recently asserted that pornography, even pornography that depicts rape, is more common in movies and especially on commercial television in Japan than in the United States, and that the subjugation of women to subservient roles in Japan is much more prevalent than in the United States. Despite those characteristics of Japanese society—all of which would be conducive to rape according to feminist theory—rape rates in Japan appear to be less than one-tenth as high as in the United States.

HYPOTHESIS 5:

Rapists Should Hold Less Eqalitarian and More Pro-rape
Attitudes Toward Women than Nonrapists

According to feminist theorists, attitudinal factors are important in causing rape (e.g., Burt 1978:282; Alder, 1985:308) (as will be pointed out in Chapter 4, this is also the case for most social learning theorists). Before discussing the research evidence directly bearing on this hypothesis, terminology needs to be given some attention. In particular, it should be pointed out that the concept of rape myths has been used in ways that can be misleading.

In coining the term, Burt (1980) defined *rape myths* as prejudicial, stereo-typed, or false beliefs about rape, rape victims, and rapists. Even though the word *myth* normally implies that the belief being referenced is simply untrue, Burt's inclusion of "prejudicial" and "stereotyped" in the definition allowed her to include, whether intentionally or not, some statements with considerable elements of truth. For example, the following statement is identified as a rape myth: "In the majority of rapes, the victim is promiscuous or has a bad reputation." While such terms as *promiscuous* and *bad reputation* would be hard to define with any precision, several studies have determined that victims of rape do have significantly more sex partners on average than other women (Belcastro, 1982:225; Lystad, 1982:18; Essock-Vitale & McGuire, 1985:149), and that they are more prone to drink excessively at parties than other women (Meyer, 1984; Brozan, 1986).

Another statement deemed a rape myth in the Burt scale is: "Many women have an unconscious wish to be raped, and may then unconsciously set up a situation in which they are likely to be attacked." As will be discussed in more detail in Chapter 5 (Hypothesis 4), significant numbers of women report at least occasionally fantasizing about being raped (e.g., Masters & Johnson, 1979:183; Goodchilds & Zellman, 1984:242; Price & Miller, 1984; Bond & Mosher, 1986; Loren & Weeks, 1986:33; Wilson, 1987). While this fantasizing may not perfectly resemble the typical predatory rape, or even the usual date rape (especially in terms of the physical attractiveness of the assailant), and for women to report it, it would have to be a conscious, not an unconscious, desire, to simply say that persons who agree with this statement are subscribing to a *myth* is, at the very least, misleading.

While not specifically categorized as a rape myth, in a related vein, the following statement has been identified as one indicating the acceptance of interpersonal violence toward women: "Many times a woman will pretend she doesn't want to have intercourse because she doesn't want to seem loose, but she's really hoping the man will force her" (Burt, 1983:138). In fact, a recent study found that approximately a third of all women surveyed reported on at least one occasion having said "No" when they were actually willing to engage in sexual intercourse with a date, and that the main reason they initially refused was to avoid appearing overly promiscuous (Muehlenhard & Hollabaugh, 1988). Similarly, Loren and Weeks (1986:33) found that 60% of women report sometimes *fantasizing* about giving in to sexual intercourse after some initial resistance. Many male respondents who score high on what Burt considers a scale of acceptance of interpersonal violence, therefore, may do so, not because they approve of males using force to have sex with their dates, but simply from knowing (or at least strongly suspecting) that, in fact, the statement in question is essentially true (unless by the word *force* one means only those acts that cause significant pain and injury). To make the statement reflective of a respondent's approval of interpersonal violence toward women, it definitely needs to be more carefully phrased.

The purpose of noting the preceding problems with attitudinal research measures on rape and violence toward women is not to single out Burt's research as uniquely defective, but to show that the most widely used measure of attitudes toward rape and violence toward women appears to contain substantial flaws—flaws that may help to explain inconsistencies in the research findings to be reviewed. In addition, the previous comments lead to the recommendation that future research on attitudes regarding such topics as rape, violence toward women, and equality in sex roles should take more care than they have in the past to separate strictly attitudinal items from items that, in fact, fairly accurately depict reality (whether the typical liberal-minded social scientist approves of that reality or not).

With these remarks in mind, the research directly bearing on this fifth feminist hypothesis will now be reviewed. In a study that compared a group of rapists with a sample of police officers and a sample of social workers, Burt (1978) found that police officers scored highest, social workers lowest, and rapists intermediate in their endorsement of rape myths. In a later study, Burt (1983) found a group of convicted rapists to be more supportive of men's use of violence in interpersonal relationships with women than were persons in the general population. However, this second study did not analyze the general population sample according to sex; and, inasmuch as males appear to have higher rape myth acceptance scores than females (Ashton, 1982), it is possible that the rapists attitudes in Burt's second study differed only from females in the general population, not from other males in the general population, in rape myth acceptance.

Kanin (1969) reported that date rapists hold more to a double standard with respect to appropriate sexual behavior than other males. Similarly, several recent studies have found that males who judge themselves to have a relatively high probability of committing rape are more likely to agree with stereotypic statements about appropriate sex roles and to subscribe to more rape myths than males who see themselves as minimally likely to commit rape (Malamuth, 1981, 1983; Check & Malamuth, 1983, 1985:418; Malamuth & Check, 1983; also see Tieger, 1981; Koss & Leonard, 1984:222). Also, supporting the hypothesis, Alder (1985:318) found that rape offenders were more likely than other males to hold attitudes that justified sexual victimization of women by men. Even though these studies all found rape-prone males holding a variety of "sexist" attitudes to a greater degree than other males, it should be mentioned that the differences were not of major magnitude.

On the negative side, one study that compared the attitudes of convicted rapists with those of males imprisoned for other offenses failed to find any significant differences between these two groups in their attitudes toward women and toward women's rights (Howells & Wright, 1978). Also, two studies of date rapists concluded that these males did not subscribe to more rape myths, or to more traditional sex role attitudes than males with no history of date rape (Ageton, 1982:137; Rapaport & Burkhart, 1984:220).

Overall, the evidence (while tilted on the side of supporting the hypothesis) is mixed, and is in need of additional research attention. In conducting future research in this area of attitudes toward rape and rape probability, greater care should be devoted to designing valid attitudinal measures than has typified past research.

GENERAL ASSESSMENT OF SUPPORT FOR HYPOTHESES DERIVED FROM THE FEMINIST THEORY

As an overall assessment of how well hypotheses derived from the feminist theory of rape have been shown to accurately predict observations, both strengths and weaknesses are apparent. In terms of strengths, rape does appear to be related to sex disparities in sociopolitical and economic affairs (although not in the sense that the risks of rape are lessened by lowering sex disparities in political and economic power, but rather the reverse).

Concerning the hypothesis that an increased exposure to pornography makes males more likely to rape, the evidence is mixed with regard to nonviolent forms of pornography, but generally indicating that at least long-term exposure to extremely explicit pornography may increase general tendencies to behave aggressively toward women and decrease the seriousness with which males view rape. (More will be said about strictly violent forms of pornography in the next chapter since this bears more precisely on the social learning theory of rape than on the feminist theory.)

Regarding weaknesses, the feminist theory seems to considerably underestimate the degree to which rape is sexually motivated, and perhaps overestimates the degree to which "sexist attitudes" are important in inclining males to commit rape.

4

THE SOCIAL LEARNING THEORY: HYPOTHESES AND EVIDENCE

The following hypotheses are among those that can be derived from the social learning theory of rape.

HYPOTHESIS 1:

Rapists Should Hold Attitudes that Are More Favorable Toward Rape, and Toward Violence in General, than Other Men

Like feminist theorists, most proponents of social learning theory consider rape propensity to be mediated by attitudinal variables. The main difference is that whereas feminist theorists emphasize the sociopolitical and dominating aspects of male attitudes toward women, social learning theorists tend to emphasize how sexuality and violence (especially toward women) can become conceptually fused (e.g., Malamuth, 1984:31; Malamuth, Check & Briere, 1986:338), or how viewing sexual violence provides a "response schema" or "script" for engaging in rape (e.g., Huesmann & Malamuth, 1986). Thus, unlike Hypothesis 5 of the feminist theory, the present hypothesis pertains to links between rape and attitudes favorable to violence.

The empirical evidence is limited, but largely supportive of the hypothesis that rapists hold more favorable attitudes toward the use of violence, especially in interacting with females, than do other males (although the differences are modest) (Burt, 1983; Rapaport & Burkhart, 1984). In addition, Taylor and Smith (1974) reported that males who approved most strongly of various traditional sex roles were more likely to behave aggressively toward women, although two other studies have called this relationship into question (Young, Beier, Beier, & Barton, 1975; Hotaling & Sugarman, 1986).

Incidentally, reflective of the importance that social learning theorists place on attitudes in rape etiology, they usually make it a point to carefully debrief subjects after exposing them to pornography (especially violent pornography) to help rid them of any rape- or other aggression-enhancing effects caused by the exposure. Evaluations of these debriefing sessions indicate that they are quite successful, at least in terms of bringing sexist attitudes and beliefs in rape myths back to preexposure levels (Donnerstein & Hallam, 1978; Donnerstein & Berkowitz, 1981; Check, 1982; Check & Malamuth, 1984; Malamuth & Check, 1984; Linz, 1985; Malamuth & Briere, 1986:88). In fact, studies by Linz (1985) and by Krafka (1985) indicate that six months after exposure to a single debriefing session—subsequent to several hours of exposure to both R-rated "slasher" films (by male subjects) and X-rated rape depictions (by female subjects)—subjects were substantially less likely to subscribe to rape myths than they were before even taking part in the experiment (for a discussion see Donnerstein, Linz, and Penrod, 1987:183; for a review see Linz, Donnerstein, Bross, & Chapin, 1986).

HYPOTHESIS 2:

Compared to Other Males, Rapists Should Display More
Sexual Arousal to Depictions of Rape, and Even
to General Depictions of Violence (Especially
Toward Women)

To a considerable extent, social learning theorists regard rapists as males who have become accustomed to thinking of violence in a sexual context. Given such a view, one would predict that depictions of rape and violence in general (especially violence toward women) would be more sexually arousing to rapists (or potential rapists) than to other males. Evidence consistent with this deduction has come from a variety of experiments, many of which have involved attaching instruments to male subjects for measuring penile erection while they listened to descriptions of sexual episodes in a secluded chamber. Most of these studies have found that, unlike males not inclined to commit rape (who show little or no sexual arousal to rape depictions), convicted rapists exhibit essentially the same degree of arousal to verbal descriptions of rape as to descriptions of consenting sexual activity (Stoller, 1976; Abel, Barlow, Blanchard, & Guild,

1977; Barbaree, Marshall, & Lanthier, 1979; Hinton, O'Neill, & Webster, 1980; Quinsey, Chaplin & Varney, 1981; Quinsey & Chaplin, 1984; Quinsey, Chaplin & Upfold, 1984; Murphy, Haynes, Coleman, & Flanagan, 1985; Earls & Proubo, 1986). This well-confirmed observation appears to have only two significant qualifications. First, Baxter, Barbaree, and Marshall (1986) found that both convicted rapists and nonrapists (male undergraduates) exhibited greater sexual arousal to depictions of consenting sexual behavior than to depictions of rape in which the victim was vigorously resisting, with only a slight tendency for the students to be more extreme in their preference for consenting sex scenes than the rapists. Second, all of the studies cited in the discussion of this hypothesis were based upon measures of sexual arousal resulting from audiotape depictions of rape. The only study using videotape depictions of rape (Murphy, et al., 1985) found no significant differences in arousal between rapists and other males.

The same pattern of unusually high penile erection to audiotape and read depictions of sexual violence has been found for males with high proclivities to rape according to self-ratings (Malamuth, Haber, & Feshbach, 1980; Check & Malamuth, 1983; Malamuth & Check, 1983). The exception to this is that when the victim is described as expressing unmistakable abhorrence or suffering throughout the rape episode, males with a proclivity to rape react with little arousal, similar to males with no proclivity to rape (Malamuth, Feshback, & Jaffe, 1977; Malamuth & Check, 1980a, 1980b). Penile erection in response to depictions of rape also have been found to predict general violence against women (Malamuth, 1983, 1984b, in press), which have, in turn, been found to predict self-reported sexual aggression against women in a naturalistic setting (Malamuth, 1986, in press).

HYPOTHESIS 3:

Exposure to Violent Pornography Should Increase Male Propensities to Commit Rape, and to Otherwise Behave Violently Toward Women

Unlike proponents of the feminist theory of rape, who essentially view all pornography as likely to induce rape (due to its fostering of male domination and exploitative attitudes toward women) (see Chapter 3, Hypothesis 5), proponents of social learning theory tend to hypothesize that only *violent* forms of pornography are likely to enhance male propensities to rape (Donnerstein, 1985:16; Linz, Donnerstein, & Penrod, 1987a). A somewhat intermediate position has been taken by Check and Malamuth (1986:205) in their arguing that all "dehumanizing" forms of pornography may enhance rape propensities, although they are not very explicit about what "dehumanizing" pornography includes. The main exception has been Zillmann (1986), whose version of social learning theory emphasizes that even exposure to many forms of nonviolent pornography increase male tendencies to rape. As noted in Chapter 3 (Hypothesis 3), this is a highly contested issue at the present time—due in part to the obvious policy implications (Attorney General's Commission on Pornography, 1986).

Overall, considerable evidence derived in laboratory settings, usually with R- and X-rated movies, found that even exposure to nonviolent pornography increases male propensities to display subsequent aggression (Zillmann, 1971, 1979, 1986; Meyer, 1972; Donnerstein & Evans, 1975; Baron & Bell, 1977; Malamuth, Feshback, & Jaffe, 1977; Donnerstein & Hallam, 1978; Baron & Straus, 1984; Donnerstein, 1984a:92; Zillmann & Sapolsky, 1977; Zillmann & Bryant, 1986). Most of the pornography stimuli in these experiments were either R- or X-rated movies or explicit verbal depictions of sexual activity. The targets for aggression in most of these studies were other males, and usually did not involve explicit attempts to provoke the subjects (e.g., by insulting them after viewing the movies) (Linz, Donnerstein, & Penrod, 1987). Thus, one could question whether or not the above cited research had much to do with sexual aggression, per se, since the recipients of most of the aggression were other males.

As mentioned in Chapter 3 (Hypothesis 3), a number of studies found that exposure to mild forms of pornography (e.g., pin-up centerfolds) actually reduced subsequent aggression (e.g., Baron, 1974a, 1974b, Baron & Bell, 1973; Frodi, 1977; Zillmann & Sapolsky, 1977). In interpreting such findings, Linz, Donnerstein, and Penrod (1987a:101) have contended that essentially any stimuli that increase "arousal (including physical exercise) and/or negative affect" will increase the probability of aggression. Therefore, the tendency for nonviolent pornography to promote aggression may be no greater than any other emotionally arousing stimuli.

Regarding exposure to violent forms of pornography, evidence suggests that it is much more likely to incite aggression, specifically toward women, than exposure to nonviolent forms (Leonard & Taylor, 1983; Zillmann & Bryant, 1983, 1986:574; Linz, Donnerstein, & Penrod, 1987a). This has been shown to be especially true of violent pornography in which the female eventually shows signs of deriving sexual pleasure from the rape (as is fairly common in pornographic depictions of rape) (Donnerstein, 1980a, 1980b, 1983, 1984; Donnerstein & Berkowitz, 1981). Most of the experimental work on the effects of violent pornography, however, found that exposure to such stimuli seems to increase aggression toward a female only after she provoked the male subjects in some way (usually via some affront or insult) (Gray, 1982; Donnerstein & Linz, 1986).

Only recently has work begun to examine the effects of long-term (more than an hour or two) exposure to pornography (Zillmann, 1986; Linz, Donnerstein, & Penrod, 1987a:101). Also, recent studies have attempted to determine the exact nature of the apparent rape-promoting effects of violent pornography exposure. Linz, Donnerstein, and Penrod (1987a:111) have suggested that the explicitness of the sexuality may not be nearly as important as the degree to which sexuality is interwoven with aggression and violence. In particular, they argue that normally R-rated slasher films (e.g., in which a female is depicted bathing, and then mutilated and killed) may be especially likely to desensitize subjects to violence against women (see also National Institute of Mental Health, 1982:29). In a study, these researchers found that after watching 10 hours of R-rated slasher films over the course of five days, subjects substantially reduced their estimates of the degree to which the films depicted violent and/or contained subjectively "offensive"' scenes (Linz, Donnerstein, & Penrod, 1984; also see Linz, 1985).

Ethical constraints, of course, prevent experimental research from directly testing the hypothesis that exposure to various types of pornography actually increase the probability of rape. Therefore, most studies have simply looked for the effects of exposure to violent pornography in terms of changes in attitudes, sexual arousal, and the like. One study exposed subjects to violent pornography and found that the males' subsequent self-reported likelihood of committing rape had increased (Malamuth, 1981). Other studies exposed male subjects to five violent pornography movies, and found that the subjects' ratings of the degree of violence and the degree to which the films degraded women significantly diminished during the course of the experiment, suggesting an overall desensitization effect (Zillmann & Bryant, 1982, 1984; Linz, Donnerstein & Penrod, 1984; Linz, 1985). A series of experiments by Zillmann and Bryant (1982, 1983, 1984) found similar effects for what they described as very explicit, but essentially nonviolent pornography. They exposed their subjects over several hour-long sessions, and found that the subjects' ratings of the repulsiveness of depictions of sadomasochism and bestiality were significantly diminished.

Results pointing toward a somewhat different conclusion than the studies by Linz, et al., and by Zillmann and Bryant have been reported by Ceniti and Malamuth (1984; Malamuth & Ceniti, 1986). They found that the number of violent pornographic films male subjects saw did not significantly increase the level of sexual arousal the subjects felt throughout the exposure period.

Overall, evidence is largely consistent with the following conclusions: (a) Exposing males to violent forms of pornography promotes male tendencies to behave aggressively toward women when they are insulted by the target. (b) Exposing males to violent forms of pornography increases male tendencies to agree with statements about women desiring and even deserving to be raped. (c) Exposing males to nonpornographic (R-rated) films containing scenes of violence and sex also appears to have the above two effects to about the same degree (Linz, Donnerstein, & Penrod, 1987b:949). (d) One should avoid equating either experimentally contrived aggression toward women or attitudes favorable to rape with rape under any uncontrolled ("natural") conditions.

Thus, many questions remain about the effects of pornographic (and less explicit depictions) of rape on the probability of male viewers eventually committing rape. Many complex issues remain to be explored, including the possibility of short-term versus long-term effects and the possible *graduating-up effect*. This later effect will be discussed more in regard to Hypothesis 4, but roughly denotes the idea that even if the nonviolent forms of pornography do not promote rape directly, they may whet a male's appetite for the forms of pornography that do.

Another possibility that has so far received almost no systematic research attention is that pornography could enhance male propensities to commit rape (and otherwise behave aggressively toward women) by providing males with sexual desires that are not conducive to the maintenance of stable monogamous relationships (Zillmann, 1986; Shepher & Reisman, 1985:112). In other words, nearly all pornography tends to emphasize fun and excitement as associated with promiscuous (and often multiple-partner) relationships, and it could encourage significant numbers of males (and possibly females) to abandon stable monogamous relationships for the excitement of promiscuous sex. Among the fragmentary evidence supporting this possibility is a study that found that exposure to pornography made both sexes feel less love for the partners they were dating than they had felt before the exposure (Anonymous, 1983). Also, Zillmann and Bryant (1986:18) reported that exposure to pornography reduced the males' expressed satisfaction with their present girlfriends' physical attractiveness (see also Kenrick, Gutierres & Goldberg, in press). (These are points to be addressed again in a somewhat different context in Chapter 6.) Also relevant may be evidence that rape rates are unusually high for divorced women—twice as high as for women with the second highest risk of being raped, those in the marital status category of never-married women (U.S. Department of Justice, 1975). The possibility that a vicious cycle has been put into motion should be investigated, one involving (a) increasing demand for, and availability of, mild forms of pornography, (b) increasing demand for, and availability of, violent pornography, (c) increasing marital instability, and (d) increasing rape rates. Such a complex series of interconnected causal factors could conceivably exist even though short-term laboratory experiments have generally failed to find any major causal connections between exposure to nonviolent pornography and either behavior or attitudes indicative of increased rape probabilities. A series of studies by Court (1976, 1980, 1982, 1984) could be cited to support this line of reasoning. From studies of various countries, he has concluded that the legalization and spread of pornography has been too closely paralleled by increases in rape rates to be considered coincidental. However, studies by Kutchinski (1971, 1973, 1988) have concluded otherwise.

Finally, some learning theorists are directing attention to the issue of whether or not some males are inherently very susceptible to rape-promoting effects of pornography, whereas many other males are not (Donnerstein, Linz,

& Penrod, 1987:117). This line of investigation tends to support the views of Eysenck, Rushton, and other researchers specializing in the study of personality (see pp. 6–17) that genetic and neurological factors may eventually be found which make some males more prone than others to commit rape (to be discussed more in chapters 6 and 7).

HYPOTHESIS 4:

Exposure to Pornography That Degrades Women,
or Depicts Them as Subservient to Men, Should Increase
Male Propensities to Subscribe to Attitudes Conducive
to the Commission of Rape

Following Bandura's (1977) general theory of human aggression, most versions of the social learning theory of rape see many of the effects of pornography on rape probability mediated through changes in an individual's attitudes. Therefore, one would predict that exposure to pornography, especially violent pornography, would increase male tendencies to hold attitudes conducive to the commission of rape (Zillmann & Bryant, 1982; Zillmann, 1986). Linz, Donnerstein, and Penrod (1987a:103) argue that these effects could come about partially by relaying a false impression to male viewers about how eager most females are to engage in promiscuous sexual behavior, and how desirous they are of being made subservient to a number of male-stimulating-only sexual desires.

In terms of research, one of the crucial variables in altering the attitudes of viewers toward scenes of rape appears to be the female's eventual reaction. If she is shown persisting in her resistance to the attack and/or showing facial signs of disgust, the response of most viewers tends to be much different than when, midway through the rape, she gradually betrays expressions of sexual excitement and enjoyment (which is most often the case in filmed rape scenes). In the case of the latter so-called *positive-outcome rape scenes*, studies have found males increasing in their acceptance of rape myths (Malamuth and Check, 1981), and in their self-perceived likelihood of ever committing rape (Malamuch, 1981). A study by Linz (1985) found that exposing males to several hours of slasher films significantly reduced their sympathies toward the plight of rape victims. Similarly, exposing males to films containing sexual violence decreased the subjects' estimates of injury suffered by, and the "worthiness" of, victims in a simulated rape trial transcript (Zillmann, 1986). However, similar effects were achieved by exposing males to nonviolent R- and X-rated pornography.

Zillmann (1986; Zillmann & Bryant, 1986) has proposed that even the ✱ viewing of nonviolent pornography can have rape-promoting effects because males eventually graduate up to the forms of pornography containing bondage, sadomasochistic, and bestiality themes after extensive exposure and habituation to the nonviolent pornography. Studies supporting the hypothesis include ones by Zillmann and Bryant (1982, 1984), in which males were exposed to five hours of nonviolent pornography over a six-week period. When compared to their preexposure attitudes, these males were found to have become (a) more tolerant of bizarre and violent forms of pornography, (b) less supportive of sexual equality, and (c) more lenient in assigning punishment to offenders in a simulated rape trial. The attitudinal results were shown to have persisted for at least three weeks (the last time subjects were followed up) (Zillmann & Bryant, 1982). A study by Check (1985) found similar effects. In a later study, Zillmann and Bryant (1986) exposed subjects of both sexes to six one-hour explicit nonviolent pornographic movies. Supporting their graduating up hypothesis, they found that males (and, to a lesser degree, females), increased in their subsequent interest in watching pornography containing scenes of bondage, sadomasochism, and bestiality (especially among the nonstudent males drawn from the general population). Using considerably different research designs from those of Zillmann and Bryant, other researchers have not found support for the suggestion that attitudes become more sympathetic toward rape when males are exposed simply to nonviolent forms of pornography. Testing male subjects four weeks after exposure to one nonviolent pornography film, Malamuth and Ceniti (1986) found no increase in the subjects' self-assessed likelihood of committing rape. Similarly, after eight hours of exposure to various explicit nonviolent pornography (e.g., *Debbie Does Dallas*), Linz (1985) found no significant increase in the subjects' tolerance of rape, their views of women as sex objects, or their views toward victims and offenders in simulated rape trials. These findings seem to almost directly contradict evidence reported by Zillmann (1986), suggesting that more research is in order (Linz, Donnerstein, & Penrod, 1987b:951).

Finally, an important point to mention is that several studies have concluded that the apparent rape-promoting attitudinal effects of exposing males to both violent and nonviolent pornography appear to be fairly easily ameliorated by twenty-minute debriefing sessions in which the fictitious and misleading nature of the films are clearly identified to the subjects (reviewed by Linz, Donnerstein, Bross, & Chapin, 1986).

GENERAL ASSESSMENT OF SUPPORT FOR HYPOTHESES DERIVED FROM THE SOCIAL LEARNING THEORY

Overall, while more research is needed regarding the social learning theory of rape, the evidence so far has been fairly supportive of most major elements of the theory. In particular, its predictions that attitudes supportive of male propensities to rape, and to behave aggressively toward women (at least in nonsexual contexts), will be increased by exposing males to violent forms of pornography is supported by most of the available evidence. Nevertheless, the theory does not account for why some males appear to be much more attracted to pornography, especially violent pornography, than other males, or why many males who are exposed to violent pornography do not appear inclined to commit rape, or even to adopt attitudes supportive of their doing so.

One persistent, but understandable, shortcoming of the social learning theory of rape is reflected by differences of opinion among leading proponents of the theory concerning the nature of the pornographic stimuli required to increase a male viewer's probability of committing rape. Whereas some have argued that it is primarily the violent elements in pornography—and even in R-rated depictions of aggressive sexuality—that promote violence toward rape (Donnerstein, Linz, & Penrod, 1987a:107; Attorney General's Commission, 1986:329), others have contended that even nonviolent pornography has rape-promoting effects (at least indirectly by serving as a point of entry to violent pornography) (e.g., Zillmann, 1986). Given that rape, per se, cannot really be used as a dependent measure in laboratory experiments, these differences may be especially difficult to resolve.

5

THE EVOLUTIONARY THEORY: HYPOTHESES AND EVIDENCE

The following hypotheses are among those that may be derived from the evolutionary theory of rape.

HYPOTHESIS 1:

Tendencies to Rape Must Be Under Some Degree of Genetic Influence

That there must be some degree of genetic control over all traits that could have possibly evolved by natural selection is a fundamental assumption in modern evolutionary theory (Daly & Wilson, 1983:341; Snowdon, 1983:73; Hinde, 1986:15). Thus, in order for natural selection to have played a role in rape etiology, the neurological foundations for such behavior would have to have some genetic underpinnings, although these underpinnings could be quite indirect. In other words, while none of the proponents of an evolutionary theory of rape have proposed that there are simply genes that dictate that a male will or will not commit rape, all of them have assumed that genes must play a contributing role, and that the natural selection pressure for rape-promoting genes in many species could be substantial (see Thiessen, 1986:29).

If there are no specific genes for rape, how could genes still have an influence on rape probability? And, if genes are involved, how could their contribution ever be detected? Regarding the first question, it can be safely assumed that every individual human has a uniquely functioning brain, and that this uniqueness, while influenced by the environment, is partially the result of innumerable unique combinations of genes (except in the case of identical twins) (Ellis, 1982a:44). Large numbers of genes also serve to influence the functioning of endocrine glands, which are vital for regulating the synthesis and release of several important hormones known to influence brain functioning, especially with reference to sexual behavior (to be discussed in more detail in Chapter 6).

Regarding the question of how to detect the influence of genes on rape, the most common research design used to determine whether or not genetic factors contribute to variations in human behavior patterns is called an *adoption study*. The most common type of adoption study requires that fairly large numbers of individuals with a particular behavior pattern be identified—people who were adopted by a nonrelative soon after the adoptees' birth. Once the adoptees to be studied have been identified, the researcher attempts to determine how many of their rearing parents (either one or both) have the same (or similar) behavior patterns, compared to the adoptees' genetic parents. When higher proportions of the genetic parents exhibit the behavior pattern than do the rearing parents, genetic contributions to the pattern are almost certainly involved. So far, the closest to an adoption study of rape that has been conducted are adoption studies of criminality in general. Such studies have repeatedly concluded that genetic factors are playing a significant role, although certainly not to the exclusion of environmental factors (Bohman, et al., 1982; Ellis, 1982a; Rowe & Osgood, 1984; Mednick, 1985; Rowe, 1986; Cloninger & Gottesman, 1987; Mednick, Gabrielli, & Hutchings, 1987). Unfortunately, the feasibility of an adoption study of such a specific offense as rape would be much lower than for criminality in general. Considerably larger numbers of affected adoptees would have to be located to ensure that one ended up with a reliable estimate of the number of fathers who were also rapists. However, a novel type of adoption study might be especially suited for studying the possibility of genetic contributions to rape etiology. It would entail identifying women who have given birth to male children they suspect were conceived during intercourse with rapists (either date rapists or predatory rapists). Theoretically, if genetics is contributing to variations in rape, by 30 years of age or so, a greater than normal proportion of these male offspring, themselves, should have become rapists. Two comparison groups could be designated: (a) the rapist's offspring's male half-siblings, or (6) males in the general population.

Another way to at least indirectly assess the hypothesis that genetic factors contribute to rape would involve looking for examples of rape outside the human species. If such behavior, or its nonlegal equivalent (see Ellis, 1986b), could be found in nonhumans (especially in nonhumans who are closely related to humans phylogenetically), the argument that rape is genetically influenced in humans would be made more reasonable, though certainly not proven. At the very least, should examples of forced copulations outside the human species be found, it would help to exclude the involvement of linguistically mediated attitudinal variables and exposure to pornography as the sole causes of rape.

As the evolutionary theory of rape would incline one to expect, numerous examples of forced copulations (or at least attempts at such) have been reported outside the human species, and, in all instances, it was the male, not the female, who exhibited the force. While it is obvious that a judgment must be made by the observer in order to designate a copulation as having been forced or not, normally it is fairly clear that the female has either welcomed the male's sexual overtures or has at least not resisted them. In all of the following species, at least one copulation (or attempted copulation) has been witnessed in which the female was seen trying to resist the male's sexual overtures, either by trying to escape from him, or by displaying physical aggression toward him in response to his overtures.

Insects and other invertebrates (Kepner, Carter & Hess, 1933; Manning, 1967; Subramoniam, 1979; Thornhill, 1980; Cade, 1981)
Fish (Kodric-Brown, 1977; Farr, 1980)
Birds (Lorenz, 1966:211; Titman & Lowther, 1975; Barash, 1977:67; Beecher & Beecher, 1979; Gladstone, 1979:546; Mineau & Cooke, 1979, Burns, Cheng, & McKinney, 1980; Cheng, Burns, & McKinney, 1982; McKinney, Derrickson, & Mineau, 1983; Afton, 1985; Emlen & Wrege, 1986)
Nonprimate mammals (Sornson, 1974:26; Cox & LeBoeuf, 1980; Angier, 1983:81; Hogg, 1984; Ghosh, Choudhuri, & Pal, 1984)
Monkeys (Chance, 1962:108; Harlow, 1962:9; Struhsaker, 1967:287; Rowell, 1973; Goldfoot, 1977:161; Daly & Wilson, 1978:205; Ripley, 1980:378; Eaton, Modahl, & Johnson, 1981; Milton, 1985)
Gorillas (Harcourt, 1978; Nadler & Miller, 1982)
Orangutans (Fox, 1929; MacKinnon, 1974, 1979; Pitcairn, 1974:259; Coffey, 1975; Rijksen, 1975, 1978; Galdikas, 1979, 1985a, 1985b; Nadler, 1982; Maple, Zucker & Dennon, 1979; Maple, 1980; Galdikas, 1981; Konner, 1982:189; Mitani, 1985; Schurmann & Van Hooff, 1986)
Chimpanzees (Pitcairn, 1974:259; Goodall, et al., 1979:49; Nishida, 1979; Fox, 1980:91; Tutin & McGinnis, 1981; de Waal, 1982:175; Nadler, 1988:156)

This list of species in which forced copulations (or at least attempted forced copulations) have been observed does not mean that force is *typically* employed in these species. In all but one of the species identified, forced copulations appear to be much less common than voluntary copulations. Only among orangutans are a substantial proportion (possibly even most) males prone to copulate in the face of obvious resistance by the female for at least a portion of the males' lives. According to several accounts, adolescent and young adult male orangutans are more likely to try to copulate while the female is actively resisting than they are prone to engage in mutually consenting sex; but, for older males, females generally show few signs of resistance to male sexual overtures (Quinsey, 1984:87; Galdikas, 1985b; Jolly, 1985:277; Mitani, 1985; Crawford & Galdikas, 1986; Smuts, 1987:391).

While these observations of forced sex by males in many species besides humans constitutes support for the evolutionary hypothesis that some genetic factors underlie human propensities to rape (Theissen, 1986:11), it is, of course, only indirect evidence.

In addition, it may be relevant to note that genetic factors appear to influence the sex drive in several animal species (Hafez & Schein, 1962; Fraser, 1974), including humans (Eysenck, 1976; Martin, Eaves & Eysenck, 1977; Barash, 1979:26). Assuming that rape is at least partially sexually motivated (see pp. 22–23), this evidence would also support the view that genetic factors underlie some of the variation in human male tendencies to commit rape.

Overall, evidence is contrary to Persell's (1984:588) recent assertion that rape is a uniquely human phenomenon. Forceful attempts to copulate, while not the norm in any species (except among young postpubertal orangutans), has been observed in many species, with males invariably being the main perpetrator. None of this proves that some genetic factors contribute to male propensities to rape among humans, but it does make the hypothesis more credible, especially when considered in conjunction with the evidence that criminal behavior in general appears to be influenced by genetic factors.

HYPOTHESIS 2:

Forced Copulations Should Impregnate Victims, at Least Enough to Offset Whatever Risks Rapists Have of Being Punished for Their Offenses

A fundamental premise of the evolutionary theory of rape is that, in order for rape to have evolved by natural selection, there must be a significant probability that the assailant will impregnate the victim. Proponents and critics alike agree that if this probability is insignificant, and has been so historically, rape could not have evolved by natural selection (Harding, 1985; Thiessen, 1986).

Unfortunately, the risk of pregnancy from rape is difficult to assess (Theissen, 1986:28). This is in part because most rapes are not officially reported, and those that are reported are rarely followed up nine months later. In addition, rape victims often are otherwise sexually active around the time of the rape incident (Belcastro, 1982:225).

Harding (1985:51) reviewed some of the evidence regarding the risk of pregnancy from predatory rape, and concluded that risks were too low for such behavior to have evolved by natural selection. However, most other researchers who have examined this issue have concluded that, while the probabilities of pregnancy may not be as high as in the case of voluntary sexual intercourse, they are not at all insignificant (Schiff, 1972; Feldman, 1975; Goldstein, 1976; Lamborn, 1976:369; Shields & Shields, 1983; Thornhill & Thornhill, 1983:155 & 163; Thiessen, 1986:28).

One study in Denver, Colorado, estimated that 3% of rapes result in pregnancy (MacDonald, 1971:92), and a study in Washington, D.C. estimated the risk to be 2% (Hayman, Stewart, Lewis, & Grant, 1972). However, in an earlier report, these latter researchers were able to document only 1 pregnancy out of 232 incidences of rape that could be definitely attributed to the attack (Hayman, Lewis, Stewart, & Grant, 1967:500). In a study of rapes in 26 large United States cities, McDermott (1979) reported that 3% of the victims attributed a pregnancy to the attack. This latter study is especially noteworthy because (a) it was based upon victimization surveys—which pick up roughly three to four times as many rapes as are reported to police (see Chapter 1)—and, (b) the crimes reported to surveyers cover up to six months prior to the interview, long enough for pregnancies to have been detected.

Finally, Brownmiller (1975:80–84) pieced together information about wartime rapes during the 1971 Pakistani-Bengalie conflict, which brought her to estimate that as many as 25,000 pregnancies occurred to 400,000 rape victims at the hands of invading soldiers, a pregnancy rate of 6.3%. Inasmuch as most wartime rapes involve several offenders attacking a single victim (sometimes over the course of several days), the pregnancy risk would be higher than the risk from a single incident. Finally, in a study of 250 child abuse cases by Vincent DeFrancis (cited by Brownmiller, 1975:279), 60% reportedly involved forced copulation. Among these victims, 29 pregnancies were reported, a rate of 11.6%. In these cases, also, the pregnancy risks were probably unusually high because they reflect the result of multiple copulations over an extended period of time, rather than a single rape episode.

For comparative purposes, a single act of voluntary sexual intercourse (without the use of contraception) for women in their 20s has about a 2%–4% probability of resulting in pregnancy (Lader, 1966:158). Whether or not a rapist's genes can be passed on in a predatory rape at a sufficient frequency to allow the "rape-promoting" genes to increase their representation in succeeding generations would depend upon (a) how often the offenders ejaculated (a point to be returned to shortly), (b) whether or not effective contraception was being used by the victim, and (c) whether or not abortions (including "morning after" abortions) were readily available to, and used by, the victims (see Lamborn, 1976:369).

Another point to consider regarding the reproductive consequences of rape, and its possible genetic underpinnings, is how often rapists engage in voluntary sexual intercourse. If they do so at levels comparable to males in general, and then supplement their voluntary sexual intercourse with forced copulations, their reproductive success could actually be higher than for males who do not commit rape. The available evidence suggests that most rapists engage in a great deal of voluntary sexual intercourse, possibly, even more than do males in general. At least for predatory rapists who are or have been married once, both their marital intercourse frequency and their experiences with extramarital affairs seems unusually high (Le Maire, 1956; Gebhard, Gagnon, Pomeroy, & Christenson, 1965; Goldstein, 1973). Regarding acquaintance rapists (at least according to anonymous self-reports), several studies have found them to have had greater numbers of sex partners than males in the general population of comparable age (Kanin, 1967a:429; 1983, 1985; Koss, Leonard, Beezley, & Oros, 1985). Thus, even if rape per se is only occasionally successful from a reproductive standpoint, males who are prone to occasionally resort to force when all other attempts to copulate fail, may be just as successful reproductively, and possibly even more so, than males who do not rape. This disturbing possibility could be checked by asking both predatory rapists and date rapists how many pregnancies they believe (or suspect) they have caused, and compare their estimates to estimates made by males who have not committed rape.

A separate point needs to be developed in the case of acquaintance rape that may bear substantially upon the possible reproductive advantages and disadvantages of this behavior. It involves the possibility that, unlike predatory rapists, acquaintance rapists may fairly often secure long-term sexual access to their victims. To explain this possibility requires introducing the concept of *trauma-induced bonding and dependency*. Many animals who are physically traumatized in a social situation often become intensely bonded to whomever induced the trauma (Scott, 1963; Sackett, 1968:320; Walster & Bersheid, 1971; Mills & Mintz, 1972; Rajecki, Lamb, & Obmascher, 1978). This phenomenon may have evolved to help ensure that dependent infants remain proximal to their parents even if they are disciplined by them, and it has been documented in a variety of species (Rajecki, Lamb, & Obmascher, 1978). Trauma-induced bonding has recently been invoked to help explain why battered wives often do not leave their husbands, even after repeated attacks (Dutton & Painter, 1981; Painter & Dutton, 1985). A study by Wilson and Durrenberger (1982) reported results that could be interpreted as suggesting that the same phenomenon may occur in the case of many date-rape victims. Wilson and Durrenberger found that 39% of date-rape victims reported continuing to date their assailant after the assault, compared to only 12% of the females who successfully thwarted a date-rape attempt. Possibly, male aggression in a sexual context serves to intensify trauma-induced bonding by the victim, thereby providing the attacker with a sex partner far beyond the rape incident itself (Eaton, Modahl, & Johnson, 1981:161). Along similar lines, Russell (1984:162) reported that some women have been found to marry men who raped them. Thus, despite claims that the statement "rape sometimes leads to a prolonged romance" is a myth (e.g., Burt, 1980; Malamuth & Check, 1985), there is some evidence that at least rape by acquaintances may induce some long-term emotional attachment to the offender by the victim. (For a more extended discussion of so-called rape myths, see pp. 29–31.)

Regarding predatory rape, Harding (1985:49) argued that one of the main reasons such rapes very rarely result in pregnancy is that only about half of predatory rapists actually ejaculate (Anonymous, 1977; Katz & Mazur, 1979; Nass, Libby, & Fisher, 1981; Masters, Johnson, & Kolodny, 1982; Shaalan, El-Akabaoui, & El-Kott, 1983). Harding reasoned that such an observation not only supports the view that sex is not a prime motivation for rape, but that it also challenges the notion that natural selection could have favored rape. Another interpretation of the substantial ejaculatory failure of many rapists, however, would be entirely consistent with evolutionary theory. It involves hypothesizing that at least one female counterstrategy to rape has evolved, and that this strategy serves to hinder male ejaculation. In accordance with this hypothesis, studies in several species have revealed various physiological responses by females to unwanted sexual intercourse that seem to inhibit male tendency to ejaculate and/or to prevent their sperm from reaching the ovum (Benshoof & Thornhill, 1979; Thornhill, 1983:785; Johnson, 1985:644). In some species, this appears to include female tendencies to remain tense and nonresponsive during intercourse, and/or not to attain orgasm (Fox & Fox, 1967; Austin, 1975). One of the functions of female sexual responsiveness during copulation, generally, and their attainment of orgasm, specifically, appears to be to increase the chances of conception, first, by stimulating the male to ejaculate forcefully, and, second, via muscular contractions tending to draw sperm deeper into the womb (Kavanagh, 1983).

The most detailed research on possible female counterstrategies to forced sex has been with orangutans. Kavanagh (1983:189) reported that female orangutans were considerably less prone to attain orgasm when subjected to forced copulation than when they engaged in mutually motivated sex. Also supporting this view, Crawford and Galdikas (1986) reported that, similar to observations in humans, about half of all forced copulations among orangutans showed no signs of male ejaculation. Furthermore, MacKinnon (1979) reported that the rate of pregnancy in orangutans resulting from forced copulations was considerably lower than the rate of pregnancy resulting from voluntary sex (see also Kavanagh, 1983:189).

In summary, evidence is still sketchy but, contrary to the view of some critics (e.g., Baron, 1985; Harding, 1985), it is largely consistent with the view that pregnancy is a significant risk in the case of human rape, even though the probabilities are probably lower than in the case of voluntary copulations. This is despite views, reportedly prevalent in medieval times, that pregnancy was a significant indication that sex had been engaged in voluntarily (presumably because God would not permit a conception except when He had approved of the union) (Carter, 1986:170). The possibility that rape of acquaintances may serve to secure long-term sexual access is in need of additional research, but suggests that date rapes may have some insidious reproductive consequences that predatory rapes have to a considerably lower degree.

HYPOTHESIS 3:

Rape Victims Should Be Primarily
of Reproductive Age

In order for rape to have evolved by natural selection, rapists would be strongly inclined to direct their attacks toward victims of reproductive age (Thornhill, Thornhill, & Dizinno, 1986:118; Thornhill & Thornhill, 1987:284).

Evidence relevant to this hypothesis is voluminous, and in accordance with the hypothesis. Without exception, studies throughout the world have found that, while rape victims can be of any age, their ages are heavily concentrated between 13 and 35 (Hayman, Lewis, Stewart, & Grant, 1967:499; Hayman, Stewart, Lewis, & Grant, 1968:1023; Amir, 1971:52; MacDonald, 1971; Hayman, Lanza, Fuentes, & Algor, 1972; New South Wales Bureau of Crime Statistics, 1974; Chappell, Geis, Schafer, & Siegel, 1977; Hindelang & Davis, 1977:368; Queen's Bench Foundation, 1978:771; West, Roy, & Nickols, 1978; Katz & Mazur, 1979:38; McDermott, 1979:5; Shaalan, El-Akabaoui, & El-Kott, 1983:279; Russell, 1984:50; U. S. Department of Justice, 1985; Pandey, 1986:176; Koss, Gidycz, & Wisniewski, 1987:163). This age range coincides closely with the period of life when human females are more likely to bear offspring (Frisch, 1980; Bongaarts & Potter, 1983:55), as the evolutionary theory predicts.

HYPOTHESIS 4:

Rape Should Be Vigorously Resisted by Victims, Especially
When the Offender Is Someone to Whom the Females Are
Not Sexually Attracted

Given that females devote considerable time and energy to gestating offspring and males do not, natural selection has favored females who are more cautious and finicky in choosing sex partners, relative to males (Leakey & Lewin, 1978:231; Hagen, 1979; Thornhill, 1980:52, 1983:784). Evolutionists reason that females who are prone to prefer males who are likely to assist in rearing offspring will leave more offspring in subsequent generations than other females (Batten, 1982; Buss, 1987:340). The more parental care that is required to successfully rear an offspring, the more natural selection should favor female preferences for males prone to assist the female. That females have evolved such discriminatory tendencies comes from the following observations:

1. In several species, females are more likely to mate with males who have established territories (in which the couples subsequently live and rear their young) than with males who are without territories (Verner & Willson, 1966; Kummer, 1968; Orians, 1969; Watson & Moss, 1972; Pleszczynska, 1978).

2. In a number of species, females are prone to only copulate with males (especially for the first time) after food offerings have been made (a phenomenon known as *nuptial feeding* or *courtship feeding*) (Bristowe & Locket, 1926; Lack, 1940; Calder, 1967; Thornhill, 1976, 1979, 1981; Boggs & Gilbert, 1979; Gwynne, 1982; Takahata, Hasegawa, & Nishida, 1984:230; Austad & Thornhill, 1986; Sakaluk, 1986). While most of the documented instances are among insects, and male insects do not commonly make significant parental investments after their offspring have been conceived, among other species (birds and mammals), females presumably use nuptial feeding to effectively test males so as to weed out those least likely to assist in long-term offspring care.

It is worth noting that these remarkable female preferences do not appear to be socially conditioned in the species in which they are found, that is, they are largely unlearned. Both seem to help females effectively discriminate against males who are either unable or unwilling to provide for the female and the offspring she bears. Presumably, females whose brains have functioned in ways that incline them to discriminate in these ways have tended to leave more descendents in subsequent generations than females who copulate rather indiscriminantly, or who prefer males who are actually disinclined to procure territories or to display nuptial feeding tendencies.

Along these lines, some have speculated that a major reproductive function of courtship is to help suppress the usual aversive reactions animals exhibit in response to their personal space being invaded by strangers and subsequently being touched by them (Tinbergen, 1965; Morris, 1970). For this reason, rape has been classified as a male courtship disorder (along with exhibitionism, voyeurism and froutage) (Freund, in press). *Courtship disorders* are largely male behavior patterns in which certain aspects of the evolved courtship process are either exaggerated or short-circuited far beyond their reproductive utility. As to why courtship disorders would be largely a male phenomenon, it may be argued that there are far fewer reproductive disadvantages to exaggerating and short-circuiting most aspects of courtship for males than for females.

Overall, one can see how forced copulations by males, if successful, effectively circumvents any evolutionary advantages females would derive from attempting to confine their copulations only to males who are able and willing to provide for them and their offspring following insemination. In essence, according to the evolutionary theory of rape, females have come to use their sexuality as a way of attracting and retaining males who will provide for them and their offspring, and rape directly frustrates this female strategy. Thus, rape should be vigorously resisted by female victims (Gladstone, 1979:553; Thornhill & Thornhill, 1983).

In regard to humans, there is considerable evidence that most females have an extreme aversion to being raped, especially when the offenders are strangers

(Murphy, 1959; LeVine, 1977; Glazer-Schuster, 1979). One survey reported that most women feared rape more than almost any other crime, even murder (Anonymous, 1981). Also, reports from rape crisis centers have found that fairly long-term and severe emotional traumas often accompany rape victimization (Shainess, 1976; Burgess & Holmstrom, 1977; McCahill, Meyer, & Fischman, 1979). Despite this supportive evidence, many studies indicate that significant minorities of women have sexual fantasies about being raped (Hariton & Singer, 1974; Hunt, 1974; Schmidt, 1974; Broude & Green, 1976; Masters & Johnson, 1979:183; Goodchilds & Zellman, 1984:242; Price & Miller, 1984; Knafo & Jaffe, 1984:460; Price, Allensworth, & Hillman, 1985; Bozzi, 1985; Krafka, 1985; Bond & Mosher, 1986; Wilson, 1987).

To reconcile the studies supporting the hypothesis with those suggesting that many women fantasize about being raped, it should be noted that most women probably do not have rape fantasies. Women who do appear to primarily fantasize the offender as being an idealized male to whom they are strongly attracted prior to the assault, and from whom they are not concerned about being seriously injured. Thus, while possibly as many as 40% of women do seem to find pleasure in fantasizing about being forced to have sex (Loren & Weeks, 1986:33)—presumably, when injury risks are minimal and the attacker is someone to whom they are (or would be) highly attracted—evidence still supports the hypothesis that most women abhor the idea of being raped (especially by strangers), and are strongly motivated to avoid and resist rape.

Evidence of similar female disdain for unwanted sexual overtures by males have come from other primate species. This evidence includes several accounts of females responding with open-mouth threats and with vigorous chasing of males who make unwelcomed mounting attempts (Bielert, 1974; Sorenson, 1974:26; Goldfoot, Slob, Scheffler, Robinson, Wiegand, & Cords, 1975).

HYPOTHESIS 5:

Rapists (Especially Those Who Assault Strangers) Should Be Less Likely than Other Males to Attract Voluntary Sex Partners

Even though rape may constitute one of the options available to males for leaving offspring in the next generation, it appears to be a less certain method for passing genes on to future generations—and one involving considerable risk to the offender—relative to taking the time to attract and mate with voluntary sex partners (Thornhill & Thornhill, 1983:137). If so, rape should be associated with difficulty in attracting voluntary sex partners. Pertinent evidence, though fragmentary, appears to support the hypothesis. Masters and Greaves (1967) reported that significant facial deformities were three times more common among convicted rapists than among the general male population (although only slightly greater than among the general prison population among whom the rapists were found). Also, most studies have found convicted rapists exhibiting unusually poor social skills in interacting with members of the opposite sex (Barlow, Abel, Blanchard, Bristow, & Young, 1977; Clark & Lewis, 1977; Abel, Blanchard, & Becker, 1978; Groth, 1979:107; Whitman & Quinsey, 1981; for contrary evidence see Segal & Marshall, 1985:61).

Inasmuch as women in all societies tend to prefer males of high social status over those of low status (or at least males who exhibit capabilities to attain high social status) (Barash, 1977a:291; Faux & Miller, 1984; Hill, 1984)—presumably because of their disproportionate control over resources—the evolutionary theory would lead one to expect unusually high rates of rape by low-status males (Thornhill & Thornhill, 1983:150; Theissen, 1986). Consistent with this expectation, several studies have found predatory rapists to be lower in social status than males generally, based upon a variety of social status indicators (Svalastoga, 1962; Amir, 1971:71; Chappell & Singer, 1977; Clark & Lewis, 1977:196; Dietz, 1978; Rabkin, 1979; Thornhill & Thornhill, 1983:154; Segal & Marshall, 1985). However, regarding rapes occurring among dating couples, no significant tendencies have been found for rapists to be of lower social status than nonrapists (Smithyman, 1978; Alder, 1985). While this latter observation appears inconsistent with the evolutionary theory, one should note that samples in these two latter studies were derived from college student populations, wherein the variability in social status tends to be limited. Also, because date rapists tend to run considerably lower risks of punishment than predatory rapists (see Chapter 1), many of the causes of rape among persons who are dating could differ from the causes of rape committed by strangers (Glaser, 1978; Deming & Eppy, 1981; Check & Malamuth, 1985:420).

GENERAL ASSESSMENT OF SUPPORT FOR HYPOTHESES DERIVED FROM THE EVOLUTIONARY THEORY

Overall, the weight of evidence bearing upon the evolutionary theory of rape is supportive of the theory. Contrary to assertions by some of the theory's critics, there is evidence that the risks of pregnancy by rape victims are significant. The evolutionary theory accurately predict that the vast majority of rape victims are of primary reproductive age (roughly in their mid-teens to late 30s) throughout the world. While the evidence pertaining to the rate at which rapists may be passing on their genes to subsequent generations relative to other males remains fragmentary, their overall level of sexual activity with numerous sex partners may actually exceed that of males generally.

In closing, it should be noted that some critics of the evolutionary theory of rape have simply maintained that there is little support for the view that rape is anything more than a socially learned phenomenon (Hite, 1981; Sanday, 1981:5;

Schwendinger & Schwendinger, 1983:217; Baron, 1985; Harding, 1985). Besides tending to base their conclusions on very superficial reviews of the relevant evidence, these critics have depicted the evolutionary theory of rape in all-or-nothing terms. In fact, many proponents of the evolutionary theory have emphasized that, while learning, situational, and social structural factors are bound to influence rape probabilities, none of these influences preclude the involvement of evolutionary factors (see especially Gibson, Linden & Johnson, 1980:63; Thornhill & Thornhill, 1983).

In the chapter to follow, a fourth theory of rape will be presented which specifically hypothesizes the involvement of an interplay of social learning and biological variables as responsible for rape. In essence, this theory will argue that, while rape is learned behavior, for evolutionary reasons, some males are genetically (and neurological) much more disposed to acquire and to be reinforced for employing raping techniques in attempting to copulate than other males.

6

A SYNTHESIZED THEORY
OF RAPE

Up to this point, three theories of rape have been described, and their major strengths and weaknesses outlined in terms of how well hypotheses derived from each theory are supported by the available research.

The feminist theory contends that rape is largely the result of male domination in sociopolitical and economic affairs and subsequent use of sexual intimidation and exploitation by males to maintain their supremacy. The social learning theory argues that frequent exposure to attitudes supportive of rape or demeaning toward women, or the repeated pairing of erotic stimuli (e.g., pornography) with violent stimuli gradually causes many males to become callous toward women's needs and desires, and insensitive toward violence and/or to actually associate violence with sexual pleasure. Finally, the evolutionary theory holds that rape is an extreme response to natural selection pressure upon males to be more assertive than females in their efforts to copulate, particularly with numerous sex partners.

In Chapters 3 to 5, research pertaining to each theory was individually reviewed, and from this evidence, the conclusion was reached that none of the theories was clearly superior to the other two in predicting all that is currently known about rape. Instead, each theory seemed to contribute significantly to understanding rape by making empirically supported predictions that the other two theories did not make.

A major strength of the feminist theory derives from its emphasis upon a relationship existing between probabilities of rape and power/dominance relationships between the sexes. Another possible strength of the feminist theory is that it most clearly predicts that exposure to many forms of pornography, not just violent forms, will enhance tendencies for at least some men to behave aggressively toward women. (Calling this a "possible strength" is in light of controversy related to the ambiguity in empirical support for the hypothesis, as discussed in Chapter 3, Hypothesis 3 and Chapter 4, Hypothesis 3.) The feminist view that, from a motivational standpoint, rape is an essentially "pseudo-sexual act," however, appears to be considerably overdrawn, although nonsexual motives may still be significant. Also, the failure of the feminist theory to specify precisely what the effects would be of lessening status disparities between the sexes (i.e., whether it would increase or decrease male probabilities of rape) was a significant deficiency.

Social learning theory contains major strengths in predicting that various "sexist" attitudes (even those that appear to have substantial elements of truth), as well as exposure to violent pornography, would increase male tendencies to commit rape and to otherwise behave aggressively toward women. The most obvious shortcoming of social learning theory was that it failed to explain individual variations in male tendencies to be aroused by violent forms of pornography or to imitate what they had seen (see Eysenck, 1984). Also, should evidence continue to indicate that exposing at least some males to essentially all forms of pornography (not just violent forms) increases their tendencies to rape, the social learning theory would need to be considered additionally deficient.

The primary strengths of the evolutionary theory of rape were that it leads one to expect rape victims to be primarily of reproductive age, and that similar forceful attempts to copulate would be found among males in many nonhuman species. By postulating some genetic basis for rape, evolutionary theory also provided a basis for predicting that there would be individual variation in male tendencies to commit rape which are independent of exposure to pornography, sex role training, or other sociopolitical environmental variables (identified by the other two theories). Nevertheless, most evolutionary theorists have thus far failed to specify the nature of any genetic factors which might vary among males to incline them toward sexual assault. In other words, evolutionary theorists so far have concentrated upon identifying natural selection pressure which might have differentially favored the evolution of rape (the so-called *distal causes*) (Rushton, 1988), instead of specifying the actual genetic, neurochemical, and more immediate environmental circumstances (the so-called *proximate causes*) that might be involved. This point will be elaborated later in this chapter.

While all three of the theories reviewed so far are relatively new, and probably will be refined in the future to better match empirical observations, in this chapter a fourth theory will be advocated. This fourth theory contains major elements of all three of the other theories, as well as ideas drawn from the long-term interests of this writer in the influence of sex hormones on brain functioning (Ellis, 1978, 1982). Because the theory to be advocated has been explicitly designed to draw upon the strengths (and avoid the weaknesses) of the other three theories, and, at the same time, incorporate some key neurohormonal concepts, it will be called the *synthesized theory of rape* (for want of a more descriptive term).

THE SYNTHESIZED THEORY

Early in Chapter 3 the point was made that no scientific theory is simply true or false; instead, the most one can ever say for a theory is that it seems to be better than any other theory yet devised for explaining a particular phenomenon. "Better" in a scientific sense is judged primarily in terms of how well a theory predicts what is empirically observed with reference to the phenomenon targeted for explanation. The major propositions of the synthesized theory may be roughly summarized as follows: First, two drives, not one, underlie most rapes—the sex drive, and the drive to possess and control (the latter will be defined shortly). Second, the actual techniques involved in committing rape are largely learned, although not all males are equally disposed to learning the techniques involved. Third, from an evolutionary standpoint, males have been favored by natural selection for readily learning methods of procuring multiple sex partners, with many of the methods involving deception and some methods incorporating the use of force. Fourth, at the level of brain functioning, varying tendencies to rape result from exposing the brain to various high (male-typical) regimens of androgens (and other sex hormones). Each of these four propositions will be explored in some detail.

PROPOSITION 1:

Both the Sex Drive and a Drive to Possess and Control Motivate Rape

Elsewhere, evidence has been reviewed upholding the view that humans share with other animals a largely unlearned drive to possess and control (Ellis, 1985). This drive—herein called the *drive to possess and control*—may be as compelling for most animals as are the sex and hunger drives, and may be even more difficult to satiate (see Beagelhole, 1932:134; Furby, 1987). This proposal is contrary to the views of such eighteenth-century philosophers as Rousseau (1964:141) and Bentham (1931:113), both of whom asserted that ownership and property were exclusively human phenomenon and entirely contingent upon written law. The present view is that concepts such as ownership and property refer to social processes which are widespread in the animal kingdom, and that human property laws are actually written *expressions* of the drive to possess and control among humans rather than their underlying cause (Ellis, 1985).

Nonhuman animals rely upon *non*linguistic methods for proclaimed ownership over things and for recognizing the declarations of conspecifics (i.e., members of their own species) with whom they socially interact. Nonlinguistic methods include (a) caching, burying, or otherwise hoarding resources (Andersson & Krebs, 1978; Dewsbury, 1978:53; Roberts, 1979; Smith & Reichmann, 1984), (b) maintaining proximity to resources and guarding them (Kummer, 1973), and (c) using a variety of techniques known as *marking* (Lumia, Westervelt, & Reider, 1975:1091; Rasmussen & Rasmussen, 1979:443; Jolly, 1985:142). The objects toward which the drive to possess and control is directed include such obvious resources as food, water, shelter, and territory (Hinde, 1956; Klopfer, 1969; Dewsbury, 1978:53), as well as conspecifics such as offspring and sex partners (Phillips, Cox, Kakolewski, & Valentstein, 1969; Richard & Schulman, 1982; Wilson & Daly, 1985:60; Belk, 1988:51). Attempts to possess and control sex partners as property have been found in many species (Maslow, 1940; Furby, 1978; Sachser & Hendrichs, 1982). For example, male rats who have been allowed to copulate and cohabitate with a female for an extended period will much more vigorously resist territorial intrusion by an alien male rat than will male rats simply allowed to occupy an identical territory for the same period of time containing no female (Albert, Walsh, Gozalka, Siemens, & Lovie, 1986; Albert, Dyson, & Walsh, 1987). Likewise, male mockingbirds with female mates were observed chasing off male intruders from their territories more regularly than males who had not yet acquired a mate (Lewin, 1987:1522). Among primates, attempts to possess and control sex partners are especially well documented in baboons (Chance, 1962:108; Kummer, 1967:66; 1968:36; Zuckerman, 1981:418; Smuts, 1987:398), and in chimpanzees (Tutin, 1979; McGinnis, 1979:436; Tutin & McGuinnis, 1981). The main differences between "conspecific possessions" and other forms of possessions are that "ownership" in the former sense tends to be more tentative and reciprocal in nature, rather than long-term and one-sided (Sigg & Falett, 1985).

In humans, evidence is substantial that males and females are often extremely possessive toward one another as far as mutual control over sexual behavior is concerned (i.e., Spiro, 1977:151; Paterson, 1979; Dutton & Painter, 1981:145; Collins, 1982:119; Hirschon, 1984; Eibl-Eibesfeldt, 1987:24; Stets & Pirog-Good, 1987:245). Collins (1975:234, 1982:121) called the results of such behavior *erotic* or *sexual property*, meaning more or less exclusive access to the sexual behavior of another human being (see also La-Free, 1982:325).

Even though Collins implied that only humans attempt to establish and retain sexual property, the proposal here is that such attempts are actually found in many, if not most, nonhuman species. If so, what is called *sexual behavior* (both in humans and in many other species) is motivated not simply by the sex drive, but also by a second drive—the drive to possess and control. The first drive essentially gives rise to copulation and foreplay, and the second drive is primarily responsible for the bonding aspects of relationships between members of the opposite sex. Viewing sexual behavior as motivated by two drives instead of one is similar to Maslow's (1935a, 1935b, 1940; Maslow & Flanzbaum, 1936) two-drive theory of sexuality, except that he called the second drive the *dominance drive*. His description of the dominance drive, in fact, is very much in accordance with the idea that one sex attempts to retain more or less exclusive sexual access to a member of the opposite sex. Presumably, the drive to possess and control sexual property is especially strong during early stages of courtship, when the permanence of all property arrangements between members of the opposite sex is especially tenuous. Another indication of how closely interconnected these two drives are comes from studies of female preferences for males with established territories and/or tendencies to nuptial feed the female before attempting to copulate with her. As mentioned earlier (Chapter 5, p. 51), in many species, males who are unable to lure a female into an established territory or who have no inclination to present the female with at least a token morsel of food before mounting her are often avoided by females even when they are sexually receptive. Presumably, female tendencies to discriminate in this way have been favored by natural selection as a means of effectively preventing them from mating with males who are disinclined to share their resources after offspring have been conceived. (Human tendencies to kiss with deep tongue penetration during courtship might be a vestige of this primitive nuptial feeding courtship ritual.)

Currently, it would be impossible to estimate how much each of these two drives contribute to sexual behavior with any precision, either generally, or specifically in the case of most rapes. The difficulty can be understood in part by noting that the neurological structures most involved in regulating these two drives both appear to reside in and around a relatively small, but complex, subcortical structure of the brain, called the *hypothalamus* (MacLean, 1977:316; Panksepp, 1982:413; Hart & Leedy, 1985; Robinson, Fox, & Sidman, 1985:381; Albert, Dyson, & Walsh, 1987).

The drive to possess and control both offspring and sex partners is likely to be largely responsible for such emotions as love and jealousy, thus helping to explain why human attempts to possess and control children are closely associated with feelings of love toward them (Davis, 1936). Regarding sex partners, too, the close connection between possession and love seems betrayed in such utterances as "I want you" and "Tell me you're mine." It appears that the drive to possess and control is essentially as strong in one sex as in the other, although the modes of expression and tactics used to satiate the drive—and the objects (social and nonsocial) toward which the drive is directed—may be quite different (see Charlesworth & Dzur, 1987:199). These are points to be returned to later in this chapter.

Although this first theoretical proposition has similarities to elements of the feminist theory, there are three noteworthy differences. First, while the feminist theory emphasizes a desire by males as a group (or class) to maintain supremacy over females as a group (or class), this proposed view sees the motivation largely in terms of individual males desiring to possess and control individual females. Male status and authority, then, are used, not as goals in and of themselves (as feminist theorists have suggested), but as tactics to help males compete with one another to obtain and retain possession and control over specific females (Buss, 1987:340). Second, feminist theorists see male aggression toward, and attempts to dominate, females as being a uniquely human phenomenon and culturally learned. While the *techniques* males use may be largely learned (as will be discussed shortly), the present view is that both the sex drive and the drive to possess and control are widespread in the animal kingdom (Beaglehole, 1932:134), and largely controlled by primitive brain functions that are minimally susceptible to learning (especially learning mediated through language) (see Edwards & Einhorn, 1986:334). Third, whereas proponents of the feminist theory have concentrated upon male attempts to control and dominate females, the present view is that the drive to possess and control is a motivating force behind the sexual behavior of *both* sexes (Fox, 1980:144; Collins, 1982:121), even though there appear to be differences in how males and females are prone to express their drives to possess and control and in the specific tactics they use (Buss, 1987) (as will be discussed later).

Regarding rape, evidence supporting the view that the drive to possess and control is often a significant motivating force behind such behavior will be reviewed in terms of the following four arguments:

1. Rape has been historically recognized as a property offense in many societies.
2. As other male mammals sometimes do after copulating, some rapists exhibit a compulsion to urine-mark their victims.
3. Both sexes associate higher probabilities of rape to circumstances in which the male repeatedly pays for the dates that a couple has.
4. Rape sometimes traumatizes victims to such a degree that it induces a bonding response to the offender, thus reinforcing the raping behavior by helping to satiate the offender's drive to possess and control sex partners.

The development of each of these four arguments follows.

First, many of the legal precedents pertaining to rape considered it a property offense in which force was sometimes used, similar to robbery and kidnapping (Bonger, 1936:154; Smith, 1974; Porter, 1986:217). The word *rape* is derived from the Latin word *rapere*, and later the Roman word *raptus*, both meaning to seize or abduct. This root for the word *rape* is especially clear in the case of statutory rape, where violence plays no role. As to whose property rights are being violated, rape laws have never been entirely clear. In the case of statutory rape, since it is normally parents who bring charges, one may assume that they still assume control over their daughter's sexuality (or at least wish to do so) (Russell, 1982:258). In the case of most forceful rape, the proprietary control over sexuality would more often be attributed to the victim herself than in the case of statutory rape. Some feminist theorists have similarly argued that rape often reflects male attempts to usurp a woman's right to control her own sexuality, and thus may be tantamount to an offense against what Collins has called *sexual property* in which violence is essentially only tactical (e.g., Griffin, 1971; Betries, 1972; Clark & Lewis, 1977:130; Rafter & Natalizia, 1981). Schwendinger and Schwendinger (1982, 1983:79), however, have criticized this view, maintaining that rapists are not at all interested in a particular female's sexuality, but only the maintenance of sociopolitical power and domination over women generally.

A second line of evidence supporting the view that the drive to possess and control partially motivates rape comes from evidence that 3%–4% of rapists attempt to urinate on their victims (or the victim's clothing) following the rape (Homstrom & Burgess, 1980). Working from a feminist perspective, Homstrom and Burgess interpreted this as evidence of the hostility and contempt that rapists feel toward women. While this interpretation cannot be dismissed out of hand, urination has rarely, if ever, been considered an expression of hostility and contempt; instead, spitting and regurgitation have been (Rozin & Fallon, 1987). Urination *is*, however, commonly used in a number of species in marking, not only with respect to inanimate objects (Wickler, 1969; Thiessen, Owen & Lindzey, 1971; Farr, Andrews & Kline, 1978), but also sometimes in the case of conspecifics (Taylor, Haller & Barko, 1983; Taylor, Griffin & Rupich, 1988).

Even though it may seem incredible to contend that human rapists are exhibiting a primitive marking response toward their victim, the following four arguments are offered to support this view:

1. Marking is a behavior pattern much more common among males than females in virtually every species ever studied (e.g., Jolly, 1966; Maruniak, Owen, Bronson, Desjardins, 1975; Kleiman & Mack, 1980; French & Cleveland, 1984). Among males in which it is found, conspecific marking tendencies are postively correlated with aggressiveness tendencies (Taylor et al., 1988).
2. The neurological control of both the sex drive and the drive to possess and control appear to be in and around the hypothalamus. A sexual orgasm is

essentially a seizure localized to the hypothalamic region of the brain (Kinsey, Pomeroy, Martin, & Gebhard, 1953:631; Masovich & Tallaferro, 1954; Currier, Little, Suess, & Andy, 1971; Heath, 1972; also see Meo, Bilo & Straiano, 1985). During the refractory period, some fairly bizarre and primitive reflexes under hypothalamic-limbic control may sometimes be discharged, including ones associated with the drive to possess and control.

3. In a number of nonhuman primates, males display an erect (or semierect) penis while asserting dominance over a conspecific, as well as during courtship (Ploog, 1967; Jones & Frei, 1979). Under both conditions, these displays are sometimes followed by excreting small quantities of urine or sperm (Petter, 1962:280; Ploog, 1971:79; Zillmann, 1984:33).

4. In at least two other primate species—a species of lemur (Petter, 1965; Jolly, 1966) and the woolly monkey (Milton, 1985b)—males have been observed urinating on sex partners, usually soon after copulating with them. Urinating on sex partners has not been directly linked to forced copulations in either of these species, but the woolly monkey is the only species of primate other than humans in which forced copulations by more than one male at a time (*gang rape*) has been observed (Milton, 1985a:55). While numbers were inadequate for their making reliable comparisons, data compiled by Holmstrom and Burgess (1980:431) did indicate that the practice of urinating on victims was more common for gang rapes than for rapes committed by lone offenders. Especially when other males are in the vicinity, and the priority of access to a female is not clear, marking tendencies may be especially likely to be reflexively discharged during and after orgasm in the form of what has been called a *fixed action pattern* (meaning a complex series of largely unlearned behavior patterns that, once begun, tend to continue in a specific order until completed) (Gould, 1982:37).

A third line of evidence that rape is often manifesting both a drive to possess and control and the sex drive (rather than *simply* the sex drive) comes from a study in which both male and female subjects predicted a greater likelihood of rape occurring in hypothetical scenarios if the male paid for the date than if a dating couple shared expenses (Muehlenhard, Friedman, & Thomas, 1985). While feminist theorists might explain this observation in terms of dominance and power relationships between the sexes, the synthesized theory would account for it in terms of most people sensing that an inherent connection exists (albeit not necessarily causal in nature) between the extent of a male's resource offerings during courtship and female's willingness to exclusively copulate with him (at least eventually) (see Hite, 1981:477; Russell, 1982:256).

The fourth line of evidence that rape emanates partially from the drive to possess and control was alluded to in Chapter 5 (Hypothesis 2) during a discussion of what is known as *trauma-induced bonding*. Assuming that the drive to possess and control is motivating rape to a substantial degree, and that victims sometimes respond by forming an emotional attachment to the offender (much as children sometimes do to an abusive parent), the offender's actions could, in fact, be reinforced by helping to satiate his drive to possess and control. In terms of humans, the main research bearing directly on this point comes from finding that female date-rape victims were more likely to continue dating their assailants than were victims of unsuccessful rape attempts (Wilson & Durrenberger, 1982), and that significant numbers of rape victims actually even marry their assailants (Russell, 1982:246). Outside the human species, a study of forced copulations among orangutans reached a similar conclusion. Specifically, Rijksen (1978) asserted that the female victims often seemed to become emotionally dependent upon the male attacker after a sexual assault (discussed by Nadler, Herndon, & Wallis, 1986:371). Various investigations have suggested how trauma-induced bonding may work at the neurochemical level. First, it is relevant to note that subjecting males to mild shock, and especially to a warning sign that has been frequently associated (paired) with impending shock, in the presence of an estrogen-primed female typically enhanced sexual activity (relative to the mere presence of an estrogen-primed female) (Barfield & Sachs, 1968; Crowley, Popolow, & Ward, 1973). While studies of female rats under similar conditions are unavailable, they would likely show similar effects. This is because mild to moderate pain, and/or threat of pain—by way of its inducing a mild fear response—typically enhances sexual arousal (at least when experienced in the vicinity of an appropriate conspecific of the opposite sex) (Zillmann, 1986). For example, an experiment by Hoon, Wincze, and Hoon (1977) among women found that emotional distress (induced by viewing a graphic depiction of a fatal automobile accident) facilitated capillary engorgement in the vagina during subsequent viewing of erotic films beyond mere exposure to the films; such engorgement is clearly indicative of sexual arousal (Masters & Johnson, 1966).

More importantly, from the standpoint of long-term bonding (rather than short-term sexual excitement), studies with humans have indicated that both males and females tend to experience heightened attraction to members of the opposite sex when frightened shortly before they initially meet (Walster & Berscheid, 1971; Dutton & Aron, 1974; Dienstbier, 1979), although at least one study failed to replicate this observation (Kenrick, Cialdini, & Linder, 1979).

As to the relevant neurochemistry, some evidence points toward phenylethylamine (PEA) as a neurotransmitter whose elevated levels may be crucial for engendering intense feelings of attachment and commitment to conspecifics (see Adler & Carey, 1980). PEA, sometimes regarded as an "endogenous amphetamine," has been found to trigger or sustain a highly pleasurable level of alertness and excitement (Sabelli, Fawcett, Gusovsky, Javaid, Edwards, & Jeffriess, 1983). Hypothetically, any social stimuli in the vicinity of an individual whose PEA levels suddenly rise might become paired with the elevated PEA "rush." Another possible neurochemical pathway for trauma-induced bonding effects of rape involves opioids (or endorphins), natural opiates that are released sometimes in response to stress (Amir, Brown, & Amit, 1980; Kulkarni, 1980). While the effects are complex, small increases in the level of opioids in the brain appear to be associated with subjective feelings of social attachment and bonding (Panksep, Siviy, & Normansell, 1985).

Should all of these admittedly fragmentary lines of investigation be correct and linked together as herein argued, the following crucial events could sometimes occur to induce a bonding response by a rape victim to her attacker:

1. Motivated by both a sex drive and a drive to possess and control, many males may come to experiment occasionally with various forceful tactics in their attempts to procure and regain access to sex partners.
2. Aggressive tactics may sometimes be more successful than nonaggressive tactics if they produce a mild or moderate level of anxiety in the female victim, provided they stimulate various parasympathetic neuronal pathways which engorge and sensitize the vaginal wall.
3. Also triggered by mild to moderate stress could be the release of PEA and other neurochemicals associated with pleasurable sensations (e.g., endorphins) which serve to induce and/or reinforce a bonding/dependency response to a rapist by the victim.

Theoretically, this bonding phenomenon would be largely confined to date rape, first, because the level of fear experienced by most predatory rape victims would exceed moderate levels, and, second, because the chances of bonding to a stranger would be less than to someone with whom some familiarity and affection had already been established.

In summary, while it is possible that the drive to possess and control is more pronounced in humans than in other species (Eibl-Eibesfeldt, 1987:24), nonetheless, the drive appears to be widespread among mammals. Presumably this drive evolved and has attained such prevalence because animals with it have a reproductive advantage over those who lack it, especially in environments where competition over resources is keen (Buss, 1984:1143). This is not to say that the most intense levels of the drive to possess and control have been favored by natural selection (any more than the most intense levels of the sex or hunger drives have been naturally selected), but only to assert that at least moderately high levels are favored over low to nonexistent levels. As far as conspecifics are concerned, one can understand why, from an evolutionary standpoint, offspring and sex partners are major targets of the drive to possess and control. Here, it is proposed that forceful copulatory tactics sometimes reinforce the offender, not only in terms of intermittent sexual gratification, but also in terms of occasionally helping to satiate the drive to possess and control as it pertains to sex partners. More on the learning and reinforcement of forceful copulatory tactics will be presented in the second proposition.

PROPOSITION 2:

Most of the Behavior Surrounding the Commission of Rape Is Learned Experientially Through Operant Conditioning, Rather than as a Result of Modeling or Changes in Attitudes

While the motivations for rape appear to be essentially derived from the combined effect of two largely unlearned drives, the behavior surrounding the commission of rape—herein called *raping techniques*—are hypothesized to be largely learned. Even though it would be impossible to identify all of the ways raping techniques are learned, the present theory assumes that both experiential and ideational factors are involved, although the former are the most important and fundamental.

Experiential learning of raping techniques comes about from actually attempting rape (or various preludes to rape) and subsequently refining those attempts based upon victim responses. According to operant conditioning principles (Skinner, 1953), in order for any experiential learning to become a sustained part of the behavioral repertoire of an individual (assuming a motivational basis for it), the behavior must be at least intermittently reinforced. Reinforcement for initiating and refining raping techniques should be based primarily on the two main drives underlying sexual behavior, that is, either the pleasure derived from copulating, or the satisfaction gained from possessing and controlling access to the sexuality of members of the opposite sex (albeit usually in a reciprocal fashion). Thus, at fairly proximate levels of analysis (see Rushton, 1988), the present theory assumes that rape is prevalent in human societies to the degree that it is (or at least has been) effective in satiating one or both of the drives which underlie sexual behavior.

Ideational learning of raping techniques primarily consists of considering and mentally rehearsing one or more raping scenarios. The inspiration for such rehearsals may come about in a variety of ways, such as from watching depictions of forced sex in movies or other mass media, or reading about it in books, or by learning attitudes and beliefs favorable to rape from associates. Ideational learning of raping techniques, therefore, may result from exposure to depictions, attitudes, and beliefs favorable to rape, regardless of their truth or falsehood. In order for ideational variables to lead to persistent raping behavior, however, it is assumed that experiential reinforcement (as previously described) must be involved.

Because of its emphasis upon experiential learning (mainly via operant conditioning), the present theory considers most of the aggression surrounding the commission of rape as primarily tactical, rather than a goal in itself. If so, raping techniques (like the use of aggression generally) should be fairly quickly abandoned unless their use at least occasionally satiates one or both of the drives hypothesized to motivate rape (see Rowe & Herstand, 1986:116). While qualifications to this proposition will be identified, overall it implies that the prevalence of rape is, to a substantial degree, a function of the effectiveness of raping techniques in securing copulatory access and/or in gaining a long-term sex partner. Purely ideational factors (e.g., acquiring sexist attitudes or mentally rehearsing and then committing rape after viewing rape depictions) would only play a minor role, and would be largely confined to males who have had little interactive sexual experience.

Most of the evidence that aggressive behavior and dominating behavior are essentially tactical, rather than the goals of most rapists, was reviewed in Chapter 3 (pp. 22–23). However, additional evidence comes from studies of violence among dating or married couples which is not of a raping nature. Large proportions of both sexes self-report the use of violence during courtship (Sigelman, Berry, & Wiles, 1984; Bogal-Albritten & Albritten, 1985). The most common set of circumstances surrounding such violence is concern over the partner sexually interacting with someone else, or being interested in doing so (Stets & Pirog-Good, 1987). Similarly, among married (and cohabitating) couples, the most common cause of violence throughout the world involves suspicion of infidelity (Bolton & Bolton, 1975; Daly, Wilson, & Wehorst, 1982; Wilson & Daly, 1985). The present view is that these are additional examples of violence being used, not as an end in itself, but as a tactic for helping to maintain possession and control over a desired sex partner. According to the synthesized theory of rape, most instances of courtship and marital violence, like most rapes, are largely tactical (or instrumental) manifestations of the drive to possess and control sexual property.

As to why males would use aggressive tactics in attempting to copulate and prevent other males from doing so to a greater degree than females would, the theory assumes that (a) the male sex drive is stronger than the female sex drive, and (b) the tendency for males to direct their drive to possess and control specifically toward multiple sex partners is greater than for females. Overall, even though males appear to be much more inclined than females to orient their drive toward the possession and control of multiple sex partners rather than just one (Betzig, 1982), the drive to possess and control appears quite strong in both sexes, and aggression is fairly often used by both males and females to help prevent other members of their sex from sexual access to their sex partners (Straus, Gelles, & Steinmetz, 1980; Stets & Pirog-Good, 1987).

While ideational learning is seen as secondary to experiential learning, the role of ideational learning in rape etiology may have increased in recent years in countries where explicit depictions of sexuality have become widely disseminated. The main ways exposure to pornography may contribute to rape, according to the present theoretical scheme, are as follows:

1. Some males who come to use forceful tactics in attempting to copulate and/ or secure a bonding commitment from a sex partner may have never thought of trying various aggressive tactics (or never thought that such tactics might work) if it were not for having seen them pornographically portrayed.
2. Given the speed with which most individuals in pornography proceed to copulate with minimal foreplay, males exposed to pornography may come to significantly underestimate the time and commitment needed to obtain voluntary copulatory access from most females. Theoretically, this would be more true of males who are least, rather than most, sexually experienced.
3. Because pornography fairly often involves female models who are above average in physical attractiveness, exposure to pornography could contribute to rape by diminishing the perceived "value" of females with which most males seek to copulate. Lowered valuation of a courtship partner may reduce the amount of time the male is willing to commit to courting her before seriously attempting to copulate. Consistent with this view, a recent study found that exposure to nude photographs appearing in a popular men's magazine caused members of both sexes to at least temporarily feel less love for the partners they were dating than they had felt before the exposure (Anonymous, 1983). Similarly, Zillmann and Bryant (1986:18 [1982]) reported that exposure to pornography reduced the male's expressed satisfaction with their present girlfriend's physical attractiveness (see also Kenrick, Gutierres, & Goldberg, in press). Such a notion that viewing much of the currently available pornography serves to lower the perceived value of sex partners might also help explain why women of lower social status appear to be more frequently victimized by rape than women of higher social status (Kanin, 1969).

As far as attitudes and beliefs favorable to rape are concerned, they too could possibly increase the probability of rape, but largely only to the degree that they contain at least an element of truth. For example, men who believe that women sometimes say "No" when they really mean "Yes" could be reinforced with more sexual experiences that males who assume that "No" means simply that. As discussed in Chapter 3 (pp. 29–30), this is because significant numbers of women who are willing to have sexual intercourse do report initially saying "No" so as not to appear overly promiscuous to their dates. Males who continued to "push" these females with at least mild physical force when confronted with their initial refusal would be intermittently reinforced (in operant conditioning terms) with sexual intercourse. Given the power of copulation as a primary reinforcer, a single success could serve to sustain the use of such tactics on numerous sucessive occasions. Similarly, given that some women derive pleasure from being forced to copulate—albeit rarely by strangers to whom they have no prior attraction (see p. 52)—males who believe that there are occasions when some women want to be forced into copulating would be occasionally reinforced for exhibiting raping behavior. Intermittently reinforced behavior appears to be especially resistant to extinction, at least among humans (Spence, 1966:456), and, presumably, this would be even more true of rape if no significant punishment was made contingent upon the behavior.

This second proposition borrows from ideas put forth by social learning theorists, although with two significant differences. First, whereas social learning theorists have concentrated on the role of imitation and attitudinal learning as causes of rape, the synthesized theory emphasizes the role of experiential learning, which would largely occur while interacting with members of the opposite sex and would require at least occasional reinforcement. The synthesized theory sees attitudinal and modeling factors as playing, at most, only a secondary role in rape etiology, and then only in the case of young or relatively inexperienced males who are still looking for effective ways of satiating their sex drive and their drives to possess and control sex partners. Second, whereas a number of learning theorists have assumed that pro-rape attitudes and beliefs have essentially no basis in truth (i.e., are "myths"), the present theory assumes that many pro-rape attitudes and beliefs contain at least an element of truth.

PROPOSITION 3:

As a Result of Natural Selection, Males Have Stronger
Sex Drives Than Females, and Are More Likely to Orient
Their Drives to Possess and Control Toward Multiple Sex
Partners, While Females Have Evolved Tendencies
to Resist Copulating Until Courting Males Exhibit
Evidence of Having Made Long-Term Commitments
to the Female and Any Offspring She May Bear

In accordance with the evolutionary theory, the synthesized theory of rape considers sex differences in tendencies to rape and to resist being raped both favored by natural selection. These sex differences can be understood as emanating from the fact that males need only copulate to the point of ejaculating in order to reproduce, whereas a female must sustain an extended gestation period to reproduce. This much lower *parental investment* (Trivers, 1972) that males make in each offspring relative to females, plus the fact that males have greater difficulty identifying their offspring with certainty than females, means that somewhat different forms of sexual behavior should have evolved in males and females (Symons, 1979; Betzig, 1982). In particular, males who were able to copulate with multiple sex partners would be favored much more than females who did so, whereas females who limited their mating activities to partners who exhibit an ability and an inclination to provision for them and any offspring they bore would be favored more than females who did not do so.

Probably more than any other species, human reproduction is dependent upon long-term parental care being lavished upon a small number of offspring (Jolly, 1985; Rushton, 1985a). For this reason, rape among humans places females at a substantial reproductive disadvantage to the degree they are unable to judiciously choose their sex partners, and, by so doing, avoid mating with males least willing or able to make long-term commitments to provide for them and their offspring. As discussed earlier (Chapter 5, Hypothesis 4), this reasoning leads one to predict that even if no physical injury is involved, rape should be dealt with as a very serious offense by both sexes, especially when close relatives (or oneself) are victimized (Hagen, 1979:98; Evans & Scott, 1984). On average, however, one would expect females to treat rape as an even more serious offense than males (since they have the most to lose in many ways as well as reproductively by being victimized), and since their approach to reproduction is more jeopardized by rape than is the average male approach. For evidence supporting these two deductions, see Tieger (1981) and Seligman, Brockman, and Kouback (1977), respectively.

The neo-Darwinian concept of *r/K selection* (MacArthur & Wilson, 1967) has been recently proposed to help explain sex differences in overall approaches to reproduction (Masters, 1983; Ellis, 1987b), and the concept may be especially useful for understanding sex differences surrounding behavioral tendencies to display sexual aggression. Basically, an r-selected approach to reproduction emphasizes producing large numbers of offspring with little parental effort made to assure survival of any one of the offspring after the offspring have been discharged from what tends to be a short gestation period. At the other end of the continuum, K-selection emphasizes producing very few offspring, while committing great time and energy to gestation and offspring nurturing and care, thus maximizing each offspring's reproductive viability. Besides their long-term parental investment being low, r-selected animals are thought to gravitate toward a high fertility rate, short gestation periods, large litter or clutch sizes, low birth weight, high infant mortality, rapid development to sexual functioning, greater copulatory frequency outside bonded relationships, less stable bonding with sex partners, and a shorter life expectancy, compared to K-selected animals (Daly & Wilson, 1983; Rushton, 1985a; Ellis, 1987b).

Considerable evidence has been shown to support the hypothesis that male mammals are more r-selected than females of the same species (reviewed by Ellis, in press-b). With only a few exceptions in both human and nonhuman species, the numbers of males conceived was higher than the number of females. Also, male gestation lengths tended to be shorter and male fetuses tended to have higher rates of miscarriage than female fetuses. Furthermore, males appeared to have earlier onset of sexual behavior, a stronger sex drive, and a shorter life expectancy than females in virtually all species (and, in humans, in virtually all societies).

To explain why males would be more r-selected than females, one may simply say that males have been favored by natural selection to a greater degree than females for displaying r-selected traits. Furthermore, while r-selected organisms are probably no more competitive than K-selected organisms, they tend to be more competitive than K-selected organisms in direct (scrambling) ways (Gould, 1982:369). Rape may be considered an extremely direct way of competing over sexual access, one of the most important resources of all from a reproductive standpoint.

If these lines of evolutionary reasoning are correct, one would expect to find rapists (especially predatory rapists) exhibiting r-selected characteristics to an even greater degree than males in general. While research necessary to test this hypothesis remains to be conducted, considerable evidence supports the view that males with serious criminal histories in general have r-selected characteristics to a greater degree than males in the general population (Ellis, 1987b).

PROPOSITION 4:

Due to Varying Degrees and Types of Exposure of Their Brains to Androgens, Males Vary Considerably in Both Their Motivations to Rape and Their Tendencies to Learn and Use Raping Techniques

So far, the synthesized theory has proposed (a) what motivates rape, (b) how techniques for committing rape are learned, and (c) what evolutionary forces are responsible for tendencies to rape and for tendencies to resist being raped. The final element in the theory focuses upon the question of *how* rape is both motivated and learned. For the answer, attention will be turned to the brain and its functioning, an area of inquiry that has received very little attention from any of the three contemporary theories of rape.

The basic rationale for including this fourth proposition is as follows: While the synthesized theory of rape asserts that both genetic and environmental factors are involved in rape etiology, the theory acknowledges that the only way either genetic or environmental factors can possibly alter any form of behavior is by way of their influencing brain functioning (Hilgard & Bower, 1975:549; Pearson, Teicher, Shaywitz, Cohen, Young, & Anderson, 1980:717; Fuller, 1987:166). In other words, the brain is recognized as the direct controller of all behavior (whether the behavior is largely learned or unlearned), and any effects that either genetics or the environment have upon behavior must be mediated through the brain (Ellis, 1982a:44). If so, the brains of rapists, at least during the time they are in the process of planning and committing their offenses, must be functioning in ways that are significantly different than the brains of other persons.

Even though the brain is an exceedingly complex organ, and enormous gaps remain in our knowledge of how it controls behavior, enough has been learned in recent years (Gerner, 1981) to warrant speculating about some of the neurological factors responsible for intra- and inter-individual variations in raping tendencies.

In moving toward identifying the detailed nature of brain functioning patterns that would be conducive to rape, one may recall that it was documented in Chapter 5 (pp. 45–46) that, in all species where forceful attempts to copulate have been found, virtually all of the attempts were made by males. This single fact is impossible to explain neurologically without assuming that something about the functioning of male brains across a wide spectrum of species must differ from the functioning of female brains. In other words, in many species, male brains must be more prone to opt for forceful copulatory tactics than female brains.

Before postulating the nature of the brain functioning patterns which seem to be conducive to forceful attempts to copulate, three topics need to be addressed: (a) the general nature of sex differences in brain functioning, (b) the genetic and hormonal bases for these sex differences, and (c) some of the general behavioral concomitants of sex differences in brain functioning (besides forceful attempts to copulate).

1. The General Nature of Sex Differences in Brain Functioning

Studies have shown that in all mammalian species yet studied, the brains of males and females are, on average, significantly different from one another, both structurally and functionally (reviews by Kolata, 1979; Ellis, 1982b; Durden-Smith & deSimone, 1983; Wimer & Wimer, 1985:196). According to studies of nonhuman mammals, the differences include the following:

1. Varying sizes and shapes of several brain parts (Gorski, Gordon, Shryne, & Southam, 1978; Breedlove & Arnold, 1980; Lehman, Winans, & Powers, 1980; Moore, 1985; Witelson, 1985; Hines, et al., 1987);
2. The amount of dendritic branching (Greenough, Carter, Steerman, & deVoogd, 1977; Bleier, Byne, & Siggelkow, 1982; Ayoub & Greenough, 1983; Hammer & Jacobson, 1982; Hammer, 1984; Kurz, Sengelaub, & Arnold, 1986);
3. Types of synaptic structures (Raisman & Field, 1973);
4. Rates of neuronal death during gestation (Nordeen, et al., 1985);

5. Rates of brain maturation (Razavi, 1975);
6. Various brain wave patterns (Bryden, 1979; Inglis & Lawson, 1981; Ashbrook, 1984; Geschwind & Galaburda, 1985a);
7. The amounts and locations of various neurochemicals (Broverman, Klaiber, Kobavashi, & Vogel, 1968; Robinson, Sourkes, Nies, Harris, Spector, Bartlett, & Kaye, 1977; Zuckerman, 1979:373; Vaccari, 1980; Wilson, Pearson, Hunter, Tuohy, & Payne, 1986); and,
8. The degree of asymmetry in both structure and functioning in various parts of the brain (Diamond, Dowling, & Johnson, 1981; Ross, Glick, & Meibach, 1981; Nordeen & Yahr, 1982).

The possibility that humans would be the only known exception to this rule, while still a point of contention in some social science circles (see Sayers, 1982), has been laid to rest by observations of sex differences in overall brain weight, even after adjusting for sex differences in body size (Stockard, Stockard, & Sharbrough, 1978; Michalewski, Thompson, Patterson, Bowman, & Litzelman, 1980; Mochizuki, Go, Ohkubo, Thatara, & Motomura, 1982; Theilgaard, 1984); structural differences in specific areas of the brain, both in adults and in infants (Morel, 1948; Rabl, 1958; McGlone, 1980; Baack & de LaCoste-Utamsing, 1982; de Locaste-Utamsing & Holloway, 1982; Swaab & Fliers, 1985); and numerous functioning differences (Reinisch, 1974; Ketterer & Smith, 1977; Zuckerman, 1979:376; Zuckerman, Buchsbaum, Monte, & Murphy, 1980; Martineau, Tanguay, Garreau, Roux, & Lelord, 1984; Houston & McClelland, 1985), nearly all of which resemble sex differences found in other species (Hines & Gorski, 1985).

Given (a) that male brains and female brains are substantially different, and (b) that brain functioning is the most direct controller of behavior, mediating all influences from the environment, one would be surprised to find males and females responding in the same ways to the same environmental stimuli, even when reared under identical conditions (Reinisch, Gandelman, & Spiegel, 1979:234). Before attempting to identify sex differences in brain functioning which might specifically account for variations in tendencies to rape, an outline of what is known about the causes of sex differences in brain functioning is in order.

2. Causes of Sex Differences in Brain Functioning

Nonhuman animal experiments have shown that numerous complex biochemical factors contribute to sex differences in brain functioning (Goy & McEwen, 1980). Despite their complexity, nearly all of the causes can be traced to the fact that, fairly early in gestation, males and females begin to synthesize different levels of various sex hormones, which, in turn, enter and gradually alter the functioning of the developing brain (Hines & Gorski, 1985; Ellis & Ames, 1987).

While relationships between neurohormonal factors and behavior are complex and still being elucidated (Reinisch, Gandelman & Spiegel, 1979), studies have shown that androgens (the so-called male sex hormones) are especially important in affecting behavior (Durden-Smith & deSimone, 1983). However, this does not mean that a straight forward correspondence exists between the levels of androgens in an individual's brain at a given point in time and any aspects of his or her behavior. Instead, while some exceptional species appear to have been identified (Simon, Gandelman & Gray, 1984), androgens have been shown to typically influence behavior by altering brain functioning in two distinguishable, but interdependent, developmental stages. The first, called the *organizational stage*, takes place during gestation (and, for some species, but not humans, during the first few weeks after birth) (Ehrhardt, 1978:532; Hines & Gorski, 1985:76). During this time, if androgen levels are high, the brain and other body parts will be diverted away from their "default" course— which, for mammals, is feminine (Jost, Vigior, Prepin, & Perchellet, 1973; MacLusky & Naftolin, 1981:1294; von Berswordt-Wallrabe, 1983:110)— and will be masculinized/defeminized instead. In other words, mammals are basically destined to be feminine unless a set of diversionary genetic instructions are inserted into each cell's nucleus, instructions contained on the Y chromosome (Dorus, 1980; Giannandrea, 1985). These instructions cause the fetal gonads to differentiate early into testes, and thereafter begin producing relatively large quantities of testosterone and other androgens during the organizational stage of sexual differentiation (Ellis & Ames, 1987).

Even though some of the organizational effects are apparent at birth (e.g., a penis and distended testes, instead of a vaginal opening and recessed ovaries), other effects (especially those inside the nervous system) will not be fully expressed, if at all, until puberty. Puberty marks the onset of the *activational stage* of sexual differentiation. This second stage is initiated by a surge in the production of sex hormones that will essentially continue throughout adulthood (Ellis, 1982b:173). Basically, the same hormones that were responsible for producing masculine traits perinatally are those that cause other masculine traits to be fully expressed following puberty. Outside the nervous system, these masculine traits for most species include increased musculature, height, growth of body hair, and enlarged vocal cords, all of which appear to have evolved in ways that make individuals more competent (or at least more intimidating) in directly competing for resources.

Within the nervous system, several masculinizing modifications are made which tend to complement the external masculinized features. As will be explained more in the following section, these modifications appear to include ones which incline males to be less sensitive to pain, more motivated to frequently copulate, and more committed to possessing and controlling numerous elements in the external environment.

3. Major Behavioral Manifestations of Sex Differences in Brain Functioning

In order to defend the view that male brains differ from female brains in ways that increase the male's tendencies to be assertive in attempting to copulate, some of the evidence on sex differences in behavior will be briefly reviewed. A meta-analysis recently revealed 12 behavior patterns in which nearly all available studies reported substantial sex differences in a wide variety of mammals, including humans (Ellis, 1986). Three of these behavior patterns will be mentioned at this point for two reasons. First, experiments with nonhumans have shown that these behavior patterns are influenced by androgens infiltrating the nervous system. Second, these three behavior patterns can be clearly conceived of as relevant to forceful attempts to copulate. The three behavior patterns are *assertive erotic sexual behavior, status-related aggressive behavior*, and *spacing behavior*.

1. *Assertive erotic sexual behavior* refers to courtship activities fairly directly surrounding copulation, although it only minimally includes most of the long-term bonding aspects of sexual behavior (pair bonding). Studies of over a dozen mammalian species, including several species of primates, have shown that males exhibit more forceful and persistent efforts to copulate than females (reviewed by Ellis, 1986:534).
2. *Status-related aggressive behavior* refers to aggressive behavior surrounding attempts to gain or retain ready access to food, territory, or sex partners relative to other conspecifics. It does not include predatory aggression or aggression that is essentially defensive in nature. Observations of large numbers of species, including primates, have concluded that, on average, males exhibit more status-related aggression than females (reviewed by Ellis, 1986:526), with the possible exception of hamsters and gerbils (Floody & Pfaff, 1977:443; Beatty, 1978:41), and the spotted hyena (Hopson, 1987).
3. *Spacing behavior* includes the procurement, marking, patrolling, and defending of space. The space itself may immediately surround its defender, called *personal space*, or may be a relatively fixed geographical area, called a *territory*. In studies of many species of mammals, spacing behavior—especially in territorial terms—has been found to be considerably more common in males than in females, both in nonhuman primates and in nonprimate mammals (reviewed by Ellis, 1986:529).

Laboratory experiments conducted over the years have confirmed that the main causes of the average sex differences in the display of these three behavior patterns are neurohormonal in nature. By and large, these neurohormonal causes involve the effects of varying regimens of sex hormones (especially androgens) upon brain functioning. Specifically, exposing the brains of females to high (male-typical) levels of various androgens have been shown to increase the sex drive, status-related aggression, and the drive to possess and control (at least in terms of territoriality). On the other hand, exposing the brains of males to low (female-typical) levels of various androgens tend to decrease their sex drives, their status-related aggression, and their drives to possess and control (Ellis, 1986:524–529). Overall, while none of these behavior patterns are likely to be exhibited unless they are provoked by "appropriate" environmental stimuli, the main factors responsible for average sex differences in the display of these three behavior patterns are neurohormonal in nature.

HYPOTHESIZING TWO NEUROLOGICAL CAUSES OF SEX DIFFERENCES IN PROPENSITIES TO RAPE

Having outlined the role of sex hormones in producing sex differences in brain functioning and, thereby, in assertive sexuality, status-related aggression, and territoriality, the relevance of such information to rape etiology now may be addressed. It will be argued that two areas of brain functioning are important in rape etiology: (a) hypothalamic-limbic functioning underlying the sex drive and the drive to possess and control, and (b) reticular activating processes underlying general sensitivity to the environment.

1. *Hypothalamic-limbic structures* lie deep within the interior of the mammalian brain, and are where most social emotions are fundamentally regulated, including those surrounding the sex drive (Sachs, 1978; Edwards & Einhorn, 1986) and the drives to possess and control (Yahr, 1983; 163). Studies among mammals generally (Hart & Leedy, 1985), and humans specifically (Swaab & Fliers, 1985) have shown that the hypothalamic-limbic structures are sexually dimophic. With certain parts of the hypothalamus chemically inactivated, or surgically disconnected from areas of the neocortex that primarily control most coordinated muscular movements, essentially all sexual motivation disappears (Edwards & Einhorn, 1985), and territorial marking behavior is greatly inhibited (Hart, 1974). From this, it may be inferred that the hypothalamic-limbic structures—even though they comprise less than one-tenth of the entire area of the human brain—fundamentally motivate all behavior involved in copulation (Andy, 1977; Andy, Kurimoto, Velamat, & Peeler, 1983; Lehman, Winans & Powers, 1980; Purins & Langevin, 1985) and in attempting to maintain more or less exclusive access to sex partners (and other important resources) (Chance, 1962:125; MacLean, 1985).

The role of the hypothalamic-limbic structures in rape etiology is hypothesized to involve tendencies toward (a) hypersexuality, and (b) extreme possessiveness of sex partners. *Hypersexuality* refers to tendencies to be preoccupied with engaging in sexual behavior, particularly copulation, and/or to actually engage in such behavior to an unusual degree. *Extreme possessiveness* refers to a strong inclination to impulsively seize things in close proximity, or otherwise try to quickly possess and control desired objects (including sex partners).

The synthesized theory of rape postulates that exposing the hypothalamic-limbic structures to various high (male-typical) androgen regimens increases the probability of both hypersexuality and extreme possessiveness. Given that, within male and female populations, androgen levels are quite varied from one individual to another (Bartke, Musto, Cardwell & Behrmen, 1973), and, even within individuals, varied over time (Doering, Brodie, Kraemer, Becker, & Hamburg, 1974; Doering, Kraemer, Brodie, & Hamburg, 1975; Dohler & Wuttge, 1975; Weisz & Ward, 1980), there must be an infinite number of possible androgen regimens. Many relatively slight variations in the timing of the presence of high and low androgen regimens during critical periods of neuro-organization could substantially alter subsequent behavior. The present line of reasoning leads one to expect a wide diversity of hypersexuality and extremely possessive tendencies, not only between the sexes, but within them as well. Given that the perinatal period of life is when androgen regimens have their most lasting, irreversible effects upon brain functioning (Ellis, 1982b; Ellis & Ames, 1987), it is hypothesized that at some time during the organizational stage (perhaps limited to only a few days), if androgen levels (especially testosterone and its aromatized metabolite, estradiol) are unusually high, the hypothalamic-limbic structures will be permanently organized to display hypersexuality and extreme possessiveness toward multiple sex partners following the onset of puberty. Either alone or especially together, these two behavioral tendencies are hypothesized to increase the chances of rape being committed during adolescence and adulthood.

2. *Reticular activating processes* are hypothesized to play an important role in rape etiology, not from the standpoint of motivation (as was the case for the hypothalamic-limbic structures just discussed), but primarily in terms of sensitivity to aversive feedback from victims and to the prospects of criminal sanctions for committing rape.

The reticular formation (also called the *reticular activating system*) is a diffuse bundle of neurons located primarily in the upper portion of the brain stem, but with neurons also extending into essentially all other parts of the brain (Ellingson, 1956:2; Joseph, Forrest, Fiducia, Como, & Siegel, 1981; Heilman, Bowers, & Valenstein, 1985:384). While an individual is awake, the reticular formation typically monitors all incoming stimuli. Chemoelectrical traces of stimuli that it registers as being sufficiently novel and/or intense will be transmitted to higher brain centers for interpretation and a coordinated response. However, traces that are highly routine tend to dissipate within the reticular formation itself (McCleary & Moore, 1965; Eysenck, 1977:86).

Humans (and other animals) appear to vary considerably in the degree to which their reticular formations treat incoming stimuli as novel and intense (Mehrabian, 1976; Zuckerman, 1979). Individuals with reticular formation functioning that quickly treats a class of incoming stimuli as routine and, thus, no longer requiring the attention of higher brain processes, are said to *habituate* quickly. Evidence indicates that, relative to females, males have brains that incline them to seek more intense levels of stimulation and to habituate more quickly to most types of stimuli at a given intensity. This sex difference has been documented both in humans (Spock, 1964; Kagan, 1971; Ketterer & Smith, 1977; Eisdorfer, Doerr & Follette, 1980) and in nonhumans (Rosenblum, 1974:139). Among humans, sometimes within only a few days after birth, males have been shown to be less sensitive than females to tactile stimuli (Ottolenghi, 1896; Gilbert, 1897; Di Mattei, 1901; Gullickson & Crowell, 1964; Redmond, Baulu, Murphy, Loriaux & Zeigler, 1976), to odors (Doty, Shaman, Applebaum, Giberson, Sikorski, & Rosenberg, 1984:1441), to tastes (Cain, 1981:55; Murphy, 1983;49), and to sounds (McGuinness, 1972; Shepherd-Look, 1982:417). The only sensory modality in which male sensitivity may be somewhat keener than that of females has to do with visual stimuli (McGuinness, 1980).

Some of these sex differences can be understood in terms of the concept of augmenting-reducing. To widely varying degrees, some persons tend to respond to incoming stimuli with brain wave patterns suggesting a tendency to "exaggerate" the meaningfulness of the stimuli; such persons are called *augmenters*. Others respond to incoming stimuli in ways suggesting a tendency to quickly "diminish" the meaningfulness of most of the stimuli they encounter, and they are called *reducers* (Lukas & Siegel, 1977; Zuckerman, Buchsbaum, Monte, & Murphy, 1980). Studies have shown that, for all ages, greater proportions of males are reducers, and greater proportions of females are augmenters (Buchsbaum & Pfefferbaum, 1971; Zuckerman, 1979:376; Rosenfeld & Rosenfeld, 1976b:9; Zuckerman, Buchsbaum, Monte, & Murphy, 1980). More generally, when they are compared to males, females have been shown to neurologically respond to most incoming stimuli with greater amplitude (Shagass & Schartz, 1965; Eeg-Olofson, 1971; Matousek & Peterson, 1973; Martineau, Tanguay, Garreau, Roux, and Lelord, 1984). While many biochemicals appear to be responsible for sex differences in reticular formation functioning (thus altering an individual's responsiveness to environmental stimuli), most, if not all, of these biohemicals are probably triggered by brain exposure to androgens (and their metabolites) (Zuckerman, Buchsbaum, Monte, & Murphy, 1980:203; Ellis, 1987a:508). Variations in reticular formation functioning—as revealed through more rapid habituation (and tendencies to be reducers, rather than augmenters of stimuli)—appears to help explain several pan-species sex differences in behavior, including the following:

1. tendencies for males to tolerate pain at higher intensities than females, both in humans (Galton, 1894; U.S. Public Health Service, 1970:9; Mechanic, 1975;357; Bachsbaum, 1978:98; McGrew, 1979:443), and in nonhuman mammals (Pare, 1969; Beatty & Beatty, 1970; Marks & Hobbs, 1972; Beatty & Fessler, 1976; Gandelman, 1983);
2. tendencies for males to require more trials than females to learn most avoidance conditioning tasks, both in humans (Durrett, 1962:61; Spence & Spence, 1966; Minton, Kagan, & Levine, 1971), and in nonhuman mammals (Sackett, 1974:145; Farres, 1976; Hauser & Gandelaman, 1983; Mactutus & Tilson, 1984);
3. tendencies for males to be less fearful of novel or threatening environments than females, both in humans (Hersen, 1972:38; Stern & Bender, 1974:254; Bem, 1975:59; Shaver & Freedman, 1976:29; Burke & Weir, 1978; Neufeld, 1978; Scarr, Webber, Weinberg, & Wittig, 1981:891), and in nonhuman mammals (Levine & Broadhurst, 1963; Joffe, et al., 1972; Blizard, Lippman, & Chen, 1973; Archer, 1977a, Gray, 1971, Gray & Buffery, 1971); and,
4. tendencies for males to be more prone toward sensation-seeking and risk-taking activities than females, both in humans (Zuckerman, 1974; Ridgeway & Russell, 1980; Zuckerman & Neeb, 1980; Galizio, Rosenthal, & Stein, 1983; Ball, Farnill, & Wangeman, 1984), and in nonhuman mammals—at least as inferred from higher rates of accidental injuries (Neville, 1972; Dittus, 1980:282; Galdikas, 1979:216).

Basically, it is being proposed that, due to their higher exposure to androgens, males have reticular formation functioning patterns that differ from females in ways that incline males to tolerate higher levels of noxious stimuli before being diverted from whatever activities they are motivated to pursue. Concerning rape, the noxious stimuli for offenders would presumably be of two types: (a) expressions of suffering and revulsion by victims, and (b) imposition of penalties by the victim, her relatives and friends, or the criminal justice system. According to the theory being proposed, the commission of rape is made most probable by a reticular formation that is less sensitive to environmental stimuli, especially stimuli of a social nature.

In summary, two fairly specific neurological factors—both of which appear to be affected by androgens—are hypothesized to influence an individual's tendencies to commit rape. One surrounds the functioning of the hypothalamic-limbic system, and the other involves the reticular formation. Concerning the former, the strengths of the sex drive and the drive to possess and control are affected. Regarding the reticular formation, an individual's sensitivity to aversive stimuli is altered. For individuals whose brains are exposed to high levels of androgens during the organizational phases of brain development, it is hypothesized that they tend to have both strong sex drives and drives to possess and control multiple sex partners, as well as low sensitivities to the aversive consequences of their actions. Low sensitivity to aversive consequences of their actions means that affected individuals will have a strong tendency to try to satiate their two basic drives surrounding sexual behavior with minimal concern for the suffering they cause, or for the prospects of being punished.

According to the synthesized theory, average sex differences in these two brain functioning patterns account for the high prevalence of rape offenses in males, and its virtual absence in females. In addition, variability in both of these brain functioning patterns among males are hypothesized to be responsible for much of the intramale variability in rape probabilities.

SUMMARY

The synthesized theory can be stated in terms of four propositions. In simplified form, they are:

1. Rape is sexually motivated, and, as all sexual behavior tends to be, is motivated by (a) a drive for erotic sexual experiences (the sex drive), and (b) a drive for bonded sexual relationships (the drive to possess and control one or more sex partners).
2. While the motivation for sex is almost entirely the result of unlearned neurological processes, the actual techniques involved in committing rape are largely learned through operant conditioning (and only secondarily through imitation and attitudinal factors).
3. Natural selection has favored stronger sex drives and stronger tendencies to orient drives to possess and control multiple sex partners in males than in females, while females have been strongly favored for resisting forceful copulatory tactics because it effectively prevents them from discriminating in favor of males who will help care for offspring after they have been conceived.
4. Exposure of the brain to androgens tends to produce strong sex drives and strong tendencies to attempt to possess and control multiple sex partners, while it also helps to reduce sensitivity to any aversive consequences of one's actions.

In the next chapter, a graphic model of the synthesized theory will be presented.

Before closing this chapter, it would be worthwhile to return momentarily to issues raised in concluding Chapter 2 in response to comments by Eysenck and Rushton regarding their proposal that a fourth theory of rape already exists. The reader will recall that what these two individuals had in mind was a personality or trait theory that saw genetics contributing to brain functioning patterns in ways that produced variations in personality, some of which produced variations in tendencies to commit rape. At this point, the reader can see that the synthesized theory I have outlined brings one to similar conclusions. It assumes that genetic factors help control the degree to which the brain is exposed to androgens (in terms of both organizational and activational levels), and that such hormonal exposure regimens produce variations in behavioral tendencies (personality) pertaining to each individual's probability of committing rape.

7

A MODEL AND GENERAL DISCUSSION OF THE SYNTHESIZED THEORY

To help elucidate the theory described in Chapter 6, this chapter elaborates on the theory by describing it in graphic form. Then, for those interested in testing the theory and contrasting its predictions with other theories of rape, proposals are made about how key concepts contained in the synthesized theory may be operationalized and incorporated into specific hypotheses.

A GRAPHIC MODEL OF THE SYNTHESIZED THEORY OF RAPE

Figure 2 presents a graphic picture of the synthesized theory's major elements. All of the terms specified in Figure 2 were defined or illustrated in Chapter 6, except for the concept of a *forced copulation threshold*. This term refers to a point along the axis beyond which individuals have a significant probability of using physical force in attempting to copulate. Figure 2 estimates that approximately 40% of males and 1% to 2% of females are likely to exceed the forced copulation threshold (although these percentages are assumed to vary from one population to another, as will be explained). Theoretically, only persons who exceed the forced copulation threshold are at risk of committing rape. The percentages used to construct Figure 2 should be regarded as estimates applicable to the current United States population, and may need to be changed once detailed data are collected. Experimenting with various ways of operationalizing the concept is certainly in order, but for the present discussion, the information used in making the estimates was as follows: For males, the estimate of

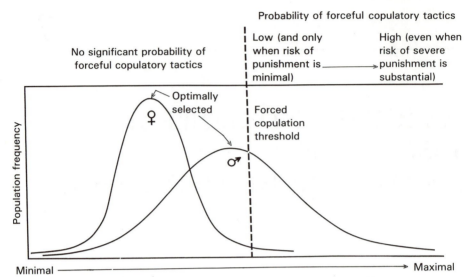

Probability of forceful copulatory tactics

FIGURE 2

40% was based upon evidence that essentially half of all males surveyed thought they could imagine circumstances under which they might ever try to force a female to copulate, provided they could be assured of never being punished for doing so (Malamuth, Haber, & Feshback, 1980; Briere, Malamuth, & Ceniti, 1981). Since a number of these males probably only had in mind such rare circumstances as when a female agreed to have sex, disrobed, engaged in prolonged petting, and then teasingly changed her mind (see Deisher, Wenet, Paperny, Clark, & Fehrenbach, 1982), 50% is probably on the high side of the most realistic estimate of the proportion of United States males at significant risk of committing rape (see also Russell, 1988:43). A 40% figure is also quite close to a recent United State college survey which found that 39.5% of males sometimes fantasized about forcing someone to have sex with them (Loren & Weeks, 1986:33).

Regarding females, a 1% estimate for the United States was derived from observations that about 0.8% of arrests and 0.2% of imprisonments for forcible rape are female offenders (National Council on Crime and Delinquency, 1976/77; Russell, 1984:67). Since males are probably more reluctant to bring charges of rape than females (Muehlenhard & Cook, 1987:72), the assumption is that these official statistics provide an estimate on the low side for female rape offenders. In addition, surveys among women report that in about 0.7% of rapes, the assailant was another women (Russell, 1984; P. A. Brand, University of Vermont, personal correspondence, April 16, 1988). Overall, a 1% estimate for the probability of rape by females in the United States seems resonable. Nevertheless, the question of female propensities to commit rape may be considerably higher, and deserves research attention in light of Loren and Weeks (1986:33) finding that 9.6% of U.S. college females sometimes fantasized about forcing a member of the opposite sex to have sex.

Basically, saying that those who exceed the forced copulation threshold have a significant risk of committing rape means that every individual to the right of the forced copulation threshold has at least a significant (1%) chance of experimenting with forceful copulatory tactics each time an opportunity presents itself, and an individual's noncoercive sexual overtures are rebuffed. Of course, individuals at the most extreme right end of the continuum have a probability of committing rape that is virtually certain (100%). Opportunities would present themselves mainly in the form of individuals being alone with and proximate to a person to whom they are sexually attracted. Therefore, individuals who are only slightly to the right of the forced copulation threshold can be expected to attempt rape only rarely, even when given numerous opportunities, and even then, to do so only if risks of punishment seem minimal and when nonforceful tactics have been tried without success. The further to the right of the forced copulation threshold an individual is, the higher the probability of his or her attempting rape, even when environmental conditions are not particularly conducive to reinforcing such behavior, and even before he or she has exhausted nonforecful options in attempting to copulate. Overall, while only persons at the extreme right end of the continuum are virtually certain to repeatedly experiment with forceful copulatory tactics, all individuals to the right of the forced copulation threshold are *at risk* of becoming rape offenders.

Theoretically, an individual's position along the axis is basically determined by the combined effect of two sets of brain functioning patterns. One of these emanate primarily from the hypothalamus, and has to do with motivating sexual behavior in two respects:—(a) by intensifying the sex drive, and (b) by orienting the drive to possess and control multiple sex partners. The other brain functioning pattern is largely seated in the reticular formation, and involves the alteration of an individual's sesitivity to the suffering of others (as well as sensitivity to stimuli generally). According to the synthesized theory, persons most prone to employ forceful tactics in attempting to copulate are relatively insensitive to the suffering of others (see Truscott & Fehr, 1986).

As shown in Figure 2, the more these two sets of brain functioning patterns are to the right of the forced copulation threshold, the more likely an individual is to commit rape. Theoretically, brain functioning patterns are pushed to the right by exposing the brain to high androgen regimens. However, as will be explained more later in this chapter, this is not to say that there should be a simple correspondence between an individual's circulating androgen levels and his (or her) rape probabilities.

According to the synthesized theory, the peaks (or means) of both the female and male distributions represent what has been optimally favored by natural selection in terms of each sex's sex drive, drive to possess and control sex partners, and reticular formation functioning. In other words, the average male has been naturally selected for having a stronger sex drive, orienting his drive to possess and control multiple sex partners, and having less sensitivity to the suffering of others than the average female. Nevertheless, there is considerable variation about the means for both sexes, presumably at least in part because variation provides a hedge against future changes in natural selection pressures (Haldane, 1985). The greater dispersion about the mean for males than for females, while not essential for the theory, was assumed in accordance with evidence that males exhibit greater variability than females do in a number of behavioral and physiological traits (Cattell, 1903; H. Ellis, 1934:436; Heim, 1970; Hutt,1972:89; Abramowicz & Richardson, 1975; Shields, 1975; Daly & Wilson, 1978:81; Lehrke, 1978), albeit not all (Charlesworth & Dzur, 1987:199). Theoretically, what has been optimally selected for each sex will vary somewhat from one population to another, but it should never be to the degree that the means for the two sexes would converge. Also, according to the synthesized theory, human populations may differ considerably among one another in terms of the percentages of both sexes surpassing the forced copulation threshold.

Variations in the two brain functioning patterns represented along the axis are assumed to be largely the result of the actions of sex hormones (especially androgens) upon the brain. As noted in Proposition 4 (pp. 70–75), basically, the more one's brain is exposed to high levels of androgens (especially during crucial periods of the neuro-organizational stage of brain development), the further to the right along the axis brain functioning will be following puberty (and, to some extent, possibly even before puberty). Moving away from the evolutionary level of analysis to a more proximate level, the average differences between males and females in brain functioning should be the result of variations in the degree (and timing) of exposure of the brain to sex hormones, particularly androgens. Regarding causes of within-sex variation in these two brain functioning patterns, many complex causal variables are likely to be involved, but androgens probably still play a central role. Androgen levels are influenced not only by genetic factors, but also by such environmental factors as exposure of the mother to drugs and stress during pregnancy (see Ellis & Ames, 1987).

In considering the involvement of environmental factors in rape etiology, one should keep in mind that the theory assumes that only individuals to the right of the forced copulation threshold are at risk of ever committing rape, and that this group is comprised of very few females (none of whom are at risk of being chronic predatory rapists). Regarding environmental variables, the synthesized theory contends that whether or not persons at risk actually do attempt rape primarily depends upon (a) being proximate to a sexually attractive con-specific, (b) the kind of past success they have had in satiating their sex drive or drives to possess and control both with and without the use of force, (c) the assessment of the potential risks of being punished for using varying degrees of forceful tactics, and, (d) for individuals with little sexual experience, the degree of exposure to "role models" and instructions for how to deal with sexual arousal. For individuals who are only slightly to the right of the forced copula-tion threshold, only a few combinations of the above categories of environmen-tal circumstances would ever cause rape, and they only in the course of court-ship. For individuals far to the right of the forced copulation threshold (which only consists of males), the commission of rape may be quite common, even when there is little or no prior intimacy between the offender and victim, even without role models or instructions conducive to rape, and ultimately even irrespective of the severity or certainty of punishment for committing rape. Theoretically, the first group of potential rapists should be much more numer-ous than the second in all societies, and should be largely responsible for date (or acquaintance) rape. The second group primarily consist of the predatory rapists. They should be more extreme than either date rapists, and certainly more than males in general regarding the strength of their sex drives, in their drives to possess and control multiple sex partners, and/or in being insensitive to the pain and suffering they cause others.

Regarding variations from one population to another, the involvement of all of the same categories of causes that are hypothesized to be responsible for variations between and within the sexes for a given population should be involved—that is, genetics, natural selection, neurological, hormonal, and so-cial environmental factors. While this is bound to be controversial, the synthe-sized theory thus implies that greater proportions of some racial (including ethnic) groups may exceed the forced copulation threshold than others. In other words, due to varying natural selection pressures, operating over countless generations, the distribution curves for some populations may have shifted fur-ther to the right than for other populations, resulting in greater proportions exceeding the forced copulation threshold. This will be discussed in more detail later in this chapter.

CONCEPTS CENTRAL TO THE SYNTHESIZED THEORY

For those interested in assessing its elegance, many testable hypotheses may be derived from the synthesized theory of rape. To ensure objectivity, most of the derivations and testing of a scientific theory should be done by persons other than the theory's major proponent. Therefore, most of what will be offered here will consist of general guidelines for deriving and testing hypotheses from the theory. These guidelines are organized around the theory's key variables, which have been grouped into two classes, called *first* and *second order variables*. Basically, the distinction is that the first order variables tend to be more basic (like primary colors) than the second order variables, although the second order variables are generally much more apparent in everyday experience (like the nonprimary colors). The first order variables consist of (a) genetic and evolutionary variables, (b) brain functioning variables, (c) hormonal variables, and (d) the forced copulation threshold variable. The second order variables consist of (e) motivational and learning variables, (f) individual differences and racial variables, (g) social stratification variables, and (h) societal reaction variables.

A. Genetic and Evolutionary Variables

Social learning theorists are largely silent on the question of any genetic or evolutionary factors underlying people's tendencies to rape, and feminist theorists have been quite insistent that these sorts of factors are not important for understanding rape (Blackman, 1985:116).

The synthesized theory concurs with the evolutionary theory of rape that genetic and evolutionary factors play a key role in rape etiology. As with the evolutionary theory, this does not mean that the synthesized theory hypothesizes the existence of specific "rape genes" (Thiessen, 1986:29). More than likely, quite a number of genes contribute to variation in rape propensities, and nearly all these genes are probably linked to motivational or learning variables. For example, some genes could contribute by increasing an individual's desires for sex with numerous sex partners, and other genes could contribute by preventing individuals from quickly learning a wide spectrum of techniques for satiating their sex drive other than the most obvious (e.g., through the use of force). Genes could also cause variations in male probabilities of rape by altering the degree to which males are aroused by various types and degrees of sexual provocation, for example, the clothing attire of females. Still other genes could contribute by giving males physical appearances that adversely affect their probabilities of attracting voluntary sex partners. Theoretically, even genes of victims could contribute to variabilility in rape by affecting their sex drive, or their tendency to be attracted to males with varying degrees of rape propensity.

If the above proposals seem farfetched, readers should consult a number of recent articles and books outlining the evidence that genes affect a wide diversity of behavioral tendencies (e.g., Scarr, Webber, Weinberg, & Witting, 1981; Ellis, 1982; Durden-Smith & deSimone, 1983; Holden, 1985; Rowe, 1986; Kalat, 1988; Rose, Koskenvuo, Kaprio, Sarna, & Langinvainio, 1988), including even minor eccentricities of human personality (e.g., Kovach, 1980; Holden, 1980, 1987; Davis, 1987) and even a number of attitudes and vocational interests (Holden, 1987:598). Also, the evidence is now all but certain that genetic factors contribute to variations in criminality in general (Ellis,

1982a; Taylor, 1984; Rowe 1986; Cloninger & Gottesman, 1987; Mednick, Gabrielli, & Hutchings, 1984, 1987).

As to how genes make contributions to these behavior patterns and preferences, several lines of research point to brain functioning patterns. Regarding criminality, persons with high probabilities seem to differ from those with low probabilities in part by neurological processes which make the former less sensitive to incoming stimuli than the latter (e.g., Mednick & Hutchings, 1978; Ellis, 1987a; Raine, 1988; Moffitt, 1988; Nachshon, 1988). As alluded to in the Conclusions to Chapter 2, the brains of persons who are most prone toward criminality appear to be somewhat less sensitive to aversive aspects of the environment than are the brains of people in general (see Ellis, 1987a). This makes them harder to condition through the use of, or threat of, punishment. The same factors may make them less attuned to the abhorrence felt by individuals with whom they wish to copulate as forceful tactics begin to be employed.

Recent theorizing by Zuckerman (1983, 1984) may have identified some of the actual neurochemistry underlying a general insensitivity to environmental stimuli and a preference for unusually high levels of stimulation. He proposed that a set of neurotransmitters called the *catecholamines* (primarily epinepherine, and norepinepherine) may be below a level that "feels good" for some persons, while they linger at levels that are "just right" for others, and possibly even "too high" for others. A study by Zuckerman and Litle (1986) lended support to this deduction by suggesting that those with a chronic need to raise their catecholamine levels to their most comfortable level may come to use a variety of means, including watching violent, fear-provoking, and erotic films. If engaging in crimes, including the commission of rape, has similar catecholamine-increasing effects, one can begin to see that links between the watching of pornography (violent and otherwise) and tendencies to commit rape may be explained without necessarily assuming that the pornography exposure is actually causing any increases in rape probabilities. More will be said about the involvement of the brain in rape etiology in the following section.

If, as the synthesized theory suggests, both rape and other victimful offenses are part of an r-selected approach to reproduction (Ellis, 1987b), some of the same genes that contribute to rape may be contributing to criminal behavior more generally. In terms of evolutionary factors, the synthesized theory of rape perceives males as being more forceful than the average female in attempting to copulate because having many sex partners is much more likely to be favored by natural selection among males than among females. At the same time, natural selection would favor females who resisted being forced to copulate until the male had exhibited the ability and the inclination to provision for her and any offspring she produces (Thornhill & Thornhill, 1983:155). Theoretically, these somewhat conflicting natural selection pressures have resulted in a complex set of courtship and mating strategies of which rape has evolved as one unfortunate component.

Returning to genetic factors underlying variations in tendencies to rape, the synthesized theory would lead one to hypothesize that some of the genes involved in rape etiology would have to be located on the Y chromosome, thus helping to account for why males are so consistently more prone to use forceful tactics than females. Nevertheless, there is no reason to think that genes located on the autosomes, and possibly even on the X chromosome, are not also involved. Also, for reasons to be explained more later, the synthesized theory would cause one to expect that genes that increase the probability of rape should be more heavily concentrated in the lower than in the upper or middle social strata.

B. Brain Functioning Variables

An indispensible element in the synthesized theory is the propostion that, on average, the brains of rapists must function differently than the brains of nonrapists, at least in the proximity of members of the opposite sex. While this is certainly a testable proposition, the differences may prove to be subtle and difficult to establish under controlled laboratory conditions.

Differences associated with variations in male tendencies to commit rape should be concentrated in some of the more primitive areas of the brain where the largely unlearned sex drive and the drive to possess and control emanate and where the sensitivity to environmental stimuli reside. Nevertheless, inasmuch as learning actual raping techniques (or alternatives to them) are involved, higher brain centers may also contribute to individual variability in tendencies to commit rape.

Theoretically, whatever neurological differences are found associated with variations in rape probabilities, they should be more extreme in the case of predatory rapists than in the case of date rapists.

C. Hormonal Variables

According to the synthesized theory, sex hormones—especially androgens (and estradiol)—should play a key role in rape etiology. One obvious role should be by sexually differentiating the brain, thereby producing virtually all of the average sex differences in assertive sexuality. Another role should be in the sense of producing intramale variability in assertive sexuality. In this second respect, one should not expect to find the way androgens contribute to rape etiology such that one could simply measure the levels of one or more of these hormones at a given point in time and predict how likely a male is to commit rape over the next few years. In fact, a few studies have attempted to correlate the level of testosterone (and other androgens) of various categories of rapists, and to compare their levels with those of other criminals or with noncriminal males (Rada, Laws, & Kellner, 1976; Rada, Laws, Kellner, Stivastava, & Peake, 1983;

Langevin, 1985). While some significant findings in predicted directions have been found, they have been weak and not always replicated. For the synthesized theory, these findings are not of major relevance since the theory postulates that the permanent structural and cellular changes in brain functioning which occur during brain organization (in humans, prior to birth) are more crucial to rape etiology than the levels circulating following puberty (unless the latter drop extremely low). In other words, given that nearly all males appear to regularly produce more that twice the level of most androgens needed to fully activate their nervous systems following puberty (Ellis, 1982:187), there is little reason to expect that measuring activational levels will be very helpful in predicting rape probabilities.

D. Forced Copulation Threshold Variable

The concept of a *forced copulation threshold* was introduced as a key element in the synthesized theory in order to account for the fact that many, and possibly most, males (and almost all females) appear to have no significant probability of committing rape under any conceivable circumstances. Without arguing that there is an absolutely perfect dividing line between those who could and those who could not commit rape, the theory assumes that, for all practical purposes, this is the case. The theory also assumes that because of genetic and natural selection factors, the precentage of each sex which can be found on each side of this threshold will vary from one population to another, although never to the extent that in any population would the proportion of females crossing the threshold ever come close to the number of males who do so.

The forced copulation threshold was created to help explain why some individuals (almost entirely males) appear to be fairly easily aroused by depictions of rape, and are thereby motivated to learn and experiment with the use of raping techniques (e.g., via viewing pornographic rape scenes), while other individuals are not. Thus, according to the synthesized theory, individuals who do not exceed the forced copulation threshold feel such aversion to the use of force for the purpose of satiating their sexual motivation that, no matter how strong their sexual motivation may be, and no matter how much exposure they may have to pro-rape attitudes and to realistic rape depictions, the commission of rape would still be essentially impossible.

While the synthesized theory can accommodate many separate male and female distribution curves, the curves displayed in Figure 2 specifically hypothesized that somewhat less than half of all males (plus a tiny proportion of females) are at risk of committing rape. While each human population should have somewhat different proportions of its members surpassing the forced copulation threshold, the theory maintains that one could never identify a population in which anything close to equal proportions of males and females would do so. Theoretically, individuals who surpass the forced copulation threshold will commit rape whenever they encounter the appropriate mix of (a) provocative circumstances, (b) encouragement to experiment with forceful copulatory tactics, (c) the degree of resistance encountered in prior attempts to employ forceful tactics, and (d) the probability of being caught and punished for rape being fairly low. No matter how conducive the environment is for the remainder of males and females (those to the left of the forced copulation threshold), the likelihood of their using forceful tactics in attempting to copulate is essentially zero.

The factors responsible for determining which individuals cross the forced copulation threshold and which do not are genetic factors (some of which must be contained on the Y chromosome), and neurological and hormonal factors (some of which must involve androgens).

E. Motivational and Learning Variables

While feminist theory and, to a lesser degree, social learning theory have held that rape is an act of aggression and domination rather than a sexual act (Persell, 1984:586) or an act of reproductive significance (Blackman, 1985:116), the synthesized theory contends that rape is largely sexually motivated and that it has had, and continues to have, significant reporductive consequences.

According to the synthesized theory, rape is sexually motivated in two respects. First, copulation and orgasm, per se, tend to be powerful primary reinforcers of whatever behavior makes these experiences possible (Russell, 1988:51), and thus the judicious use of raping techniques would be frequently reinforced. Second, in the broad sense, sexuality is purported to include bonding tendencies between sex partners—tendencies that also are hypothesized to play a fundamental role in rape motivation. On average males are hypothesized to be more strongly reinforced than females for exhibiting behavior leading up to copulation and orgasm (i.e., males have a stronger sex drive than females). And, while both sexes are hypothesized to be somewhat equally reinforced for exhibiting behavior culminating in the possession and control of the sexual activities of a desired sex partner, males are hypothesized to be more motivated to extend this possession and control to multiple sex partners. The combined effect of these two aspects of sexual motivation is hypothesized to be that members of each sex learn tactics for satiating their sexual motivations, and that for individuals who exceed the forced copulation threshold (largely males), some of the tactics are likely to involve the use of force. Thus, the primary reinforcement for rape comes not only from the pleasures associated with copulation, but also sometimes from securing and/or retaining exclusive sexual access to a sex partner. While this sexual-bonding-of-the-victim effect of rape definitely needs additional research, the theory contends that rape victims are often so extremely traumatized by the experience (see Frank & Anderson,

1987) that a bonding response to whomever is in the vicinity at the time (i.e., the rapist) is sometimes induced.

From the perspective of the synthesized theory, rape is essentially a set of learned tactics involving the use of physical force—tactics that are motivated by both the short-term (copulatory) and long-term (bonding) aspects of human sexuality. Theoretically, both the short-and long-term aspects of sexual motivation are minimally learned, and the motivation for rape is essentially no different than the motivation underlying sexual gratification in general. Partial support for this view comes from evidence that drugs known as *anti-androgens* have been found to greatly reduce rapists continuation of all sexual behavior (Rada, 1978; Spodak, Falck, & Rappeport, 1978; Walker, Meyer, Emory, & Rubin, 1984) (because, in clinically prescribed dosages, they tend to dramatically deplete testosterone production and/or androgen uptake by the brain) while only minimally reducing their general aggressiveness (Bradford, 1983:167; Rees, Bonsall, & Michael, 1986).

According to the synthesized theory, the motivation for rape is, so to speak, "hard-wired" into the brain by numerous genetic programs that, in most cases, have survived countless generations of natural selection. The only major qualification to the idea that rape represents learned tactics employed to help satiate one or both aspects of an individual's sexual motivation has to do with brain seizures in and around the hypothalamus. As mentioned earlier (p. 62), such seizures may occasionally trigger rape with minimal learning and forethought, in the form of what has been called *fixed action patterns*. In other words, it is conceivable that a small percentage of rapes are triggered by seizures in primitive parts of the brain where sexual behavior is motivated. These seizures could be brought on by physical or chemical insults, by viral infections, or by emotional stress (including emotional stress associated with events leading up to copulation) (see Monroe, 1986).

Learning variables are important in the synthesized theory, although the types of learning emphasized are somewhat different from those emphasized in the feminist and social learning theories. Rather than focusing upon attitudinal and imitative learning, the synthesized theory primarily emphasizes learning through operant conditioning. According to the synthesized theory, since the motivation behind rape is largely sexual and unlearned, the learning of raping techniques would take place primarily during direct interactions with members of the opposite sex. Attitudinal and imitative learning would still be seen as contributing to rape, but only for males who are beyond the forced copulation threshold with minimal sexual experience. As soon as they have gained copulatory experiences, these experiences, per se, should largely determine how much force the males use, not the linguistically mediated attitudes they express, or the rape (and other sexually violent) depictions they see.

While similarities should not be overlooked between the synthesized theory's concept of the *drive to possess and control* and the feminist concept of *aggression and domination over sex partners,* the latter tends to be largely depicted in economic and political terms, and as being an end in itself. In the synthesized theory, economic and political power would be best relegated simply to the the level of tactical maneuvers that many males use to gain and retain access to sex partners. As a set of major alternative tactics to gaining copulatory access through force, male attainment of economic and political power (i.e., social status) would have been favored as part of a process called *sexual selection.* The term refers to a subcategory of *natural selection* in which the main selective pressure eminates from within the species, either from competition within one's own sex, or from preferences by members of the opposite sex, or from both (O'Donald, 1980; Ryan, 1980:523; Lewin, 1984). Given that females have evolved strong biases toward mating with high rather than low-status males (all else being equal), most high-status males will have sufficient opportunities to pass their genes on to future generations without resorting to forceful tactics.

F. Individual Differences and Racial Variables

Given that the synthesized theory postulates the involvement of genetic, evolutionary, neurological, and hormonal factors in rape etiology, one cannot escape deducing that these factors are important in explaining individual variations in male tendencies to rape. These same factors would also incline one to suspect that there will be racial variations in propensities to rape.

Race refers to evolved subspecies variations in a number of morphological traits (e.g., skin, hair, and eye color, hair texture, and a variety of facial features), variations that are genetically based (Scriver, Laberge, Clow, & Fraser, 1978; McConville, Soudek, Sroka, Cote, & Boagtberry, 1983:9), and that tend to be maintained in identifiable populations over countless generations by assortive mating (Eckland, 1967; Jensen, 1975:215). *Assortive mating* refers to tendencies for both sexes to mate selectively within their species, and to thereby to maintain at least a fair degree of reproductive isolation, either through geopolitical or social mechanisms, from other subspecies populations.

Overall, three major racial groups have been widely recognized—blacks, whites, and Orientals (Ogborn & Nimkoff, 1958:94; Goldsby, 1971:31; Osborne, 1971:166; Wallace, Garrison, & Knowler, 1985:152)—although a large proportion of humans, especially in modern and/or newly colonized countries, are actually racial (and, especially, ethnic) hybrids (Workman, 1973; Thomas, 1984:396).

Postulating the involvement of genetic, evolutionary, neurological, and hormonal factors would incline one to hypothesize that rape will be more prevalent in some racial groups than in others. To see how this hypothesis would be derived, one needs to consider the following:

1. Physical traits used to distinguish various races are, in the final analysis, the culmination of genetic factors having responded to natural selection pressures that have been localized to whatever region of the world the ancestors of a particular racial group inhabited over numerous generations in relative reproductive isolation (Campbell, 1985:471; Scriver, Laberge, Clow, & Fraser, 1978; McConville, et al., 1983:9).
2. Average racial differences have been identified in various brain functioning patterns (Thompson, Bogen, & March, 1979; TenHouten, 1980; Denno, Meijs, Nachshon, & Aurand, 1982; Nachshon, Denno, & Aurand, 1983; McShane, Risse, & Rubens, 1984; Geschwind & Galabruda, 1985b).
3. Average racial differences have been found in sex hormone levels and functioning patterns (Freeman, 1934; Nylander, 1973; Soma, Takayama, Kiyokawa, Akaeda, & Tokoro, 1975; Campbell, 1988:501; also see Ellis, in press-a).

If genetic, evolutionary, neurological, and hormonal factors are all important in rape etiology, and if all of these factors vary according to race, it is most likely that, on average, not all racial groups will have the same proportions of their members disposed to commit rape. Put in terms depicted in Figure 2, the synthesized theory leads one to expect that, for both sexes, races will vary in their distributions along the x-axis. Theoretically, as will be explained shortly, the racial groups that are most prone to exceed the forced copulation threshold should be those with the greatest proportions of males in the lowest social strata. (Incidentally, to the degree that *ethnicity* refers to subracial groups (see Mourant, Kopec, & Domaniewska-Sobczak, 1978), the synthesized theory would also lead to the hypothesis that genetic factors underlie ethnic variations in rape probabilities.)

Before proceeding further, an emotionally sensitive and socially important issue should be raised: Theories asserting that genetic factors are responsible for race variations in behavior risk being denounced as *racist* (Freedman, 1979b:170). As critics consider making that charge against the present theory, they are asked to note that, in the strictest sense, *racism* does not include the idea that genetic and neurohormonal factors contribute to racial variations in behavior. Instead, it denotes (a) feelings of intolerance and superiority that some people harbor toward members of racial groups other than their own (Nelson & Jurmain, 1982:205; Campbell, 1985:488), and, possibly also, (b) the belief that individuals should be legally treated differently because of the racial categories into which they happen to fit (or at least best fit) (Havender, 1978; for an extended discussion see Ellis 1987b:163).

To determine which racial groups have the highest and the lowest rape rates, the synthesized theory suggests that one should look for racial variation in characteristics that are r/K-selected (see Chapter 6, Proposition 3). Extensive evidence indicates that, of the three major racial groups, blacks are more r-selected than whites and that whites are more so than Orientals (Rushton, 1985a, Ellis, 1987b; Rushton & Bogaert, 1987). More precisely, wherever these three racial groups have been found living in roughly the same environmental habitats, when blacks are compared to whites, and especially when they are compared to Orientals, they have (a) higher fertility rates, (b) shorter gestation lengths, (c) higher twinning rates, (d) lower birth weights, (e) higher infant mortality rates, (f) earlier onset of coitus, (g) highest coital frequencies, (h) less stable bonds with sex partners, (i) lower parental investment (as indicated by child abuse and abandonment), and (j) shorter life expectancies (reviewed by Ellis, 1987b:159).

If (a) blacks are more r-selected than whites, and whites in turn are more r-selected than Orientals, and (b) forced copulations are more characteristic of r-selected organisms, then blacks should have higher rape rates than whites, and whites in turn should have higher rates than Orientals. In looking for empirical evidence relevant to this deduction, comparisons involving Orientals were not found, but those pertaining to blacks and whites all support the deduction (Johnson, 1941; Bonger, 1943; Korn & McCorkle, 1959:232; Amir, 1971:44; Curtis, 1974; McDermott, 1979). If, as the theory implies, these differences are genetically based and neurohormonally mediated, the race differences should be found in nearly all societies where comparisons are made, and should remain roughly similar over time. This would be the case unless, of course, quite consequential natural (or artificial) selection pressure is causing one or more racial groups to shift to a new average position along the r/K continuum.

To further defend the proposal that rape probabilities are likely to be higher for some racial groups than the others, not simply because of environmental factors, but because of genetic and neurohormonal factors, a number of recent scientific reports can be cited. These reports have concluded that genetic and/or neurohormonal factors are probably responsible for significant racial variations in a number of behavioral phenomena besides rape, including the following:

Alcohol consumption patterns and/or alcoholism (Wolff, 1972; Ewing, Rouse & Pellizzari, 1974; Schwitters, Johnson, McClearn, & Wilson, 1982:1259; Seto, Tricomi, Goodwin, Kolodney, & Sullivan, 1978; Madden, 1984:334; Chan, 1986:99; Sue, 1987:64)

General activity levels (Freedman, 1979a, 1979b; Freedman & DeBoer, 1979; Weisfeld, 1982:225);

Intelligence and intellectual functioning (Jensen, 1975, 1985; Nurcombe, 1976:47; Heyns, 1978:83; Lynn, 1978: Willerman, 1979; Reynolds, McBride, & Gibson, 1981; Lynn, 1987);

Personality traits such as extroversion and neuroticism (Rushton, 1984, 1985b, 1987; Freedman & Deboer, 1979:588);

Various aspects of sexual behavior, including strength of the sex drive (Rushton & Bogaert, 1987);and

Serious criminality (Wilson & Herrnstein, 1985:457; Ellis, 1986b; Whitney, in press).

Even ethnic (subracial) variations for some of these traits may be influenced by genetic factors (see Schwitters, Johnson, McClearn, & Wilson, 1982; Park, Huang, Nagoshi, Yuen, Johnson, Ching, & Bowman, 1984).

While ethical principles and societal policies can (and should) never be directly deduced from a scientific theory, given the importance of the present topic, the reader is asked to ponder the ethical implications of the argument just made. One policy implication might be that, in order to reduce rape, all relatively r-selected racial groups should be reduced in numbers. Of course, that begs such questions as, by how much, and by what means? Then, of course, one would need to decide what to do with individuals of mixed racial ancestry, and whether or not to extend the policy to various subracial groups. Recalling the unfortunate legacy of Nazi Germany's attempt to diminish the prevalence of Jews because Jews exhibited a number of traits that leaders of the Nazi movement wanted to eliminate (Blacker, 1952:141; Kevles, 1985; Allen, 1988:9) should forewarn anyone of the ethical dilemmas and practical pitfalls incumbered by the application of a social science theory that sees biological factors contributing to variations in important aspects of behavior.

Also, while reducing, and eventually eliminating rape is certainly something that almost everyone would agree should be pursued, most people would also consider it desirable to reduce many diseases that are known to be more prevalent in some races than in others at least in part because of genetic factors. For example, mainly for genetic reasons, whites appear to be more susceptible than other racial groups to:

Parkinson's disease (Chandra, Bharucha, & Schoenberg, 1984);
Anorexia nervosa (Pumariega, Edwards, & Michell, 1984);
Phenylketonuria excesses and deficiencies (Campbell, 1988:501);
Tay-sachs disease (especially among Jews) (Myrianthopoulos & Aronson, 1966; Shaw & Smith, 1969; Meyrowitz & Hogikyan, 1986);
Spina bifida (especially among British and Irish) (Ghosh, Woo, & Poon, 1981); and,
Colley's anemia (especially among Italians and Spanish) (Culliton, 1972).

Blacks appear to be more genetically susceptible than other racial groups to:

High blood pressure and *hypertension* (Phillips & Burch, 1960; Florey & Cuadrado, 1968; Howard & Holman, 1970; Tyroler, 1977, 1980; Voors, Berenson, Dalferes, Webber, & Shuler, 1979);
Sickle-cell anemia (Campbell, 1988:88);

Systemic lupus erythematosus (Damon, 1971:67); and,
Tuberculosis (Harvald & Hauge, 1965).

And, Orientals seem to exhibit an unusually high genetic susceptibility to:

Esophagus, stomach, and liver cancer (Damon, 1971:63);
Acatalasia and *Oguchi's disease* (Japanese and Koreans, in particular) (Noble, 1978:327);
Serious deficiencies in alpha-thalassemia and glucose-6-phospate dehydrogenase (Scriver, Laberge, Clow, & Fraser, 1978); and,
Spontaneous occlusion of the circle of Willis (at least among Japanese) (Kudo, 1968).

If one were to try to reduce the prevalence of these diseases by eliminating the racial groups with the greatest genetic vulnerability to them, none of the major racial groups would be left! (All of the less prevalent racial groups also probably have unusually high susceptibilities to one or more diseases, as well (Damon, 1971).

So, what use should be made of the hypothesis that some racial and subracial groups may be more genetically predisposed to rape than others? Four recommendations are offered here: First, no one should consider the hypothesis at this point as being anything more than an unproven deduction from a theory that needs a great deal of empirical scrutiny.

Second, if the hypothesis is true, in attempting to identify the underlying causes of rape, if should be helpful to have a wide diversity of more or less exclusively intrabreeding populations to compare. Sooner or later, all explanations of rape will need to focus a great deal of attention on neurohormonal mechanisms (as discussed earlier in this and the preceding chapter). Inasmuch as the races differ on average in neurohormonal functioning (see p. 93), these differences may hold a key to understanding how genetics are involved in rape etiology, not only with respect to racial differences, but in regard to intraracial variations, as well.

Third, if genetic factors partially determine racial variations in rape probability, such evidence may be helpful in attempting to identify DNA markers for rape propensity. This is because, in the initial stages of searching for DNA markers for a trait, it is often important to be able to identify reproductively isolated populations whose display of the trait varies to the greatest degrees (see Mourant, Kopec, & Domaniewska-Sobczak, 1978; Kolata, 1987:1140). Basically, *DNA markers* refer to specific segments along chromosomes which directly contribute to the expression of a particular trait (Smith, Kimberling, Pennington, & Lubs, 1983). Substantial progress has been made in recent years in identifying various genetic markers for a number of human disease conditions, including ones involving brain functioning and behavior:

Huntington's disease (Gusella, et. al., 1984; Gilliam, et. al., 1987);
Depression (Maugh, 1981);
Reading disabilities (Smith, Kimberling, Pennington, & Lubs, 1983);
Down's syndrome (Allore, et. al., 1988);
Lesch-Nyhan disease (Martin, 1987:770); and
Alcoholism (Shaw, Stimmel, & Lieber, 1976).

Even so, the more genes that are involved in determining the expression of a trait, usually the harder it is to locate DNA markers for that trait; and it could be that rape propensity is very much of a polygenic, rather than a monogenic, trait.

Fourth, the establishment of a genetic basis for either racial variation, or individual variation, in rape etiology, should foster a spirit of tolerance for those groups or individuals who are most affected. Tolerance, of course, does not mean that the behavior per se should be tolerated; nor does it mean that reasonable efforts should not be taken to minimize the commission of rape, even if that requires incarcerating those with the highest probability of recidivating (until effective alternative methods of preventing rape recidivism are devised). As far as incarcerating those individuals or groups who simply have high *probabilities* of committing rape, the presumption of innocence until proven otherwise must be honored (although this presumption need not preclude the development of noncoercive programs designed to reduce the probability of rape among individuals and groups with the greatest risks).

G. Social Stratification Variables

As in the case of the feminist theory, which emphasizes the relative status of the offender and the victim (or of males and females, as groups of people within the society as a whole), the synthesized theory largely focuses on the social status of offenders. The synthesized theory predicts that rape probabilities will be inversely correlated with social status, especially when the status of males themselves (rather than the status of their parents or guardians) are at issue, and provided that most of the subjects being studied are not just middle- and upper-status males (as explained below). This hypothesis emanates from noting that females should have evolved tendencies to prefer mating with males who are likely to be dependable providers. Thus, females appear to be more keenly aware than males of the social status (and status potential) of prospective mates.

Not only do females appear attracted to mates on the basis of status indicators (such as income, occupational status, or educational attainment) more than males are, but on the basis of personal characteristics indicative of the probability of attaining high social status (such as high motivation, self-confidence, and intelligence) (Buss, 1987). Among various nonhuman species, also, females appear prone to shun mating with males of low status (Kleiman, 1978; Lancaster, 1979:61; McGinnis, 1979; Appleby, 1982), particularly during estrus, when they are most likely to conceive (Hausfater, 1975).

While the synthesized theory predicts that most male characteristics indicative of low social status (or low potential for attaining social status) should be inversely correlated with rape probabilities, especially among humans living in modern industrial societies, there may be little difference in the likelihood of middle- and upper-status males being stable long-term providers for their spouses and children. Only large proportions of males in the lowest social strata would be quite undependable in this regard, thus providing substantial selection pressure against females who mate with them.

Faced with female discrimination against them in mating preferences, lower-status males, in turn, may have been selected more than upper- and middle-status males for taking advantage of more marginal reproductive opportunities (despite the additional risks that might be involved). Theoretically, these more marginal reproductive opportunities would include the use of varying degrees of force (although deception during courtship probably would also be more favored in the lower than the upper and middle strata). For reasons discussed in Chapter 5, Hypothesis 2, predatory rape is probably much more marginal in its reproductive payoff, and riskier in terms of the offender being apprehended and incarcerated, than date rape. Thus, the synthesized theory would predict that predatory rape would be especially heavily concentrated among lower-status males. In other words, from the standpoint of Figure 2, lower-status males should have a frequency distribution which is farther to the right along the x-axis than upper- and middle-status males, and this would place greater proportions of lower status males beyond the forced copulation threshold than for other males.

H. Societal Reaction Variables

To be complete, any theory of criminal behavior must eventually address the issue of *why* the behavior in question is considered criminal. In other words, why is rape or any other behavior considered so repugnant that most people comprising a society, and/or its legislators, institute criminal laws against the behavior? Over the years, some have contended that criminal behavior is more or less arbitrarily designated (e.g., Becker, 1963; Chapman, 1968; for discussion see Hindelang, 1978), or is designated on the basis of being contrary to the interests of the rich and powerful within a particular society (e.g., Chambliss, 1974; Quinney, 1974; Michalowski, 1985). In defense of such "relativist" views on the origins of criminal laws, examples have been cited of several criminal statutes that have been passed against behavior that, in another society (or, within a society at another point in time), was not illegal (Ginsberg, 1965:213; Wilson, 1976:83; Wells, 1980:166; Sigvardsson, Cloninger, Gohman, & von Knorring, 1982:1253). A fairly extensive review of this topic, however, revealed that all of these inconsistencies pertain to so-called *victimless crimes,* rather than to *victimful crimes* (Ellis, 1988:526). The basic distinction between victimless and victimful crimes is that, in the first case, it is difficult to clearly identify a victim, and, in the second case, a victim is apparent. Rape (excluding statutory rape) is obviously a victimful offense, and, like other victimful offenses, throughout the world, it is universally condemned, especially when a close relative or friend is victimized (Ellis, 1988:528).

The synthesized theory would basically account for the universal condemnation of rape by maintaining that most humans have evolved inclinations to attend to events that are highly relevant to their reproductive interests, and changes in a community's rape risks would certainly be relevant. Societies in which most members fail to treat rape as a serious offense would probably effectively permit more and more rape offenders to pass greater and greater proportions of their genes on to future generations. This would result in an ever-increasing inability of females to discriminate in their choice of sex partners on the basis of the male's probability of remaining with the female to help her care for whatever offspring they jointly produce. Presumably, such societies would reach a point where extinction of its members would be a real prospect, given that human evolution, perhaps more than the evolution of any other species, has been contingent upon intense, long-term parental investment.

While there are bound to be substantial ranges within which rape can exist in a society before the society's members risk extinction, and there ranges may be broader under some ecological and/or technological circumstances than others, the ranges are still unlikely to include societies in which rape is evident in more than 1% or 2% of all copulations. Thus, the synthesized theory of rape could be fundamentally disproven if even one thriving human society could be located in which rape was anything close to the common mode of copulation.

As to how the actual process of societal condemantion and punishment of rape evolved, theoretically, it should have appeared long before the advent of writing (and therefore of written laws). Some evidence along these lines may be gleaned from a recent review article on how nonhuman primates seem to suppress what was termed the *nonlegal equivalent of aggressive criminal behavior* (Ellis, 1986). In it, a discussion was devoted to what has been variously called peace-keeping, policing, order maintenance, and control behavior, which has been observed in many nonhuman primate species (e.g., Kawamura, 1967; Lemmon, 1971; Burton, 1972; Talmage-Riggs & Anschel, 1973; Eaton, 1976; Cheney, 1977; Horwich & Wurman, 1978; de Waal, 1978, 1982). Typically, this behavior consists of high-ranking males vigilantly patrolling their societal group, and immediately rushing to intervene in any social disturbance, usually on behalf of whichever individual seems to be losing (Bernstein, 1966; Eaton, 1976). While in small societies of primates (those under 50 or so), the leader (or alpha) male usually performs most peace-keeping functions, in many of the larger nonhuman primate societies, the peace-keepers are typically age cohorts of the alpha male who helped him dislodge the former leader, called beta males (Burton, 1972; Eaton, 1976).

From an evolutionary standpoint, the stakes that both alpha and beta males have in maintaining order within their society is, first, to protect the females with whom they frequently copulate, and, second, to protect the offspring that these females bear. One can see how such a social system would be favored by natural selection, and how it could be a primitive forerunner of human law enforcement activities (Pospisil, 1972:12; Alexander, 1979; de Waal, 1982; Ellis, 1986:65). No instances were found of alpha or beta males attempting to prevent a sexual assault. However, there have been several observations of these males harassing other males whenever they attempt to copulate (e.g., Hall & DeVore, 1965:65; Hanby & Brown, 1974; MacKinnon, 1974; Tutin, 1979).

It seems fair to conclude from the above evidence that (a) animals (especially primates) other than ourselves have a sense of acceptable and unacceptable social behavior under various conditions, (b) much of what they punish as unacceptable social behavior is similar to what we punish (and may include what we call *rape),* and (c) both their and our tendencies to do so may have evolved due to natural selection. Based upon this and other evidence, several social scietists in recent years have argued that many animal species have a basic moral sense as well as a sense of outrage when limits of "fair play" are exceeded, even if they themselves are not directly harmed by the excess (e.g., Kummer, 1978:34; Gruter, 1979; Boehm, 1982). If so, many human notions of right and wrong may not be simply the result of our social training and reinforcement (Huxley & Huxley, 1947; Waddington, 1961; Lorenz, 1966:235; Willhoite, 1981:244; Goodall, 1983; Alexander, 1986; Richards, 1988; Ellis, in press-c).

Overall, the synthesized theory contends that the outrage nearly all humans feel when they learn that someone they know has been raped, or otherwise criminally victimized in a serious way, is a minimally learned emotional response. We and many other social animals are likely to inherently sense that, left unchecked, such actions threaten to unravel a delicately woven social fabric upon which the proliferation of our genes (and those of our relatives) depends (Wilson, 1975:3; Carmen, 1987:201). This proposal is contrary to the views of social scientists—and even literary figures such as Mark Twain (Van der Zanden, 1978:385)—who have contended that human morality is socially conditioned (Lindsey, 1980:213; Kohlberg, 1976) and found in no other species but ours (Diamond, 1985:82). However, it is consistent with arguments by a number of other social scientists who see much of the variability in human morality as (a) due to genetic influences (Hartmann, 1962:6; Hare, 1970:101; Campbell, 1975), and (b) something our species shares with many other creatures (despite the inability of other creatures to express their moral sense verbally) (Lorenz, 1966, 1971; Carmen, 1987). If so, the laws pertaining to rape and other crimes are likely to be founded upon largely unlearned moral principles. This does not mean that every nuance in rape statutes are genetically programmed, but only that the basic blueprint is substantially influenced by DNA molecules—molecules, it should be remembered, that program the structure and much of the functioning of our brains.

SUMMARY

In general terms, the synthesized theory postulates that a number of variables are important in rape etiology. These may be conceived of in terms of two levels of scientific analysis. At the most fundamental level are genetic, evolutionary, neurological, and hormonal variables. At a more experiential level are motivational and learning variables, individual and group differences, stratification variables, and variability in societal reactions to rape. Collectively, these variables are hypothesized to interact in ways that have produced substantial variability in human raping tendencies.

Even though linguistic and visual portrayals of sexual behavior should not be major determinants of variations in male rape probabilities, the theory leads one to suspect that such variables could play a secondary role in rape etiology. Before being specific in this regard, readers should keep in mind two important qualifications: First, theoretically, only males who surpass the forced copulation threshold should be affected by any environmental experiences in terms of altering rape probabilities. Second, persons who surpass the forced copulation threshold are probably somewhat more attracted to pornography—especially provocative (including violent) forms of pornography—than are other males. (Thus, the theory would predict a positive correlation between pornography exposure and male rape probabilities simply because of self-selection, not because pornography exposure causes rape.) In other words, individuals who have a very strong sex drive and drive to possess and control sex partners, or who are very insensitive to stimuli would probably prefer viewing highly varied and provocative sexual stimuli, and would also be more likely to commit rape. Thus, studies that have found statistical associations between rape probability or attitudes favorable to rape, on the one hand, and amount of exposure to pornography, on the other hand (e.g., Baron & Straus, 1984; Malamuth & Check, 1985; Scott & Schwalm, 1988a; see also Russell, 1988:66), are likely to be *largely* reflecting a self-selection factor rather than the causal effects of exposure to pornography. To see how this deduction differs from the feminist and social learning theories of rape, see Russell (1988).

Nevertheless, theoretically, there are at least two ways exposure to mass media portrayals of sexual behavior might increase rape probabilities for males surpassing the forced copulation threshold. First, from an evolutionary standpoint, courtship and mating are fundamentally exchange processes in which the reproductive assets of a male are traded for the reproductive assets of a female. Anything that diminishes the perceived value of either participant in the exchange in the eyes of the other should lower the investment made by the perceiver. Keeping in mind that copulatory access, per se, is probably the main objective for most courting males (see Collins, 1975:252), and that this would be especially true for males who exceed the forced copulation threshold, one can predict that any lowering of the perceived value of the female being courted will increase the likelihood of his rushing through the courtship process in order to establish a copulatory relationship. Exposure to pornography in which female actresses/models are perceived as more sexually attractive than the female being courted could have this effect.

Second, the synthesized theory predicts that exposure to linguistic or visual portrayals of sexual activity could increase the probability of rape for males who exceed the forced copulation threshold if they are relatively inexperienced sexually. While the theory assumes that operant learning principles primarily determine how much force a male above the forced copulation threshold will use—prior to this male having acquired such experiences—he may rely upon images produced by verbal descriptions or visual means to guide his attempts to gain copulatory access. Exposure to pornography that depicts raping techniques could increase the chances of such a male committing rape. However, as soon as he gains sexual experience, whether or not he continues to use forceful copulatory tactics should depend primarily upon his ability to attract voluntary sex partners, upon the degree of success he has with the forceful copulatory tactics, and upon whether or not he is punished for using them. Inasmuch as a recent survey conducted by J. Bryant (see Russell, 1988:55) disclosed that 84% of high school students had seen at least one X-rated movie, and that at least 13% of these movies involved some degree of sexual aggression (Palys, 1986:26), rape-promoting effects of pornography exposure could be of some consequence for youthful males, although the main causes theoretically lie elsewhere.

In summary, regarding the effects of pornography, the synthesized theory views such vicarious experiences as, at most, playing only a secondary role in rape etiology. Much more important would be the learning derived from the actual use of raping techniques. Regarding attitudinal factors, while they may correlate with raping behavior, the synthesized theory does not see them as being significant in causing rape.

In the final chapter, brief summaries of the feminist, the social learning, the evolutionary, and the synthesized theories of rape are presented, followed by a few concluding remarks about the future of scientific efforts to understand and prevent rape, and to treat rape offenders and victims.

8

SUMMARY AND EPILOGUE

This book has been devoted to reviewing scientific attempts to understand the causes of rape. The review was initially oriented around the three theories of rape that have been proposed in the social science literature over the past 15 years. The feminist theory essentially sees rape as "a pseudosexual act" used by males to intimidate and dominate women. Support for it came from evidence that rape appeared related to sex disparities in socioeconomic and political arenas, although the direction of the disparities seemed contrary to what most feminists theorists have hypothesized. Specifically, it appears that lessening the disparities is associated with increased rape risks. Additional value in the feminist theory of rape is reflected in its emphasis upon connections between male tendencies to rape and their tendencies to display aggression, although the theory is probably incorrect in its implication that aggression and domination are the actual goals of most rapists.

The social learning theory postulates that rape is the result of male acquisition of attitudes and vicarious learning experiences (e.g., through the mass media) favorable to males behaving aggressively toward women. Consistent with this theory was evidence that attitudes favorable toward rape and toward the general use of violence toward women was associated with higher rape probability. Also supportive of the social learning theory was evidence that rapists were more prone to respond sexually to depictions of rape and aggression toward women than were other males.

According to the evolutionary theory, rape is an extreme response to natural selection pressure which has favored male assertiveness in attempting to copulate with numerous sex partners, and has favored females who resist male attempts to control their sexual behavior. The theory was supported by observations of forced copulations by males in many nonhuman species (suggesting the possibility of a genetic basis for male raping tendencies). Also favorable to the evolutionary theory was evidence that pregnancy risks, while probably lower than for voluntary sexual intercourse, are still significant (at least where birth control and abortion are not widely utilized by rape victims). In addition, the fact that the vast majority of rape victims throughout the world are of reproductive age is predicted by the evolutionary theory.

After reviewing the evidence both favoring and disfavoring hypotheses derived from the preceding three theories, a new theory was proposed—one based upon what was judged to be the main strengths of the other three theories. In addition, the new theory incorporated neurohormonal concepts so that it would be *neurologically specific,* a feature considered vital for elegant theories of behavior (Ellis, 1979, 1982:58).

In the briefest terms, the new theory argues that rape, like sexual behavior generally, is motivated by two largely unlearned and closely linked drives—the sex drive and the drive to possess and control (especially in regard to sex partners). While the motivation behind rape is assumed to be largely unlearned, the actual techniques and strategies involved in committing rape are believed to be learned (largely through operant conditioning, rather than through attitudes and imitation). From an evolutionary standpoint, the tendency to commit rape is seen as resulting from natural selection favoring a relatively strong sex drive and a drive to possess and control directed toward multiple sex partners. The natural selection pressure for these two drives was hypothesized to be more intense for males than for females, primarily because males can reproduce without committing time and energy to the gestation process, whereas females cannot escape this time and energy investment in reproduction.

The neurology underlying both the motivational and the learning processes surrounding rape are hypothesized to be intimately linked with the effects of sex hormones upon brain functioning (especially androgens and estradiol). Theoretically, to the degree that an individual's brain is exposed to high (male-typical) levels of androgens (especially prior to birth), the individual (a) should have an intense sex drive, and will orient his or her drive to possess and control toward multiple sex partners, and (b) should be relatively insensitive to aversive stimuli following the onset of puberty. However, because of a great deal of variability in male-typical levels of these sex hormones (both in terms of the levels of these hormones and the exact critical timing of their infiltration of various parts of the brain), males will exhibit considerable variability in regard to these neurological conditions (and females will also, to a lesser degree). Overall, exposing the brain to certain still-to-be-specified male-typical sex hormone regimens is postulated to increase the probability of an individual being very forceful in attempting to copulate and not easily deterred by any aversive consequences of those attempts.

The theory contends that, following the onset of puberty, when sexuality is fully activated (by the same hormones that helped to sexually differentiate the brain prior to birth), many males (and a few females) cross a theoretical point called the *forced copulation threshold.* Those males (and females) who only slightly surpass the forced copulation threshold are largely responsible for acquaintance rapes, but could, under some circumstances (e.g., during wartime when the prospects of punishment might be virtually nonexistent), commit predatory rape. Males who greatly surpass the forced copulation threshold should primarily be those who commit the vast majority of predatory rapes. Theoretically, their sex drives and/or drives to possess and control multiple sex partners should be unusually strong, and/or their sensitivities to aversive aspects of their environment (especially their social environment) should be low.

Somewhat more analytically, the synthesized theory can be stated in terms of the following four propositions.

1. *Motivational factors.* Rape, like most other forms of sexual behavior, is the expression of two largely unlearned drives—the sex drive and the drive to possess and control sex partners.
2. *Learning factors.* The techniques involved in committing rape are largely learned through operant conditioning, and the main reinforcement for learning such techniques are the pleasures associated with copulation and foreplay, and with possessing and controlling sexual access to sex partners. The learning of attitudes favorable to rape and tendencies to imitate rape depictions are hypothesized to play only secondary and indirect roles in rape etiology (and, even then, only in the case of individuals surpassing the forced copulation threshold).
3. *Evolutionary factors.* Due to natural selection, males have evolved relatively strong sex drives, greater tendencies to orient their drives to possess and control toward multiple sex partners, and lowered sensitivities to the aversive features of their environments. Females, on the other hand, have evolved tendencies to resist copulating except with males who demonstrate an abilty and a long-term willingness to provision for offspring and the females who bore them. Thus, individuals who are most likely to employ raping techniques are males who are least capable of making long-term provisioning commitments to sex partners and/or are least inclined to do so.
4. *Neurohormonal factors.* Androgens and other sex hormones alter brain functioning in and around the hypothalamus in ways that facilitate the sex drive and orient the drive to possess and control away from offspring and toward sex partners. In addition, androgens alter brain functioning in and around the reticular formation in ways that lower an individual's sensitivity

to the environment. Thus, exposing brains to relatively high androgen regimens (largely perinatally) eventually motivates individuals to copulate with multiple sex partners, and inclines them to be relatively insensitive to the suffering and distress inflicted upon others in the course of their learning and using forceful copulatory tactics.

While the merits of the synthesized theory remain to be determined, it should not be a complete surprise to find that it is better at "predicting" most of what is currently known about rape than its three predecessors since the synthesized theory was formulated after shortcomings of the other three had been systematically identified. As detailed in Chapter 7, however, there are many hypotheses that may be derived from the synthesized theory which should allow *its* strengths and weaknesses to eventually become apparent.

Among the topics that have been largely avoided throughout this book are those having to do with preventing rape and treating rape offenders and rape victims. The reason is that despite the progress that has been made in scientifically understanding rape in recent years, this understanding still is a long way from justifying a reliance upon any specific theory to guide the design of prevention and treatment programs. This, of course, will be a disappointment to those who must deal with rape and its aftermath as immediate practical problems, but it is in the best interest of all concerned that scientific theories not be applied before their scientific merits have been well established in largely innocuous and inconsequential ways.

In closing, it is hoped that, at the very least, this book will stand as a tribute to the extraordinary commitment that large numbers of social scientists have made in recent years to understanding rape and its etiology. In addition to the sheer magnitude of the research, what seems to have made the work in this area particularly fruitful is that so much of the research has been "theory driven" rather than simply the result of random curiosity. Even when theories are found to be defective (as virtually all are sooner or later), they still are very helpful for channeling research in ways that facilitate the accumulation and assimilation of scientific knowledge.

REFERENCES

Abel, G. G., Barlow, D. H., Blanchard, E. B., & Guild, D. (1977). The components of rapists' sexual arousal. *Archives of General Psychiatry, 34,* 895–908.

Abramowicz, H. K., & Richardson, S. A. (1975). Epidemiology of severe mental retardation in children: Community studies. *American Journal of Mental Deficiency. 80,* 18–39.

Abramson, P. R., & Hayashi, H. (1984). Pornography in Japan: Cross-cultural and theoretical considerations. In N. E. Malamuth & E. Donnerstein (Eds.), *Pornography and sexual aggression* (pp. 173–183). New York: Academic Press.

Adler, J., & Carey, J. (1980, Feb 25). The science of love. *Newsweek,* pp. 89–90.

Afton, A. D. (1985). Forced copulation as a reproductive strategy of male lesser scaup: A field test of some predictions. *Behavior, 92,* 146–167.

Ageton, S. S. (1982). *Sexual assault among adolescents.* Lexington, MA: Lexington Books.

Albert, D. J., Dyson, E. M., & Walsh, M. L. (1987). Intermale social aggression: Reinstatemtn in castrated rats by implants of testosterone propionate in the medial hypothalamus. *Physiology & Behavior, 39,* 555–560.

Albert, D. J., Walsh, M. L., Gorzalka, B. B., Siemens, Y., & Louie, H.

(1986). Testosterone removal in rats results in a decrease in social aggression and a loss of social dominance. *Physiology & Behavior, 36,* 401–407.

Alder, C. (1985). An exploration of self-reported sexually aggressive behavior. *Crime and Delinquency, 31,* 306–331.

Alexander, R. D. (1979). *Darwinism and human affairs.* Seattle: University of Washington Press.

Alexander, R. D. (1986). Biology and law. In M. Gruter & R. D. Masters (Eds.). *Ostracism: A social and biological phenomenon* (pp. 19–25). New York: Elsevier.

Allen, C. (1952). The problems of homosexuality. *International Journal of Sexology, 6,* 40–42.

Allen, C. L. (1988, July 11), Feats to concoct the flawless being. *Insight,* pp. 8–11.

Allen, C. M., & Straus, M. A. (1979). Resources, power, and husband-wife violence. In M. A. Straus & G. T. Hotaling (Eds.), *The social causes of husband-wife violence.* Minneapolis: Univ. of Minnesota Press.

Allore, R., O'Hanlon, D., Price, R., Neilson, K., Willard, H. F., Cox, D. R., Marks, A., & Dunn, R. J. (1988). Gene encoding the beta subunit of S100 protein is on chromosome 21: Implications for Down's syndrome. *Science, 239,* 1311–1313.

Amir, M. (1971). *Patterns in forcible rape.* Chicago: University of Chicago Press.

Amir, S., Brown, Z. W., & Amit, Z. (1980). The role of endorphins in stress: Evidence and speculation. *Neuroscience and Biobehavioral Reviews, 4,* 77–86.

Anderson, M., & Krebs, J. (1978). On the evolution of hoarding behavior. *Animal Behavior, 26,* 707–711.

Andy, O. J. (1977). Hypersexuality and limbic system seizures. *Pavlovian Journal of Biological Science, 12,* 187–228.

Andy, O. J., Kurimoto, T., Velamati, S., & Peeler, D. (1983). Limbic stimulation induced hypersexuality. *Pavlovian Journal of Biological Science, 18,* 22.

Angier, N. (1983, October). Mother nature's murderers. *Discover, 4,* pp. 78–82.

Anonymous. (1977, April 4). A new view of evolution. *Time,* p. 47.

Anonymous. (1978, April). Chimp killings: Is it the "man" in them. *Science News,* p. 276.

Anonymous, (1981, March). This is what you though about fear of crime. *Glamour,* p. 31.

Anonymous. (1983, September). Pinups and letdowns. *Psychology Today,* p. 83.

Appleby, M. C. (1982). The consequences and causes of high social rank in red deer stags. *Behavior, 80.*

Archer, J. (1977a). Sex differences in the emotional behavior of laboratory mice. *British Journal of Psychology, 68,* 125–131.

Ashbrook, J. B. (1984). Neurotheology: The working brain and the work of theology. *Zygon, 19,* 331–350.

Ashton, N. L. (1982). Validation of rape myth acceptance scale *Psychological Reports, 50,* 252.

Attorney General's Commission on Pornography. (1986). *Report of the Attorney General's Commission on Pornography: Final report.* Washington, DC: U.S. Government Printing Office.

Austad, S. N., & Thornhill, R. (1986). Female reproductive variation in a nuptial-feeding spider, *Pisaura mirabilis. Bulletin of British Arachnological Society, 7,* 48–52.

Austin, C. R. (1975). Sperm fertility, viability and persistence in the female tract. *Journal of Reproduction and Fertility, Supplement, 22,* 75–89.

Ayoub, D. M., Greenough, W. T., & Juraska, J. M. (1983). Sex differences in dendritic structure in the preoptic area of the juvenile Macaque monkey brain. *Science, 219,* 197–198.

Ayres, A. J. (1972). Types of sensory integrative disfunction among disabled learners. *American Journal of Occupational Therepy, 26,* 13–18.

Baack J.., & de LaCoste-Utamsing, C. (1982). Sexual dimorphism in fetal corpus callosum. *Society of Neuroscience Abstracts, 8,* 213.

Ball, I. L., Farnill, D., & Wangeman, J. F. (1984). Sex and age differences in sensation seeking: Some national comparisons. *British Journal of Psychology, 75,* 257–265.

Balkan, S., & Berger, R. J. (1979). The changing nature of female delinquency. In C. B. Kopp & M. Kirkpatrick (Eds.), *Becoming Female,* (pp. 207–227). New York: Plenum.

Bandura, A. (1967). Behavioral psychotherapy. *Scientific American 216,* 78–86.

Bandura, A. (1973). *Aggression: A social learning process.* Englewood Cliffs, NJ: Prentice-Hall.

Bandura, A. (1977). *Social learning theory.* Englewood Cliffs, NJ: Printice-Hall.

Bandura, A. (1978). Social learning theory of aggression. *Journal of Communication, 28,* 12–29.

Bandura, A. (1986). *Social foundations of thought and action.* Englewood Cliffs, NJ: Prentice-Hall.

Barash, D. P. (1977a). *Sociobiology and behavior.* Amsterdam: Elsevier.

Barash, D. P. (1977b). Sociobiology of rape in mallards *(anos platyhynchos):* Responses of the mated males. *Science, 197,* 788–789.

Barash, D. P. (1979). *The Whisperings Within.* New York: Harper & Row.

Barbaree, H. F., Marshall, W. L., & Lanthier, R. D. (1979). Deviant sexual arousal in rapists. *Behavioral Research and Therapy, 17:* 215–222.

Barber, R. N. (1969). Prostitution and the increasing number of convictions for rape in Queensland. *Australian and New Zealand Journal of Criminology* 2, 169–174.

Barfield, R. J., & Sachs, B. D. (1968). Sexual behavior: Stimulation by painful electrical shock to skin in male rats. *Science, 161,* 392–393.

Barlow, D. H., Abel, G. G., Blanchard, E. G., Bristow, A. R., & Young, L. D. (1977). A heterosocial skills behavior checklist for males. *Behavior Therapy, 8,* 229–239.

Barnes, G. E., Malamuth, N. M., & Check, J. V. P. (1984). Psychoticism and sexual arousal to rape depictions. *Personality and Individual Differences, 5,* 273–379.

Baron, L. (1985). Does rape contribute to reproductive success? Evaluation of sociobiological views of rape. *International Journal of Women's Studies, 8,* 266–277.

Baron, R. A. (1974a). Sexual arousal and physical aggression: The inhibiting influence of "cheesecake" and nudes. *Bulletin of the Psychonomic Society, 3,* 337–339.

Baron, R. A. (1974b). The aggression-inhibiting influence of heightened sexual arousal. *Journal of Personality and Social Psychology, 30,* 318–322.

Baron, R. A., & Bell, P. A. (1973). Effects of heightened sexual arousal on physical aggression. *Proceedings of the 81st Annual Convetion ofthe American Psychological Association, 8,* 171–172.

Baron, R. A., & Bell, P. A. (1977). Sexual arousal and aggression by males: Effects of type of erotic stimuli and prior provocation. *Journal of Personality and Social Psychology, 35,* 79–87.

Baron, R. A., & Straus, M. A. (1984). Sexual stratification, pornography, and rape in the United States. In N. M. Malamuth & E. Donnerstein (Eds.), *Pornography and Sexual Aggression* (p. 185–209). New York: Academic Press.

Barry, K. (1979). *Female sexual slavery.* Englewood Cliffs, NJ: Prentice-Hall.

Bartke, A., Musto, N., Caldwell, B. V., & Behrman, H. R. (1973). Effects of a cholesterol esterase inhibitor and of prostagladin F2a on testis cholesterol and on plasma testosterone in mice. *Prostaglandins, 3,* 97–104.

Bateman, A. J. (1948). Introasexual selection in *Drosophila. Heredity, 2,* 349–368.

Batten, M. (1982). Why men rape. *Science Digest, 90,* 64.

Baxter, D. J., Barbaree, H. E., & Marshall, W. L. (1986). Sexual responses to consenting and forced sex in a large sample of rapists and nonrapists. *Behavior Research and Therapy, 24,* 513–520.

Beach, F. A., Fleming, J. D., & Maxey, D. (1975, March). PUrsuit of intellectual orgasm. *Psychology Today,* pp. 69–77.

Beaglehole, E. (1932). *Property, a study in social psychology.* New York: Macmillan.

Beatty, W. W. (1978). DRL behavior in gerbils and hamsters of both sexes. *Bulletin of the Psychonomic Society, 11,* 41–42.

Beatty, W. W., & Beatty, P. A. (1970). Hormonal determinants of sex differences in avoidance behavior and reactivity to electric shock in rats. *Journal of Comparative and Physiological Psychology, 73,* 446–455.

Beatty, W. W., & Fessler, R. G. (1976). Ontogeny of sex differences in open-field behavior and sensitivity to electric shock in the rat. *Physiology and Behavior, 16,* 413–417.

Becker, H. S. (1963). *Outsiders.* New York: Free Press.

Beecher, M. D., & Beecher, I. M. (1979). Sociology of bank swallows: Reproductive strategy of the male. *Science, 205,* 1282–1285.

Belcastro, P. A. (1982). A comparison of latent sexual behavior patterns between raped and never raped females. *Victimology, 7,* 224–230.

Belk, R. W. (1988, July/August). My possessions myself. *Psychology Today, 22,* 50–52.

Bell, R. D., Alexander, B. M., & Schwartzman, R. J. (1983). Methylphenidate decreases local glucose metabolism in the motor cortex. *Pharmacological, Biochemistry, and Behavior, 18,* 1–5.

Bem, S. L. (1975, September). Androgyny vs. the tight little lives of fluffy women and chesty men. *Psychology Today,* pp. 58–62.

Benderly, B. L. (1982). Rape free or rape prone. *Science, 82,* 3, 40–43.

Benshoof, L., & Thornhill, R. (1979). The evolution of monogamy and concealed ovulation in humans. *Journal of Social & Biological Structures, 2,* 95–106.

Bentham, J. (1931). *The theory of legislation.* New York: Harcourt, Brace.

Ben-Veniste, R. (1971). Pornography and sex-crime: The Danish experience. *Technical Reports of the Commission on Obscenity and Pornography,* (Vol. 8). Washington, DC: U.S. Government Printing Office.

Bercovitch, F. B., Sladky, K. K., Roy, M. M., & Goy, R. W. (1987). Intersexual aggression and male sexual activity in captive rhesus macaques. *Aggressive Behavior, 13,* 347–358.

Bernard, M. L., & Bernard, J. L. (1983). Violent intimacy: The family as a model for love relationships. *Family Relations, 32,* 283–286.

Bernstein, I. S. (1966). Analysis of a key role in capuchin *(Cebus albifrons)* group. *Tulane Studies in Zoology, 13,* 49–54.

Betries, J. (1972, Summer). Rape: An act of possession. *Sweet Fire, 23,* pp. 12–16.

Betzig, L. L. (1982). Despotism and differential reproduction: A cross-cultural correlation of conflict asymmetry, hierarchy, and degree of polygyny. *Ethology and Sociobiology, 3,* 209–221.

Bielert, C. (1974). The effects of early castration and testosterone propriate treatment on the development and display of behavioral patterns by male rhesus monkeys. Unpublished doctoral dissertation, Michigan State University.

Blacker, C. P. (1952). *Eugenics: Galton and after.* Cambridge, MA: Harvard University Press.

Blackman, J. (1985). The language of sexual violence: More than a matter of semantics. In S. R. Sunday & E. Tobach (Eds.), *Violence against women* (pp. 115–128). New York: Gordian Press.

Blaszczynski, A. P. (1985, December). A winning bet: Treatment for compulsive gambling. *Psychology Today,* pp. 38–46.

Blaszczynski, A. P., Winter, S. W., & McConaghy, N. (1986). Plasma endorphin levels in pathological gambling. *Journal of Gambling Behavior, 2,* 3–14.

Bleier, R., Byne, W., & Siggelkow, I. (1982). Cytoarcyitectonic sexual dimorphisms of the medial preoptic and anterior hypothalamic areas in guinea pig, rat, hamster and mouse. *Journal of Comparative Neurology, 212,* 118–130.

Blizard, D. A., Lippman, H. R., & Chen, J. J. (1973). Neonatal androgen effects on open-field activity and sexual behavior in the female rat: The modifying influence of ovarian secretions during development. *Physiology and Behavior, 11,* 65–69.

Boehm, C. (1982). The evolutionary development of morality as an effect of dominance behavior and conflict interference. *Journal of Social and Biological Structures, 5,* 413–421.

Bogal-Albritten, R. B., & Allbritten, W. (1985). The hidden victims: Courtship violence among college students. *Journal of Student Personnel,* 201–204.

Boggs, C. L., & Gilbert, L. E. (1979). Male contribution to egg production in butterflies: Evidence for transfer of nutrients at mating. *Science, 206,* 83–84.

Bohman, M., Cloninger, R., Sigvardsson, S., & von Knorring, A. (1982). Predisposition to petty criminality in Swedish adoptees. *Archives of General Psychiatry, 39,* 1233–1241.

Bolton, R., & Bolton, C. (1975). *Conflictos en la familia Andina.* Cuzco: Centro de Estudios Andina.

Bond, S. B., & Mosher, D. L. (1986). Guided imagery of rape: Fantasy, reality, and the willing victim myth. *Journal of Sex Research, 22,* 162–183.

Bongaarts, J., & Potter, R. G. (1983). *Fertility, biology and behavior (analysis of the proximate determinants).* New York: Academic Press.

Bonger, W. A. (1916). *Criminality and economic conditions.* Bloomington: Indiana University Press (reprinted in 1936).

Bonger, W. A. (1936). *An Introduction to criminology.* London: Methuen.

Bonger, W. A. (1943). *Race and crime.* New York: Columbia University Press.

Bowker, L. H. (1979). The criminal victimization of women. *Victimonology: An International Journal, 4,* 371–384.

Bozzi, V. (1985, November). Sex and the romance reader. *Psychology Today,* p. 73.

Bradford, J. M. (1983). Research on sex offenders. *Psychiatric Clinics of North America, 6,* 715–731.

Breedlove, S. M., & Arnold, A. P. (1980). Hormone accumulation in a sexually dimorphic motor nucleus of the rat spinal cord. *Science, 210,* 564–566.

Brickman, J., & Briere, J. (1984). Incidence of rape and sexual assault inan urban Canadian population. *International Journal of Women's Studies, 7,* 195–206.

Briere, J., Malamuth, N., & Ceniti, J. (1981). Selfassessed rape proclivity: Attitudinal and sexual correlates. Paper presented at the meeting of the American Psychological Association, Los Angeles.

Briere, J., & Malamuth, N. M. (1983). Self-reported likelihood of sexually aggressive behavior: Attitudinal vs. sexual explanations. *Journal of Research in Personality, 17,* 315–323.

Bristow, W. S., & Lockett, G. H. (1926). The courtship of British lycosid spiders, and its probable significance. *Proceedings of the Zoological Society of London, 2,* 317–347.

Broude, G. J., & Green, S. J. (1976). Cross-cultural codes on twenty sexual attidudes and practices. *Ethnology, 15,* 409–428.

Broverman, D. M., Klaiber, E. L., Kobavashi, Y., & Vogel, W. (1968). Roles of activation and inhibition in sex differences in cognitive abilities. *Psychological Review, 75,* 23–50.

Brown, J. S. (1952). A comparative study of deviations from sexual mores. *American Sociological Review, 17,* 135–146.

Brownmiller, S. (1975). *Against our will: Men, women, and rape.* New York: Simon & Schuster.

Brozan, N. (1986, Feb. 17). Gang rape: A rising campus concern. *New York Times.* p. 17.

Bryden, M. P. (1979). Evidence for sex-related differences in cerebral organization. In M. A. Wittig & A. C. Petersen (Eds.), *Sex-related differences in cognitive functioning* (pp. 121–143). New York: Academic Press.

Buchsbaum, M. S. (1978, May). The sensoristat in the brain. *Psychology Today,* pp. 96–104.

Buchsbaum, M. S., & Pfefferbaum, M. A. (1971). Individual differences in stimulus intensity responses. *Psychophysiology, 8,* 600–611.

Burgess, A. W., & Holmstrom, L. L. (1977). Rape trauma syndrome. In R. Gies & G. Gies (Eds.), *Forcible rape.* New York: Columbia University Press.

Burke, R. J., & Weir, T. (1978). Sex differences in adolescent life stress, social support, and well-being. *Journal of Psychology, 98,* 277–288.

Burns, J. T., Cheng, K. M. & McKinney, F. (1980). Forced copulation in captive mallards. I. Fertilization of eggs. *Auk, 97,* 875–879.

Burstein, Paul. (1979). EEO legislation and the income of women and non-whites. *American Sociological Review, 44,* 367–391.

Burt, C. (1944). *The young delinquent.* 4th ed. New York: Appleton.

Burt, M. R. (1978). Attitudes supportive of rape in American culture. House Committee on Science and technology, Subcommittee Domestic and International Scietific Planning, Analysis and Cooperation, *Research into violent behavior: Sexual assaults* (pp. 277–322). Washington, DC: U.S. Government Printing Office.

Burt, M. R. (1980). Cultural myths and supports for rape. *Journal of Personality and Social Psychology, 38,* 217–230.

Burt, M. R. (1983). Justifying personal violence: A comparison of rapists and the general public. *Victimology, 8,* 131–150.

Burton, F. D. (1972). The integration of biology and behavior in the socialization of *Macaca sylvana* of Gibralter. In F. E. Poirier (Ed.), *Primate socialization,* (pp. 29–62). New York: Random House.

Buss, D. M. (1984). Evolutionary biology and personality psychology: Toward a conception of human nature and individual differences. *American Psychologist, 3,* 1135–1147.

Buss, D. M. (1987). Sex differences in human mate selection criteria: An evolutionary perspective. In C. Crawford, M. Smith, & D. Krebs (Eds.), *Sociobiology and psychology.* Hillsdale, NJ: Lawrence Erlbaum Associates.

Cade, W. H. (1981). Alternative male stategies: Genetic differences in crickets. *Science, 212,* 563–564.

Cain, W. S. (1981). Educating your nose. *Psychology Today, 15,* 48–56.

Calder, C. (1967). Breeding behavior of the roadrunner, *Geococcyx californianus. Aux, 84,* 597–598.

Campbell, B. G. (1987). *Humankind emerging,* (4th ed.). Boston: Little Brown.

Campbell, B. G. (1975). On the conflicts between biological and social evolution and between psychology and moral tradition. *American Psychologist, 30,* 1103–1126.

Cann, A., Calhoun, L. G., & Selby, J. W. (1981). Rape: A contemporary overview and analysis. *Journal of Social Issues, 37,* 1–4.

Carmen, I. H. (1987). Bioconstitutional politics: Toward an interdisciplinary paradigm. *Politics & the Life Sciences, 5,* 193–207.

Carneiro, R. L. (1977). A theory of the origin of the state. *Readings in anthropology 77/78* Guildford, CT: Dushkin.

Carrow, D. M. (1986). *Rape in medieval England.* Lanham, MD: University Press of America.

Cattell, J. M. (1903). A statistical study of eminent men. *Popular Science Monthly, 62,* 359–377.

Ceniti, J., & Malamuth, N. M. (1984). Effects of repeated exposure to sexually violent or nonviolent stimuli on sexual arousal to rape and nonrape depictions. *Behavior Therapy and Research, 22,* 535–548.

Chagnon, N. S. (1988). Life histories, blood revenge, and warfare in a tribal population. *Science, 239,* 985–992.

Chambliss, W. J. (1974). The state, the law and the definition of behavior as criminal or delinquent. In D. Glaser (Ed.), *Handbook of criminology.* Chicago: Rand McNally.

Chamove, A., Harlow, H. F., & Mitchell, G. D. (1967). Sex differences in the infant-directed behavior of preadolescent rhesus monkeys. *Child Development, 38,* 329–335.

Chan, A. W. K. (1986). Racial differences in alcohol sensitivity. *Alcohol and Alcoholism, 21,* 93–104.

Chance, M. R. A. (1962). Social behavior and primate evolution. In M. F. A. Montagu (Ed.), *Culture and the evolution of man* (pp. 84–130). New York: Oxford University Press.

Chandra, V., Bharucha, N. E., & Schoenberg, B. S. (1984). Mortality data for the U.S. for deaths due to and related to twenty neurologic diseases. *Neuroepidemiology, 3,* 149–168.

Chapman, D. (1968). *Sociology and the stereotype of the criminal.* London: Taverstock.

Chappell, D., Geis, G., Schafer, S., & Siegel, L. (1977). A comparative study of forcible rape offenses known to the police in Boston and Los Angeles. In D. Chappell, R. Geis, & G. Geis (Eds.), *Forcible rape: The crime, the victim, and the offender.* New York: Columbia University Press.

Chapell, D., & Singer, S. (1977). Rape in New York: A study of material in the police files and its meaning. In D. Chapell, R. Geis, & G. Geis (Eds.), *Forcible rape* (pp. 245–271). New York: Columbia University Press.

Charlesworth, W. R., & Dzur, C. (1987). Gender comparisons of preschoolers, behavior and resource utilization in group problem solving. *Child Development, 58,* 191–200.

Check, J. V. P. (1982). *Rape attitudes following participation in pornography experiments employing debriefing procedures.* Paper presented at the American Psychological Association Convention, Washington, DC.

Check, J. V. P., (1985). Hostility toward women: Some theoretical considerations. In G. W. Russell (Ed.), *Violence in intimate relationships.* Jamaica. NY: Spectrum.

Check, J. V. P., & Malamuth, N. M. (1983). Sex-role stereotyping and reactions to stranger vs. acquaintance rape. *Journal of Personality and Social Psychology, 45,* 344–356.

Check, J. V. P., & Malamuth, N. M. (1984). Can participation in pornography experiments have positive effects? *Journal of Sex Research, 20,* 14–31.

Check, J. V. P., & Malamuth, N. M. (1985). An empirical assessment of some feminist hypothesis about rape. *International Journal of Women's Studies*, *8*, 414–423.

Check, J. V. P., & Malamuth, N. M. (1986). Pornography and sexual aggression: A social learning theory analysis. *Communication Yearbook, 9*, 181–213.

Cheney, D. L. (1977). The acquisition of rank and the development of reciprocal alliances among free-ranging immature baboons. *Behavioral Ecology and Sociobiology, 2*, 303–318.

Cheng, K. M., Burns, J. T., & McKinney, F. (1982). Forced copulation in captive Mallards *(Anas Platyhynchos):* II. Temporal factors. *Animal Behavior, 30*, 695–699.

Cherlin, A., & Walters, P. B. (1981). Trends in United States men's and women's attitudes: 1972 to 1978. *American Sociological Review, 46*, 453–460.

Clark, A. B. (1978). Sex ratio and local resource competition in a prosimian primate. *Science, 201*, 163–165.

Clark, L. (1980). Pornography's challange to liberal ideology. *Canadian Forum, 3*, 9–12.

Clar, L., & Lewis, D. (1977). *Rape: The price of coercive sexuality.* Toronto: Women's Press.

Cline, V. B. (Ed.) (1974). *Where do you draw the line?* Salt Lake City, UT: Brigham Young Press.

Cloninger, C. R., & Gottesman, I. I. (1987). Genetic and environmental factors in antisocial behavior disorders. In S. A. Mednick, T. E. Moffitt, & S. A. Stock (Eds.), *The causes of crime* (pp. 92–109). Cambridge: Cambridge University Press.

Coffey, P. F. (1975). Sexual cyclicity in captive orangutans *(Pongo pygmaeus)* with some notes on sexual behavior. In the *Annual Report of the Jersey Wildlife Preservation Trust*, pp. 54–55.

Cohen, L. E., & Felson, D. J. (1979). Social changes and crime rate trends: A routine activity approach. *American Sociological Review, 44*, 588–608.

Collins, R. (1975). *Conflict sociology: Toward an explanatory science.* New York: Academic Press.

Collins, R. (1982). *Sociological Insight.* New York: Oxford University Press.

Conklin, J. E. (1986). *Criminology* (2nd ed.). New York: Macmillan.

Court, J. H. (1976). Pornography and sex-crimes: A reevaluation in the light of recent trends around the world. *International Journal of Criminology and Penology, 5*, 129–157.

Court, J. H. (1980). *Pornography and the Harmm Condition: A Response to the Report of Obscenity and Film Censorship.* Adelaide: Flinders University.

Court, J. H. (1982). Rape and trends in New South Wales: A discussion of conflicting evidence. *Australian Journal of Social Issues, 17*, 202–206.

Court, J. H. (1984). Sex and violence: A ripple effect. in N. M. Malamuth &

E. Donnerstein (Eds.), *Pornography and sexual aggression* pp. 143–172. New York: Academic Press.

Cox, C. R., & Le Boeuf, B. J. (1980). Female incitation of male competition: A mechanism in sexual selection. In J. H. Hunt (Ed.), *Selected readings in sociobiology* (pp. 320–338). New York: McGraw-Hill.

Crawford, C., & Galdikas, B. M. F. (1986). Rape in nonhuman animals: An evolutionary perspective. *Canadian Psychology, 27,* 215–230.

Crowley, W. R., Popolow, H. B., & Ward, O. B., Jr. (1973).From dud to stud: Copulatory behavior elicited through conditioned arousal in sexually inactive male rats. *Physiology and Behavior, 10,* 391–394.

Cullitan, B. J. (1972). Cooley's anemia: Special treatment for another ethnic disease. *Science, 178,* 590–593.

Currier, R. D., Little, S. C., Suess, J. F., & Andy, O. J. (1971). Sexual seizures. *Archives of Neurology, 25,* 260–264.

Curtis, L. A. (1974). *Criminal violence: National patterns and behavior.* Lexington, MA: Lexington.

Daly, M., & Wilson, M. (1978). *Sex, evolution and behavior.* North Scituate, MA: Duxbury.

Daly, M., & Wilson, M. (1980). Discriminitive parental solicitude: a biological perspective. *Journal of Marriage and the Family, 42,* 277–288.

Daly, M., & Wilson, M. (1983). *Sex, Evolution and Behavior* (2nd ed.). Belmont, CA: Wadsworth.

Daley, M, Wilson, M., & Weghorst, S. J. (1982). Male sexual jealousy. *Ethology and Sociobiology, 3,* 11–27.

Damon, A. (1971). RAce, ethnic group, and disease. In R. H. Osborne (Ed.), *The biological and social meaning of race.* San Francisco: Freeman.

Darwin, C. (1859). *The Origin of Species.* New York: Mentor (1958 reprint).

Davis, K. (1936). Jealousy and sexual property. *Social Forces, 14,* 395–405.

Davis, L. (1987, May/June). The personality genes. *Hippocrates,* 104–105.

Davis, N. J. (1975). *Sociological constructions of deviance.* Dubuque, IA: Wm. C. Brown.

Dawkins, R. (1976). *The selfish gene.* New York: Oxford University Press.

Deisher, R. W., Wenet, G. A., Paperny, D. M., Clark, T. F., & Fehrenbach, P. A. (1982). Adolescent sexual offense behavior: The role of the physician. *Journal of Adolescent Health Care, 2,* 279–286.

de Lacoste-Utamsing, C., & Holloway, R. L. (1982). Sexual dimorphism in the human corpus caltosum. *Science, 216,* 1431–1432.

Deming, M. B., & Eppy, A. (1981). The sociology of rape. *Sociology and Social Research, 65,* 357–380.

Denno, D., Meijs, B., Nachshon, I., & AUrand, S. (1982). Early cognitive function: Sex and race differences. *International Journal of Neuroscience, 16,* 159–172.

Deutsch, H. (1944). *The psychology of women: Vol. I. Girlhood.* New York: Bantam Books.

de Waal, F. B. M. (1978). Join-aggression and protective-aggression among captive *Macaca fascicularis.* In D. J. Chivers & J. Herbert (Eds.), *Recent advances in primatology, (Vol. 1.)* pp. 577–579. London: Academic Press.

de Waal, F. B. M. (1982). *Chimpanzee politics.* New York: Harper & Row.

Dewsbury, D. A. (1978). *Comparative animal behavior.* New York: McGraw-Hill.

Diamond, I. (1980). Pornography and repression: A reconsideration. *Signs, 5,* 686–701.

Diamond, J. (1985, April). Everything else you always wanted to know about sex. *Discover,* pp. 72–82.

Diamond, M. C., Dowling, G. A., & Johnson, R. E. (1981). Morphologic cerebral cortical asymmetry in male and female rats. *Experimental Neurology, 71,* 261–268.

Dienstbier, R. A. (1979). Emotion-attribution theory: Establishing roots and exploring future perspectives. In H. E. Howe & R. A. Dienstbier (Eds.), *Nebraska Symposium on Motivation* (Vol. 26, pp. 237–306). Lincoln: University of Nebraska Press.

Dietz, P. E. (1978). Social factors in rapist behavior. In R. Rada (Ed.), *Clinical aspects of the rapists.* New York: Grune and Stratton.

Dietz, P. E., & Evans, B. (1982). Pornographic imagery and prevalence of paraphilia. *American Journal of Psychiatry, 139,* 1493–1495.

Di Mattei, E. (1901). La sensibilita nei fanciulli in rapporto al sesso ed all'eta. *Archivio di Psichiatria, 22,* 207–208.

Dittus, W. P. (1980). The social regulation of primate populations: A synthesis. In D. G. Lindburg (Ed.), *The macaques: Studies in ecology, behavior and evolution* (pp. 263–286). New York: Van Nostrand Reinholt.

Di Vasto, P. V., Kaufman, A., Rosner, L. Jackson, R., Christy, J., Pearson, S., & Burgett, T. (1984). The revalence of sexually stressful events among females in the general population. *Archives of Sexual Behavior 13,* 59–67.

Doering, C. H., Brodie, H. K. H., Kraemer, H., Becker, H., & Hamburg, D. A. (1974). Plasma testosterone levels and psychologic measures in men over a two-month period. In R. C. Friedman, R. M. Richart, & R. L. Van de Wiele (Eds.), *Sex differences in behavior* (pp. 413–431). New York: Wiley.

Doering, C. H., Kraemer, H. C., Brodie, K. H., & Hamburg, D. A. (1975). A cycle of plasma testosterone in the human male. *Journal of Clinical Endocrinology and Metabolism, 40,* 495–500.

Dohler, K. D., & Wuttge, W. (1975). Changes with age in levels of serum gonadotropins, prolactin, and gonadal steroids in prepubertal male and femal rats. *Endocrinology, 97,* 898–907.

Donnerstein, E. (1980a). Pornography and violence against women. *Annals of the New York Academy of Sciences, 347,* 277–288.

Donnerstein, E. (1980b). Aggressive-erotica and violence against women. *Journal of Personality and Social Psychology, 39,* 269–277.

Donnerstein, E. (1984). Pornography: Its effect on violence against women. In N. M. Malamuth & E. Donnerstein (Eds.), *Pornography and Sexual Aggression* (pp. 53–84). New York: Academic Press.

Donnerstein, E. (1985). The effects of exposure to violent ponographic mass media images. *Engage Social Action, 13,* 16–19.

Donnerstein, E., & Barrett, G. (1978a). Eroticism and aggression. *Journal of Personality and Social Psychology, 36,* 180–188.

Donnerstein, E., & Barrett, G. (1978b). The effects of erotic stimuli on male aggression toward females. *Journal of Personality and Social Psychology, 36,* 180–188.

Donnerstein, E., & Berkowitz, L. (1981). Victim reactins in aggressive erotic films as a factor inviolence against women. *Journal of Personality and Social Psychology, 41,* 710–724.

Donnerstein, E., Donnerstein, M., & Evans, R. (1975). Erotic stimuli and aggression: Facilitation or inhibition. *Journal of Personality and Social Psychology, 32,* 237–244.

Donnerstein, E., & Hallam, J. (1978). Facilitating effects of erotica on aggression toward females. *Journal of Personality and Social Psychology, 36,* 1270–1277.

Donnerstein, E., & Linz, D. (1984, January). Sexual violence in the media: A warning. *Psychology Today,* pp. 14–15.

Donnerstein, E., & Linz, D. (1986). The question of pornography. *Psychology Today,* pp. 56–59.

Donnerstein, E., Linz, D., & Penrod, S. (1987). *The question of pornography.* New York: Free Press.

Dorus, E. (1980). Variability in the Y chromosome and variability of human behavior. *Archives of General Psychiatry, 37,* 587–594.

Doty, R. L., Shaman, P., Applebaum, S. L., Giberson, R., Sikorski, L., & Rosenberg, L. (1984). Smell identification ability: Changes with age. *Science, 226,* 1441–1443.

Durden-Smith, J., & deSimone, D. (1983). *Sex and the brain.* New York: Warner.

Durret, M. E. (1962). The relationship of early infant regulation and later behavior in play interviews. In V. H. Noll & R. P. Noll (Eds.), *Readings in educational psychology* (pp. 55–62). New York: Macmillian.

Dutton, D. G., & Aron, A. P. (1974). Some evidence for heightened sexual attraction under conditions of high anxiety. *Journal of Personality and Social Psychology, 30,* 510–517.

Dutton, D., & Painter, S. L. (1981). Traumatic bonding: The development of emotional attachments in battered women and other relationships of inter-mittent abuse. *Victimology, 6,* 139–155.

Dworkin, A. (1979). Pornography: The new terrorism. *New York University Review of Law and Social Change, 8,* 215–218.

Dworkin, A. (1981). *Pornography: Men possessing women.* New York: Peri-gee.

Dworkin, A. (1984). *Effect of pornography on women and children.* Testimony at the Hearings before the Subcommittee on Juvenile Justice of the Comm. on the Judiciary, 98th Cong., 2nd Sess., pp. 227–255.

Dworkin, A. (1985). Against the male flood: Censorship, pornography, and equality. *Harvard Women's Law Journal, 8,* 1–29.

Earls, C. M., & Proubo, J. (1986). The differentiation of francophone rapists and nonrapists using penile circumferential measures. *Criminal Justice and Behavior, 13,* 419–429.

Eaton, G. G. (1976). The social order of Japanese Macaques. *Scientific Ameri-can, 235,* 95–106.

Eaton, G. G., Modahl, K. B., & Johnson, D. F. (1981). Aggressive behavior in a confined troop of Japanese Macaques: Effects of density, season, and gender. *Aggressive Behavior, 7,* 145–164.

Eckland, B. K. (1967). Genetics and sociology: A reconsideration. *American Sociological Review, 32,* 173–194.

Edwards, D. A., & Einhorn, L. C. (1986). Preoptic and midbrain control of sexual motivation. *Physiology and Behavior, 37,* 329–335.

Eeg-Olofsson, O. (1971). The development of the EEG in normal adolescents from the ages of 16 through 21 years. *Neuro-podiatrie, 3,* 11–45.

Ehrhardt, A. A. (1978). Behavioral sequelae of prenatal hormonal exposure in animals and man. In M. A. Lipton, A. DiMascio, & K. F. Killam (Eds.), *Psychpharmacology: A generation of progress* (pp. 531–539). New York: Raven Press.

Eibl-Eibesfeldt, I. (1987). Ethologic aspects of food sharing and the roots of possession. *South African Journal of Ethology, 10,* 23–28.

Eisdorfer, C., Doerr, H. O., & Follette, W. (1980). Electrodermal reactivity: An analysis by age and sex. *Journal of Human Stress, 6,* 39–42.

Ellingson, R. J. (1956). Brain waves and problems of psychology. *Psychologi-cal Bulletin, 53,* 1–34

Ellis, E. M., Atkeson, B. M., & Calhoun, K. S. (1981). An assessment of long-term reaction to rape. *Journal of Abnormal Psychology, 90,* 263–266.

Ellis, H. (1934). *Man and woman, a study of secondary and tertiary sexual characteristics* (8th rev. ed.). London: Heinemann.

Ellis, L. (1982a). Genetics and criminal behavior: Evidence through the end of the 1970s. *Criminology, 20,* 43–66.

Ellis, L. (1982b). Developmental androgen fluctuations and the five dimensions of mammalian sex (with emphasis upon the behavioral dimension and the human species). *Ethology and Sociobiology, 3,* 171–197.

Ellis, L. (1985). On the rudiments of possessions and property. *Social Science Information, 24,* 113–143.

Ellis, L. (1986a). Evidence of neuroandrogenic etiology of sex roles from a combined analysis of human, nonhuman primate, and nonprimate mammalian studies. *Personality and Individual Differences, 7,* 519–552.

Ellis, L. (1986b). Evolution and the nonlegal equivalent of aggressive crimnal behavior. *Aggressive Behavior, 12,* 57–71.

Ellis, L. (1987a). Neurological basis of varying tendencies to learn delinquent and criminal behavior. In C. J. Braukmann & E. K. Morris (Eds.), *Behavioral approaches to crime and delinquency: Application, research and theory* (pp.499–518). New York: Plenum.

Ellis, L. (1987b). Criminal behavior and r/k selection: An extension of gene-based evolutionary theory. *Deviant Behavior, 8,* 149–176.

Ellis, L. (1987c). Religiosity and criminality from the perspective of arousal theory. *Journal of Research in Crime and Delinquency, 24,* 215–232.

Ellis, L. (in press-a). Monoamine oxidase and criminality: Identifying an apparent biological marker for antisocial behavior. *Journal of Research in Crime and Delinquency, 1991, 28,* 227–250.

Ellis, L. (in press-b). Sex differences in criminality: An explanation based on the concept of r/K selection. In L. Ellis and H. Hoffman (Eds.), *Crime in Biological, Social, and Moral Contexts.* New York: Praeger (1990).

Ellis, L. (in press-c). The evolution of collective counterstrategies to crime: From primate control behavior to the criminal justice system. In L. Ellis & H. Hoffman (Eds.), *Crime in Biological, Social, and Moral Contexts.* New York: Praeger (1990).

Ellis, L., & Ames, M. A. (1987). Neurohormonal functioning and sexual orientation: A theory of homosexuality-heterosexuality. *Psychological Bulletin, 101,* 233–258.

Ellis, L., & Beattie, C. (1983). The feminist explanation for rape: An empirical test. *Journal of Sex Research, 19,* 74–93.

Emlen, S. T., & Wrege, P. H. (1986). Forced copulations and intra-specific parasitism: Two costs of social living in the white-fronted bee-eater. *Ethology, 71,* 2–29.

Ennis, P. H. (1967). *Criminal victimization in the United States: A report of a national survey.* National Opinion Research Center (N.O.R.C.), University of Chicago, Washington, DC: U.S. Government Printing Office.

Essock-Vitale, S. M., & McGuire, M. T. (1985). Women's lives viewed from an evolutionary perspective. I. Sexual histories, reporductive success, and demographic characteristics of a random sample of American women. *Ethology and Sociobiology, 6,* 137–154.

Evans, S. S., & Scott, J. E. (1984). The seriousness of crime cross-culturally. *Criminology, 22,* 39–57.

Ewing, J. A., Rouse, B. A., & Pellizzari, E. D. (1974). Alcohol sensitivity and ethnic background. *American Journal of Psychiatry, 130,* 206–210.

Eysenck, H. J. (1967). *The biological basis of personality.* Springfield MA: C. C. Thomas.

Eysenck, H. J. (1976). *Sex and personality.* Austin: University of Texas Press.

Eysenck, H. J. (1977). *Crime and personality* (3rd ed.). London: Routledge & Kegan Paul.

Eysenck, H. J. (1984). Sex, violence, and the media: Where do we stand now? In N. M. Malamuth & E. Donnerstein (Eds.), *Pornography and sexual aggression* (pp. 305–318). New York: Academic Press.

Eysenck, H. J., & Eysenck, S. B. (1978). Psychopathy, personality and genetics. In R. D. Hare & D. Schalling (Eds.), *Psychopathic behavior: Approaches to research* (pp. 197–223). New York: Wiley.

Farley, F. (1986, May). The big T in personality. *Psychology Today,* pp. 44–52.

Farr, J. A. (1980). The effects of sexual experience and female receptivity on courtship rape decisions in male guppies, *Poecilia reticulata* (Pisces: poeciliidae). *Animal Behavior, 28,* 1195–1201.

Farr, L. A. Andrews, R. V., & Kline, M. R. (1978). Comparison of methods for estimating social rank of deer mice. *Behavioral Biology, 23,* 399–404.

Farres, A. G. (1976). Cognitive sex differences as a function of critical period exposure to testosterone in rats. (Doctoral dissertation, University of Akron). *Dissertation Abstracts, 37,* (10-B), 5423.

Faux, S. F., & Miller, H. L. (1984). Evolutionary speculations on the oligarchic development of Mormon polygyny. *Ethology and Sociobiology, 5,* 15–31.

Feild, H. S. (1978). Attitudes toward rape: A comparative analysis of police, rapists, crisis counselors and citizens. *Journal of Personality & Social Psychology, 36,* 156–179.

Feldman, S. (1975). Likelihood of pregnancy caused by rape. Medical Aspects of Human Sexuality, 9, 89.

Feldman-Summers, S., & Palmer, G. C. (1980). Rape as viewed by judges, prosecuters, and police officers. *Criminal Justice and Behavior, 7,* 19–40.

Findlay, B. (1974). The cultural context of rape. *Women's Law Review, 60,* 199–207.

Finkelhor, D., & Vilo, K. (1982). Forced sex in marriage: A preliminary research report. *Crime & Delinquency, 28,* 459–478.

Fisher, J. L., & Harris, M. B. (1976). Modeling, arousal, and aggression. *Journal of Social Psychology, 100,* 219–226.

Floody, O. R., & Pfaff, D. W. (1977). Aggressive behavior in female hamsters:

The hormonal basis for fluctuations in female aggressiveness correlated with estrous state. *Journal of Comparative and Physiological Psychology, 91,* 443–464.

Florey, C. Du V., & Cuadadro, (1968). Blood pressure in native Cape Verdeans and in Cape Verdean immigrants and their descendants living in New England. *Human Biology, 40,* 189–211.

Fox, C. A., & Fox, B. (1967). Uterine suction during orgasm. *British Medical Journal, 1,* 300–301.

Fox, H. (1929). The birth of two anthropoid apes. *Journal of Mammalogy, 10,* 37–51.

Fox, R. (1980). *The red lamp of incest.* New York: Dutton.

Frank, E., & Anderson, B. P. (1987). Psychiatric disorders in rape victims: Past history and current symptomotology. *Comprehensive Psychiatry, 28,* 77–82.

Fraser, A. F. (1974). *Farm animal behavior.* London: Ballier & Tindall.

Freedman, D. G. (1979a, January). Ethnic differences in babies. *Human Nature,* pp. 36–43.

Freedman, D. G. (1979b). *Human sociobiology.* New York: Free Press.

Freedman, D. G., & DeBoer, M. M. (1979). Biological and cultural differences in early child development. *Annual Review in Anthropology, 8,* 579–600.

Freeman, W. (1934). The weight of the endocrine glands: Biometrical studies in psychiatry. *Human Biology, 6,* 489–523.

French, J. A., & Cleveland, J. (1984). Scent-marking in the tamarin, *Seguinus Oedipus:* Sex differences and ontogeny. *Animal Behavior, 32,* 615–623.

Freund, K. (in press). Courtship disorder: A simple observation and a hypothesis. In L. Ellis & H. Hoffman (Eds.), *Evolution, the brain and criminal behavior: Explorations in biosocial criminology.* New York: Praeger.

Freund, K., Scher, H., & Hucker, S. (1983). The courtship disorders. *Archives of Sexual Behavior, 12,* 369–379.

Freund, K., Scher, H., & Hucker, S. (1984). The courtship disorders: A further investigation. *Archives of Sexual Behavior, 13,* 133–139.

Frisch, R. E. (1980). Fatness, puberty, and fertility. *Natural History, 89,* (10), 16–27.

Frodi, A. (1977). Sexual arousal, situational restrictiveness and aggressive behavior. *Journal of Research in Personality, 11,* 48–58.

Fuller, J. L. (1987). What can genes do? In C. Crawford, M. Smith, & D. Krebs (Eds.), *Sociobiology and psychology: Ideas, issues, and applications* (pp. 147–174). Hillsdale, NJ: Lawrence Erlbaum Associates.

Furby, L. (1978). Possession in humans: An exploratory study of its meaning and motivation. *Social Behavior and Personality, 6,* 49–65.

Gager, N., & Schurr, C. (1976). *Sexual assualt: Confronting rape in America.* New York: Grosset and Dunlap.

Galdikas, B. M. (1979). Orangutan adaptation at Tanjung Putiny Reserve: Mating and ecology. In D. A. Hamburg & E. R. McCown (Eds.), *The great apes,* (pp.195–233). Menlo Park, CA: Benjamin/Cummings.

Galdikas, B. M. F. (1981). Orangutan reproduction in the wild. In C. E. Graham (Ed.), *Reproductive biology of the great apes.* New York: Academic Press.

Galdikas, B. M. F. (1985a). Adult male sociality and reproductive tactics among orangutans at Tanjung Putiny. *Folia Primatologica, 45,* 9–24.

Galdikas, B. M. F. (1985b). Subadult male orangutan sociality and reproductive behavior at Tanjung Putiny. *American Journal of Primatology, 8,* 87–99.

Galizio, M., Rosenthal, D., & Stein, F. A. (1983). Sensation seeking, reinforcement, and student drug use. *Addictive Behaviors, 8,* 243–252.

Galton, F. (1894). The relative sensitivity of men and women at the nape of the neck by Webster's test. *Nature, 50,* 40–42.

Gandelman, R. (1983). Gonadal hormones and sensory function. *Neuroscience and Biobehavioral Reviews, 7,* 1–17.

Garrett, T. B., & Wright, R. (1975). Wives of rapists and incest offenders. *Journal of Sex Research, 11,* 149–157.

Gebhard, P. H., Gagnon, J. H., Pomeroy, W. B., & Christenson, C. V. (1965). *Sex offenders: An analysis of types.* New York: Harper & Row.

Gerner, M. (1981). The brain and behavior: Casting light into the "blackbox." *Psychological Reports, 49,* 51–518.

Geschwind, N., & Galaburda, A. M. (1985a). Cerebral lateralization: Biological mechanisms, associations, aand pathology: I. A hypothesis and a program for research. *Archives of Neurology, 42:* 428–459.

Geschwind, N., & Galaburda, A. M. (1985b). Cerebral lateralization: Biological mechanisms, associations, and pathology: II. A hypothesis and a program for research. *Archives of Neurology, 42,* 521–552.

Ghosh, B., Choudhuri, D. K., & Pal, B. (1984). Some aspects of the sexual behavior of stray dogs. *Applied Animal Behavior Science, 13,* 113–127.

Ghosh, A., Woo, J. S. K., & Poon, I. M. L. (1981). Neural tupe defects in Hong Kong Chinese. *Lancet, 2,* 468–469.

Giannandrea, P. F. (1985). The myth of male superiority: Its biopsychosocial importance to male psychological development. *Psychiatric Annals, 15,* 715–724.

Giarrusso, R., Johnson, P., Goodchilds, J., & Zellman, G. (1979). Adolescents' cues and signals: Sex and assault. In P. Johnson (Chair.), *Acquaintance rape and adolescent sexuality.* Symposium conducted at the meeting of the Western Psychological Association.

Gibbons, D. C. (1987), *Society, crime, and criminal behavior* (5th ed.). Englewood Cliffs, NJ: Prentice-Hall.

Gibson, L., Linden, R., & Johnson, S. (1980). A situational theory of rape. *Canadian Journal of Criminology, 22,* 51–63.

Gilbert, J. A. (1897). Researches upon children and college students. *Iowa University Studies of Psychology, 1*, 1–39.

Gilliam, T. C., Bucan, M., MacDonald, M. E., Zimmer, M., Haines, J. L., Cheng, S. V., Pohl, T. M., Meyers, R. H., Whaley, W. L., Allitto, B. A., Faryniarz, A., Wasmuth, J. J., Frischauf, A., Conneally, P. M., Lehrach, H., & Gusella, J. (1987). A DNA segment encoding two genes very tightly linked to Huntington's disease. *Science, 238*, 950–952.

Ginsberg, M. (1965). *On justice in society.* Baltimore: Penguin.

Gladstone, D. E. (1979). Promiscuity in monogamous colonial birds. *American Naturalist, 114*, 545–557.

Glaser, D. (1978). *Crime in our changing society.* New York: Holt, Reinhart & Winston.

Glazer-Schuster, I. M. (1979). *New women of Lusaka.* Palo Alto, CA: Mayfield.

Goldfoot, D. A. (1977). Sociosexual behaviors of nonhuman primates. In A. M. Schrier (Ed.), *Behavioral primatology. Volume 1* (pp. 136–180). New York: Wiley.

Goldfoot, D. A., Slob, A. K., Scheffler, G., Robinson, J. A., Wiegand, S. J., & Cords, J. (1975). Multiple ejaculations during prolonged sexual tests and lack of resultant serum testosterone increases in male stumptail macques *(M. arctoides). Archives of Sexual Behavior, 4*, 547–560.

Goldsby, R. A. (1971). *Race and races.* New York: Macmillan.

Goldschmidt, W. (1976). *Culture and behavior of the sebei.* Berkeley: University of California Press.

Goldstein, B. (1976). *Human sexuality.* New York: McGraw-Hill.

Goldstein, M. J. (1973). Exposure to erotic stimuli and sexual deviance. *Journal of Social Issues, 29*, 197–219.

Goma, M., Perez, J., & Torrubia, R. (1988). Personality variables in antisocial and prosocial disinhibitory behavior. In T. E. Moffitt & S. A. Mednick (Eds.), *Biological contributions to crime causation,* (pp. 213–222). Dordrecht: Martinus Nijoff.

Goodall, J. (1983). Order without law. In M. Gruter & P. Bohannan (Eds.), *Law and culture: The evolution of law and culture* (pp. 50–62). Santa Barbara, CA: Ross-Erikson.

Goodall, J., Bandora, A., Bergmann, E., Busse, C., Matama, H., Mpongo, E., Pierce, A., & Riss, D. (1979). Intercommunity interactions in the chimpanzee population of the Gombe National Park. In D. A. Hamburg & E. R. McCown (Eds.), *The great apes* (pp. 12–53). Melo Park, CA: Benjamin/Cummings.

Goodchilds, J. D., & Zellman, G. L. (1984). Sexual signaling and sexual aggression in adolescent relationships. In N.M. Malamuth & E. Donnerstein (Eds.), *Pornography and sexual aggression* (pp. 233–243). New York: Academic Press.

Gorski, R. A., Gordon, J. H., Shryne, J. E., & Southam, A. M. (1978). Evidence for a morphological sex difference within the medial preptic area of the rat brain. *Brain Research, 143,* 333–346.

Gould, J. L. (1982). *Ethology: The mechanisms and evolution of behavior.* New York: Norton.

Gove, W. R., Hughes, M., & Geerken, M. (1985). Are *Uniform Crime Reports* a valid indicator of the Index Crimes? An affirmative answer with minor qualifications. *Criminology, 32,* 451–501.

Goy, R. W., & McEwen, B. S. (1980). *Sexual differentiation of the brain.* Cambridge, MA: MIT Press.

Gray, J. A. (1971). Sex difference in emotional behavior in mammals including man: Endocrine bases. *Acta Psychologica, 35,* 29–46.

Gray, J. A., & Buffery, A. W. H. (1971). Sex differences in emotional and cognitive behavior in mammals including man: Adaptive and neural bases. *Acta Psychologica, 35,* 89–111.

Gray, S. H. (1982). Exposure to pornography and aggression toward women: The case of the angry male. *Social Problems 29,* 387–398.

Greenough, W. T., Carter, C. S., Steerman, C., & deVoogd, T. J. (1977). Sex differences in dendrite patterns in hamsters preoptic area. *Brain Research, 126,* 63–72.

Griffin, S. (1971, September). The all-American crime. *Ramparts,* pp. 26–35.

Groth, A. N. (1979). *Men who rape: The psychology of the offender.* New York: Plenum.

Groth, A. N., & Burgess, A. W. (1978). Rape: A pseudosexual act. *International Journal for Women's Studies, 1,* 207–210.

Groth, A. N., Burgess, A. W., & Holmstrom, L. L. (1977). Rape: Power, anger, and sexuality. *American Journal of Psychiatry, 134,* 1239–1243.

Gruter, M. (1979). The origins of legal behavior, *Journal of Social and Biological Structures, 2,* 43–51.

Guinzburg, S. (1983, September). Collegiate rape. *Psychology Today,* p. 76.

Gullickson, G. R., & Crowell, D. H. (1964). Neonatal habituation to electrotactual stimulation. *Journal of Experimental Child Psychology, 1,* 388–396.

Gusella, J. F., Tanzi, R. E., Anderson, M. A., Hobbs, W., Gibbons, K., Raschtchian, R., Gilliam, T. C., Wallace, M. R., Wexler, N. S., & Conneally, P. M. (1985). DNA markers for the nervous system disease. *Science, 225,* 1320–1326.

Guttmacher, M. (1951). *Sex offenses: The problem, causes, and prevention.* New York: Norton.

Guttmacher, M., & Weihofen, H. (1952). *Psychiatry and the law.* New York: Norton.

Gwynne, D. T. (1982). Mate selection by female katydids. (Orthoptera: Tettigoniidae, *Conocephalus nigropleurum*). *Animal Behavior, 30,* 734–738.

Hafez, E. S. E., & Shein, M. W. (1962). The behavior of cattle. In E. S. E.

Hafez (Ed.), *The behavior of domestic animals* (pp. 247–296). Baltimore: Williams & Wilkins.

Hagan, F. E. (1988). *Introduction to Criminology.* Chicago: Nelson-Hall.

Hagen, R. (1979). *The bio-sexual factor.* Garden City, NY: Doubleday.

Haldane, J. B. S. (1985). *On being the right size and other essays.* New York: Oxford University Press.

Hall, E. R., & Flannery, P. J. (1984). Prevalence and correlates of sexual assault experiences in adolescents. *Victimology: An International Journal, 9,* 398–406.

Hall, K. R., & DeVore, I. (1965). Baboon social behavior In I. DeVore (Ed.), *Primate Behavior* (pp. 53–110). New York: Holt, Rinehart & Winston.

Hammer, R. P., Jr. (1984). The sexually dimorphic region of the preoptic area in rats contains denser opiate receptor binding sites in females. *Brain, 308,* 172–176.

Hammer, R. P., Jr., & Jacobson, C. D. (1982). Sex difference in dendrites during development of the sexually dimorphic nucleus in the preoptic area. *Society Neuroscience Abstract, 8,* 197.

Hanby, J. P., & Brown, C. E. (1974). The development of sociosexual behaviors in Japanese macaques. *Behaviour, 49,* 152–196.

Harcourt, A. H. (1978). Strategies of emigration and transfer by primates, with particular reference to gorillas. *Zeitschrift für Tierpsychologie, 48,* 401–420.

Harding, C. F. (1985). Sociobiological hypotheses about rape: A critical look at the data behind the hypotheses. In S. R. Sunday & E. Tobach (Eds.), *Violence against women: A critique of the sociobiology of rape,* pp. 23–58). New York: Gordian Press.

Hare, R. D. (1970). *Psychopathy.* New York: Wiley.

Hare, R. D. (1982). Psychopathy and the personality dimensions of psychoticism, extraversion and neuroticism. *Personality and Individual Differences, 3,* 35–42.

Hariton, B., & Singer, J. (1974). Women's fantasies during sexual intercourse: Normative and theoretical implications. *Journal of Consulting and Clinical Psychology, 43,* 313–322.

Harlow, H. (1962). The heterosexual affectional system in monkeys. *American Psychologist, 17,* 1–19.

Harrison, A. A. (1969). Exposure and popularity. *Journal of Personality, 38,* 359–377.

Hart, B. L. (1974). Medial preoptic-anterior hypothalamic area and sociosexual behavior of male doges: A comparative neuropsychological analysis. *Journal of Comprehensive Physiology and Psychology, 86,* 238–249.

Hart, B. L., & Leedy, M. G. (1985). Neurological bases of male sexual behavior. In N. Adler, D. Pfaff, & R. W. Goy (Eds.), *Handbook of behavioral neurobiology, Vol. 2, Reproduction* (pp. 373–422). New York: Plenum.

Hartmann, N. (1962). *Ethik*. Berlin: Walter de Gruyter.

Harvald, B., & Hauge, H. M. (1965). Hereditary factors elucidated by twin studies. In J. V. Neel, et. al. (Eds.), *Genetics and the epidemiology of chronic disesases*. (U.S. Public Health Service, Publication No. 1163). Washington, DC: U.S. Government Printing Office.

Hauser, H., & Gandelman, R. (1983). Continquity to males in utero affects avoidance responding in adult female mice. *Science, 220,* 437–438.

Hausfater, G. (1975). Dominance and reproduction in baboons *(Papio cyno-cephalus). Contributions to Primatology, 7,* 1–150.

Havendar, W. R. (1978). Defining racism. *Science, 199,* 934.

Hayman, C. R., Lanza, C., Fuentes, R., & Algor, K. (1972). Rape in the District of Columbia. *American Journal of Obstetrics and Gynecology, 113,* 91–97.

Hayman, C. R., Lewis, F. R., Stewart, W. F., & Grant, M. (1967). A public health program for sexually assaulted females. *Public Health Reports, 82,* 497–504.

Hayman, C. R., Stewart, W. F., Lewis, F. R., & Grant, M. (1968). Sexual assault on women and children in the District of Columbia. *Public Health Reports, 83,* 1021–1028.

Heath, R. G. (1972). Pleasure and brain activity in man. *Journal of Nervous and Mental Disease, 154,* 3–17.

Heilman, K. M., Bowers, D., & Valenstein, E. (1985). Emotional disorders associated with neurological diseases. In K. M. Heilman & E. Valenstein (Eds.), *Clinical neuropsychology* (chap. 13). New York: Oxford University Press.

Heim, A. H. (1970). *Intelligence and personality.* Harmondsworth, England: Penguin.

Helmreich, R. L., Spencer, J. T., & Gibson, R. J. (1982). Sex-role attitudes: 1972–1980. *Personality and Social Psychology Bulletin, 8,* 656–663.

Herschberger, R. (1970). Is rape a myth? In B. Roskak & T. Roskak (Eds.), *Masculine-feminine: Readings in sexual mythology and the liberation of women*. New York: Harper & Row.

Hersen, M. (1972). Nightmare behavior: A review. *Psychological Bulletin, 78,* 37–48.

Heyns, B. (1978). *Summer learning and the effects of schooling*. New York: Academic Press.

Hilgard, E. R. & Bower, G. H. (1975). *Theories of Learning* (4th ed.), Englewood Cliffs, NJ: Prentice-Hall.

Hill, J. (1984). Prestige and reproductive success in man. *Ethology and Sociobiology, 5,* 77–95.

Hinde, R. A. (1956). The biological significance of territories of birds. *Ibis, 98,* 340–369.

Hinde, R. A. (1986). Some implications of evolution theory and comparative data for the study of human prosocial and aggressive behavior. In D. Olweus, J. Black, & M. Redke-Yarrow (Eds.), *Development of antisocial and prosocial behavior* (pp. 13–32). Orlando: Academic Press.

Hindelang, M. (1978). Race and involvement in common law personal crimes. *American Sociological Review, 43,* 93–109.

Hindelang, M. J., & Davis, B. L. (1977). Forcible rape in the United States: A statistical profile. In D. Chappell, R. Geis, & G. Geis (Eds.), *Forcible rape: The crime, the victim, and the offender.* New York: Columbia University Press.

Hines, M., Alsum, P., Roy, M., Gorski, R. A., & Goy, R. W. (1987). Estrogen contributions to sexual differentiation in the female guinea pig: Inflences of diethylstilbestrol and tamoxifen on neural, behavioral, and ovarian development. *Hormones and Behavior, 21,* 402–417.

Hines, M., & Gorski, R. A. (1985). Hormonal influences on the development of neural asymmetries. In F. Benson and E. Zaidel (Eds.), *The dual brain* (pp. 75–96). New York: Guilford.

Hinton, J. W., O'Neill, M. T., & Webster, S. (1980). Psychophysiological assessment of sex offenders in a security hospital. *Archives of Sexual Behavior, 9,* 205–216.

Hirschon, R. (1984). *Women and property.* New York: St. Martin's.

Hite, S. (1981). *The Hite report on male sexuality.* New York: Knopf.

Hogg, J. T. (1984). Mating in bighorn sheep: Multiple creative male strategies. *Science, 225,* 526–528.

Holden, C. (1980). Twins re-united. *Science, 80,* 54–59.

Holden, C. (1985, January). Genes, personality and alcoholism. *Psychology Today,* pp. 38–44.

Holden, C. (1987). The genetics of personality. *Science, 237,* 598–601.

Holmstrom, L. L. & Burgess, A. W. (1980). Sexual behavior of assailants during reported rapes. *Archives of Sexual Behavior, 9,* 427–439.

Hoon, P. W., Wincze, J. P., & Hoon, E. F. (1977). A test of reciprocal inhibition: Are anxiety and sexual arousal in women mutually inhibitory? *Journal of Abnormal Psychology, 86,* 65–74.

Hopson, J. L. (1987, August). Boys will be boys, girls will be... *Psychology Today,* pp. 60–66.

Hornung, C. A., McCullough, B. C., & Sugimoto, T. (1981). Status relationships in marriage: Risk factors in spouse abuse. *Journal of Marriage and the Family, 43,* 675–692.

Horwich, R. H., & Wurman, C. (1978). Socio-maternal behaviors in response to an infant birth in *Colobus guereze. Primates, 19,* 693–713.

Hotaling, G. T., & Sugarman, D. B. (1986). An analysis of risk markers in husband to wife violence: The current state of knowledge. *Violence and Victims, 1,* 101–124.

Houston, H. G., & McClelland, R. J. (1985). Age and gender contributions to intersubject variability of the auditory brainstem potentials. *Biology Psychiatry, 20,* 419–430.

Howard, J., & Holman, B. L. (1970). The effects of race and occupation on hypertension mortality. *Milbank Memorial Fund Quarterly, 48,* 263–296.

Howard, J. A. (1988). A structural approach to sexual attitudes: Interracial patterns in adolescents' judgments about sexual intimacy. *Sociological Perspectives, 31,* 88–121.

Howells, K., & Wright, E. (1978). The sexual attitudes of aggressive sexual offenders. *British Journal Criminology 18,* 170–173.

Hrdy, S. B. (1981) *The woman who never evolved.* Cambridge, MA: Harvard University Press.

Huesman, L. R., & Malamuth, N. M. (1986). Media violence and antisocial behavior: An overview. *Journal of Social Issues, 42,* 1–6.

Hunt, M. (1974). *Sexual behavior in the 1970's.* Chicago: Playboy Press.

Hursch, C., & Selkin, J. (1984). *Rape prevention research project.* Annual report of the Violence Research Unit, Division of Psychiatric Service, Department of Health and Hospitals. Denver: Denver Anti-Crime Council.

Hutt, C. (1972). *Males and females.* Harmondsworth, England: Penguin.

Huxley, T. H., & Huxley, J. S. (1947). *Touchstone for ethics.* New York: Harper.

Inglis, J., & Lawson, J. S. (1981). Sex differences in the effects of unilateral brain damage on intelligence. *Science, 212,* 693–695.

Jaffe, Y. (1974). *Sex and aggression: An intimate relationship.* Unpublished doctoral dissertation. University of California at Los Angeles.

Jaffe, Y., Malamuth, N., Feingold, J., & Fesbach, S. (1974). Sexual arousal and behavioral aggression. *Journal of Personality and Social Psychology, 30,* 759–764.

Jensen, A. R. (1975). Race and mental ability. In F. J. Ebling (Ed.), *Racial variation in man* (pp. 215–262). London: Blackwell.

Jensen, I., & Gutek, B. A. (1982). Attributions and assignments of responsibility in sexual harassment. *Journal of Social Issues, 38,* 121–136.

Joffe, J. M., Mulick, J. A., & Rawson, R. A. (1972). Effects of adrenalectomy on open-field behavior in rats. *Hormones and Behavior, 3,* 87–96.

Johnson, A. G. (1980). On the prevalence of rape in the United States. *Signs: Journal of Women in Culture and Society, 6,* 136–146.

Johnson, G. B. (1941). The Negro in crime. *The Annals of the American Academy of Political and Social Science, 217,* 93–105.

Johnson, L. K. (1985). Tactics in reproduction. *Science, 229,* 643–644.

Jolly, A. (1966). *Lemur behavior.* Chicago: University of Chicago Press.

Jolly, A. (1985). *The evolution of primate behavior* (2nd ed.). New York: MacMillan.

Jones, G. (1986). Sexual chases in sand martins *(Riparia reparia):* Cues for males to increase their reproductive success. *Behavioral Ecology and Sociobiology, 19,* 179–185.

Jones, I. H., & Frei, D. (1979). Exhibitionism—a biological hypothesis. *British Journal of Medical Psychology, 52,* 63–70.

Joseph, R., Forrest, N. M., Fiducia, D., Como, P., & Siegel, J. (1981). Electrophysiological and behavioral correlates of arousal. *Physiological Psychology, 9,* 90–95.

Jost, A., Vigior, B., Prepin, J., Perchellet, J. P. (1973). Studies on sex differentiation in mammals. *Recent Progress in Hormone Research, 29,* 1–41.

Kagan, J. (1964). Acquisition and significance of sex typing and sex role identity. In M. L. Hoffman & L. W. Hoffman (Eds.), *Review of child development research* (pp. 137–168). New York: Russell Sage Foundation.

Kagan, J. (1971). Change and continuity in infancy. New York: Wiley.

Kalat, J. W. (1988). *Biological Psychology,* 3rd Ed. Belmont, Calif.: Wadsworth.

Kanin, E. J. (1967a). An examination of sexual aggression as a response to sexual frustration. *Journal of Marriage and the Family, 3,* 428–433.

Kanin, E. J. (1967b). Reference groups and sex conduct norm violation. *Sociological Quarterly, 8,* 495–504.

Kanin, E. J. (1969). Selected dyadic aspects of male sex aggression. *Journal of Sex Research, 5,* 12–28.

Kanin, E. J. (1983). Rape as a function of relative sexual frustration. *Psychology Reports, 52,* 133–134.

Kanin, E. J. (1984). Date rape: Unofficial criminals and victims. *Victimology, 9,* 95–108.

Kanin, E. J. (1985). Date rapists: Differential sexual socialization and relative deprivation. *Archives of Sexual Behavior, 14,* 219–231.

Kanin, E., & Parcell, S. R. (1977). Sexual aggression: A second look at the offended female. *Archives of Sexual Behavior, 6,* 67–76.

Katz, S., & Mazur, M. (1979). *Understanding the rape victim: A sythesis of research findings.* New York: Wiley.

Kavanagh, M. (1983). *A complete guide to monkeys, apes, and other primates.* New York: Viking.

Kawamura, S. (1967). Aggression as studied in troops of Japanese monkeys. In C. D. Clemente & D. B. Lindsley (Eds.), *Aggression and defense, Vol. V.* (pp. 195–223). Berkeley: University of California Press.

Kenrick, D. T., Cialdini, R. B., & Linder, D. E. (1979). Misattribution under fear-producing circumstances: Four failures to replicate. *Personality and Social Psychology Bulletin, 5,* 329–334.

Kenrick, D. T., Guteirres, S. E., & Goldberg, L. (in press). Influence of popular erotica on interpersonal attraction judgments: The uglier side of pretty pictures. *Journal of Personality and Social Psychology.*

Kepner, W. A., Carter, J. S., & Hess, M. (1933). Observations upon stenostomum cesophagium. *Biological Bulletin, 64,* 405–417.

Ketterer, M. W., & Smith, B. D. (1977). Bilateral electrodermal activity, lateralized cerebral processing, and sex. *Psychophysiology, 14,* 513–516.

Kevles, D. J. (1985). *In the name of eugenics.* New York: Knopf.

King, J. C. (1971). *The biology of race.* New York: Harcourt, Brace and Jovanovich.

Kinsey, A. C., Pomeroy, W. B., Martin, C. E., & Gebhard, P. H. (1953). *Sexual behavior in the human female.* New York: Saunders.

Kinsie, P. M. (1950). Sex crimes and the prostitution racket. *Journal of Social Hygiene, 36,* 250–254.

Kirkpatrick, C., & Kanin, E. (1957). Male sex aggression on a university campus. *American Sociological Review, 22,* 52–58.

Kirkpatrick, F. G., & Veronen, L. J. (1984). *Assessing victims of rape: Methodological issues.* National Center for the Prevention and Control of Rape. (NIMH, Grant No. R01 MH 38052-01).

Kleiman, D. G. (1978). The development of pair preferences in the lion tamarin *(Leontopithecus rosalia):* Male competition or female choice? In H. Rothe, H. J. Wolters, & J. P. Hearn, (Eds.), *The biology and behavior of Marmosets.* (pp. 203–207). Gottingen: Eigenverlag-H. Rothe.

Kleiman, D. G., & Mack, D. S. (1980). Effects of age, sex and reproductive status on scent marking frequency in the golden lion tamarin *(Leontopithecus rosalia). Folia Primatologica, 33,* 1–14.

Klein, D., & Kress, J. (1976, Summer). Any woman's blues. *Crime and Social Justice,* pp. 34–47.

Klopfer, P. H. (1969). *Habitats and territories.* New York: Basic Books.

Knafo, D., & Jaffe, Y. (1984). Sexual fantasizing in males and females. *Journal of Research in Personality, 18,* 451–462.

Kodric-Brown, A. (1977). Reproductive success and the evolution of breeding territories in pupfish *(Cyprinodon). Evolution, 31,* 750–766.

Kohlberg, L. (1976). Moral stages and moralization. In T. Lickona (Ed.), *Moral development and behavior.* New York: Holt, Rinehart & Winston.

Kolata, G. B. (1979). Sex hormones and brain development. *Science, 205,* 985–987.

Kolata, G. (1987). Manic-depression gene tied to chromosome 11. *Science, 235,* 1139–1140.

Konner, M. (1982). *The tangled wing.* New York: Holt, Rinehart & Winston.

Korman, S. K., & Lester, G. R. (1982). The relationship of feminist ideology and date expense sharing to perceptions of sexual aggression in dating. *Journal of Sex Research, 18,* 114–129.

Korn, R. R., & McCorkle, L. W. (1959). *Criminology and Penology.* New York: Holt, Rinehart & Winston.

Koss, M. P. (1985). The hidden rape victim: Personality attitudes and situational characteristics. *Psychology of Women Quarterly, 9,* 193–212.

Koss, M. P., & Leonard, K. E. (1984). Sexually aggressive men: Empirical findings and theoretical implications. In N. M. Malamuth & E. Donnerstein (Eds.), *Pornography and sexual aggression,* (pp. 213–231). New York: Academic Press.

Koss, M. P., Gidycz, C. A., & Wisniewski, N. (1987). The scope of rape: Incidence and prevalence of sexual aggression and victimization in a national sample of students in higher education. *Journal of Consulting and Clinical Psychology, 55,* 162–170.

Koss, M. P., Leonard, K. E., Beezley, D. A., & Oros, C. J. (1985). Nonstranger sexual aggression: A discriminate analysis classification. *Sex roles, 12,* 981–992.

Koss, M. P., & Oros, C. (1982). Sexual experiences survey: A research instrument investigating sexual aggression and victimization. *Journal of Consulting and Clinical Psychology, 50,* 455–457.

Kovach, J. K. (1980). Medelian units of inheritance control color preferences in quail chicks. *(Coturnix japonica). Science, 207,* 549–551.

Krafka, C. L. (1985). Sexually explicit, sexually violent, and violent media: Effects of multiple naturalistic exposures and debriefing on female viewers. Unpublished doctoral dissertation. University of Wisconsin, Madison.

Kudo, T. (1968). Spontaneous occlusion of the circle of Willis: A disease apparently confined to Japanese. *Neurology, 18,* 485–496.

Kulkarni, K. (1980). Heat and other physiological stress-induced analgesia: Catecholamine mediated and noloxone reversible response. *Life Sciences, 27,* 185–188.

Kummer, H. (1967). Tripartite relations in Hanadryas baboons. In S. A. Altmann, (Ed.), *Social communication among primates.* Chicago: University of Chicago Press.

Kummer, H. (1968). *Social organization of Hamadryas baboons.* Chicago: University of Chicago Press.

Kummer, H. (1973). Dominance versus possession, an experiment on Hamadryas baboons. In E. W. Menzel (Ed.), *Precultural primate behavior.* (Symposia of the 4th International Congress of Primatology, Vol. 1). Basel: Karger.

Kurz, E. M., Sengelaub, D. R., & Arnold, A. P. (1986). Androgens regulate the dendritic length of mammalian motoneurons in adulthood. *Science, 232,* 395–398.

Kutchinski, B. (1971). Towards an exploration of the decrease in registered sex crimes in Copenhagen. *Technical report of the Commission on Obscenity and Pornography (Vol. 7).* Washington, DC: United States Government Printing Office.

Kutchinski, B. (1973). The effect of easy availability of pornography on the incidence of sex crimes: The Danish empire. *The Journal of Social Issues, 29: 3,* 163–181.

Kutchinski, B. (1988, June 16). Pornography and sexual violence: The criminological evidence from aggregated data in several countries. Paper presented at the 14th International Congress on Law and Mental Health, Montreal.

Lack, D. (1940). Pair-information in birds. *Condor, 42,* 269–286.

Lader, L. (1966). *Abortion.* Boston: Beacon.

LaFree, G. D. (1982). Male power and female victimization: Toward a theory of interracial rape. *American Journal Sociology, 88,* 311–328.

Lamborn, L. L. (1976). Compensation for the child conceived in rape. In E. C. Viano (Ed.), *Victims and society* (pp. 368–381). Washington, DC: Visage Press.

Lancaster, J. B. (1979). Sex and gender in evolutionary perspective. In H. A. Katchadourian (Ed.), *Human sexuality: A comparative and developmental perspective,* (pp. 51–80). Berkeley: University of California Press.

Langevin, R. (1985) *Erotic preferences, gender, identity, and aggression in man.* Hillsdale, NJ: Lawrence Erlbaum Associates.

Lawson, J., & Hillix, W. A. (1985, February). Coercion and seduction in robbery and rape. *Psychology Today,* pp. 50–53.

Leakey, R. E., & Lewin, R. (1978). *People of the lake.* Garden City, NY: Doubleday.

LeGrande, C. E. (1973). Rape and rape laws: Sexism in society and law. *California Law Review, 61:* 919–941.

Lehman, M. N., Winans, S. S., & Powers, J. B. (1980). Medical nucleus of the amygdula mediates chemosensory control of male hamster sexual behavior. *Science, 210,* 557–560.

Lehrke, R. (1978). A biological basis for greater male variability in intelligence. In R. Osbourne, C. Noble, & N. Weyl (Eds.), *Human variation* (pp. 171–198). New York: Academic Press.

Le Maire, L. (1956). Danish experiences regarding the castration of sexual offenders. *Journal of Criminal Law, Criminology, and Police Science, 47,* 294–310.

Lemmon, W. B. (1971). Deprivation and enrichment in the development of primates. In H. Kummer (Ed.), *Proceedings of the Third International Congress of Primatology, Vol. 3,* (pp. 108–115). Basel: S. Karger.

Leonard, K. E., & Taylor, S. P. (1983). Exposure to pornography, permissive and nonpermissive cues, and male aggression toward females. *Motivation and Emotion, 7,* 291–299.

Leshner, A. L. (1978). *An Introduction to behavioral endocrinology.* New York: Oxford University Press.

LeVine, R. A. (1977). Gusii sex offenses: Study in social control. In D. Chappell, R. Geis, & G. Geis (Eds.), *Forcible Rape: The crime, the victim and the offender,* (pp. 189–226).

Levine, S., & Broadhurst, P. L. (1963). Genetic and ontogenetic determinants of adult behavior in the rat. *Journal of Comparative and Physiological Psychology, 56,* 423–428.

Lewin, R. (1982). Darwin died at a most propitious time. *Science, 217,* 717–718.

Lewin, R. (1984). Is sexual selection a burden? *Science, 226,* 526–527.

Lewin, R. (1987). Mockingbird song aimed at mates, not rivals. *Science, 236,* 1521–1522.

Liebert, R. M., & Schwartzberg, N. S. (1977). Effects of mass media. *Annual Review of Psychology, 28,* 141–173.

Lindsey, W. L. (1880). *Mind in the lower animals: Vol. 2,* New York: Appleton.

Linz, D. G. (1985). *Sexual violence in the Media: Effects on male viewers and implications for society.* Unpublished doctoral dissertation, University of Wisconsin, Madison.

Linz, D., Donnerstein, E., Bross, M., & Chapin, M. (1986). Mitigating the effects of sexual violence in the media. In R. Blanchard (Ed.), *Advances in the study of aggressin* (Vol. 2). New York: Academic Press.

Linz, D., Donnerstein, E., & Penrod, S. (1984). The effects of multiple exposures to filmed violence against women. *Journal of Communications, 34,* 130–147.

Linz, D., Donnerstein, E. & Penrod, S. (1987a). Sexual violence in the mass media: Social psychological implications. In P. Shaver & C. Hendrick (Eds.), *Sex and gender,* (pp. 95–123). Beverly Hills: Sage.

Linz, D., Donnerstein, E., and Penrod, S. (1987b). The findings and recommendations of the Attorney General's Commission on Pornography. *American Psychologist, 42,* 946–953.

Loren, R. E. A., & Weeks, G. R. (1986). Sexual fantasies of undergraduates and their perceptions of the sexual fantasies of the opposite sex. *Journal of Sex Education and Therapy, 12,* 31–36.

Lorenz, K. (1966). *On aggression.* New York: Bantam.

Lorenz, K. (1971). *Studies in animal and human behavior. Vol. II.* Cambridge, MA: Harvard University Press.

Lott, B., Reilly, M. E., & Howard, D. R. (1982). Sexual assault and harassment: A campus community case study. *Signs: Journal of Women in Culture and Society, 8,* 296–319.

Lukas, J. H., & Siegel, J. (1977). Cortical mechanisms that augment or reduce evoked potentials in cats. *Science, 198,* 73–75.

Lumia, A. R., Westervelt, M. O., & Rieder, C. A. (1975). Effects of olfactory bulb ablation and androgen on marking and agonistic behavior in male Mongolian gerbils. *Journal of Comparative and Physiological Psychology, 89,* 1091–1099.

Lykken, D. T. (1982, September). Fearlessness. *Psychology Today*, pp. 20–28.

Lynn, R. (1978). Ethnic and racial differences in intelligence: International comparisons. In R. T. Osborne, C. E. Noble, & N. Weyl (Eds.), *Human variation: The biopsychology of age, race, sex* (pp. 261–286). New York: Academic Press.

Lynn, R. (1987). The intelligence of the Mongoloids: A psychoanalytic, evolutionary and neurological theory. *Personality and Individual Differences, 8,* 813–844.

Lystad, M. H. (1982). Sexual abuse in the home: A review of the literature. *International Journal of Family Psychiatry, 3,* 3–31.

MacArthur, R. H., & Wilson, E. O. (1967). *The theory of Island Biogeography.* Princeton, NJ: Princeton University Press.

MacDonald, J. M. (1971). *Rape offenders and their victims.* Springfield, IL: Charles C. Thomas.

MacKinnon, C. (1984). Not a moral issue. *Yale Law and Policy Review, 2,* 321–345.

MacKinnon, C. (1985). Pornography, Civil Rights, and Speech: Commentary. *Harvard Civil Rights–Civil Liberties Law Review, 20,* 1–70.

MacKinnon, C. (1986). *Feminism unmodified.* Cambridge, MA: Harvard University Press.

MacKinnon, J. (1974). The behavior and ecology of wild orangutans, *Pongo pygmaeus. Animal Behavior, 22,* 3–74.

MacKinnon, J. (1979). Reproductive behavior in wild orangutan population. In D. A. Hamburg, & E. R. McCown (Eds.), *The great apes* (pp. 257–274). Menlo Park, CA: Benjamin/Cummings.

MacKinnon, P. C. (1978). Male sexual differentiation of the brain. *Trends in Neuroscience, 1,* 136–138.

MacLean, P. D. (1977). On the evolution of three mentalities. In S. Arieti & G. Chrzanowski (Eds.), *New dimensions in psychiatry: A world view, Vol. 2,* (pp. 306–327). New York: Wiley.

MacLean, P. D. (1985). Evolutionary psychiatry and the triune brain. *Psychological Medicine, 15,* 219–221.

MacLusky, N. J., & Naftolin, F. (1981). Sexual differentiation of the central nervous system. *Science, 211,* 1294–1302.

Mactutus, C. F., & Tilson, H. A. (1984). Neonatal chlordecone exposure impairs early learning and retention of active avoidance in the rat. *Neurobehavioral Toxicology and Teratology, 6,* 75–83.

Madden, J. S. (1984). Psychiatric advances in the understanding and treatment of alcoholic dependence. *Alcohol and Alcoholism, 19:(4),* 339–353.

Magnusson, D. (1988). Antisocial behavior of boys and autonomic activity/reactivity. In T. E. Moffit & S. A. Mednick (Eds.), *Biological contributions to crime causation,* (pp. 137–146). Dordrecht: Martinus Nijhoff.

Malamuth, N. M. (1980). Testing hypotheses regarding rape: Exposure to sexual violence, sex differences, and the "normality" of rapists. *Journal of Research in Personality, 14,* 121–137.

Malamuth, N. M. (1981). Rape proclivity among males. *Journal of Social Issues, 37,* 138–157.

Malamuth, N. M. (1983). Factors associated with rape as predictors of laboratory aggression against women. *Journal of Personality and Social Psychology, 45,* 432–442.

Malamuth, N. M. (1984). Aggression against women: Cultural and individual causes. In N. M. Malamuth & E. Donnerstein (Eds.), *Pornography and sexual aggression* (pp. 19–52). New York: Academic Press.

Malamuth, N. M. (1986). Prediction of naturalistic sexual aggression. *Journal of Personality and Social Psychology, 50,* 953–962.

Malamuth, N. M. (in press). Predicting laboratory aggression against female and male target: Implications for sexual aggression. *Journal of Research in Personality.*

Malamuth, N. M., & Briere, J. (1986). Sexual violence in the media: In direct effects on aggression against women. *Journal of Social Issues, 42,* 75–92.

Malamuth, N., Briere, J., & Check, J. V. P. (1986). Sexual arousal in response to aggression: Ideology, aggressive, and sexual correlates. *Journal of Personality and Social Psychology, 50,* 330–340.

Malamuth, N. M., & Ceniti, J. (1986). Repeated exposure to violent and nonviolent pornography: Likelihood of raping ratings and laboratory aggression against women. *Aggressive Behavior, 12,* 129–137.

Malamuth, N., & Check, J. V. P. (1980a). Penile tumescence and perceptual responses to rape as a function of victim's perceived reactions. *Journal of Applied Social Psychology, 10,* 528–547.

Malamuth, N., & Check, J. V. P. (1980b). Sexual arousal to rape and consenting depictions: The importance of the woman's arousal. *Journal of Abnormal Psychology, 89,* 763–766.

Malamuth, N., & Check, J. V. P. (1981). The effects of mass media exposure on acceptance of violence against women: A field experiment. *Journal of Research in Personality, 15,* 436–446.

Malamuth, N., & Check, J. V. P. (1983). Sexual arousal to rape depictions: Individual diffences. *Journal of Abnormal Psychology, 92,* 55–67.

Malamuth, N., & Check, J. V. P. (1984). Debriefing effectiveness following exposure to rape depictions. *The Journal of Sex Research, 20,* 1–13.

Malamuth, N. M., & Check, J. V. P. (1985). The effects of aggressive pornography on beliefs in rape myths: Individual difference. *Journal of Research in Personality, 19,* 299–320.

Malamuth, N. M., Fesbach, S., & Jaffe, Y. (1977). Sexual arousal and aggression: Recent experiments and theoretical issues. *Journal of Social Issues, 33,* 110–133.

Malamuth, N., Haber, S., & Fesbach, S. (1980). Testing hypotheses regarding rape: Exposure to sexual violence, sex differences and the normality of rapists. *Journal of Research in Personality, 14,* 121–137.

Malamuth, N., Heim, M., & Feshback, S. (1980). Sexual responsiveness of college students to rape depictions: Inhibitory and disinhibitory effects. *Journal of Personality and Social Psychology, 38,* 399–408.

Malamuth, N. M., & Spinner, B. (1980). A longitudinal content analysis of sexual violence in the best-selling erotic magazines. *Journal of Sex Research, 16,* 226–237.

Malinowski, B. (1929). *The sexual life of savages in North-Western Melanesia.* New York: Eugenics.

Manning, A. (1967). The control of sexual receptivity in female drosophila. *Animal Behavior, 15,* 239–250.

Maple, T. L. (1980). *Orangutan behavior.* New York: Van Nostrand Reinhold.

Maple, T. L., Zucker, E. L., & Dennon, M. B. (1979). Cyclic proceptivity in a captive female orangutan *(Pongo pygmaeus abilii). Behavioral Processes, 4,* 53–59.

Marcus, M. (1977, October). We dream about our problems. *Psychology Today,* pp. 44–46.

Marks, H. E., & Hobbs, S. H. (1972). Changes in stimulus reactivity following gonadectomy in male and female rats of different ages. *Physiology and Behavior, 8,* 1113–1119.

Marolla, J. A., & Scully, D. H. (1979). Rape and psychiatric vocabularies of mative. In E. Gomberg & V. Franks (Eds.), *Gender and disordered behavior,* (pp. 305–320). New York: Brunner/Mazel.

Marshall, E. (1983). A controversy on *Somoa comes of age. Science, 216,* 1042–1045.

Marshall, W. L. (1984). L'avenir de la therapie behaviorale: Le behaviorisme bio-social (illustre a partir d'une theorie sur le viol). *Revue de Modification du Compartement, 14: 4,* 136–149.

Martin, J. B. (1987). Molecular genetics: Applications to the clinical neurosciences. *Science, 238,* 765–772.

Martin, N. G., Eaves, L. J., & Eysenck, H. J. (1977). Genetical, environmental and personality factors influencing the age of first sexual intercourse in twins. *Journal of Biosocial Science, 9,* 91–97.

Martineau, J., Tanguay, P., Garreau, B., Roux, S., & Lelord, G. (1984). Are there sex differences in averaged evoked responses produced by coupling sound and light in children and adults? *International Journal of Psychophysiology, 2,* 177–183.

Maruniak, J. A., Owen, K., Bronson, F. H., & Desjardins, C. (1975). Urinary marking in female house mice: Effects of ovarian steroids, sexual experience and type of stimulus. *Behavioral Biology, 13,* 211–217.

Maslow, A. H. (1935a). The role of dominance in the social and sexual behavior of infra-human primates: I. Observations at Vilas Park Zoo. *Journal of Genetics Psychology, 48,* 261–277.

Maslow, A. H. (1935b). The role of dominance in the social and sexual behavior of infra-human primates: III. A theory of sexual behavior of infra-human primates. *Journal of Genetics Psychology, 48,* 310–338.

Maslow, A. H. (1940). Dominance-quality and social behavior in infra-human primates. *Journal of Social Psychology, 11,* 313–324.

Maslow, A. H., & Flanzbaum, S. (1936). The role of dominance in the social and sexual behavior of infra-human primates: II. The experimental determination of the dominance behavior syndrome. *Journal of Genetics Psychology, 48,* 278–309.

Mason, K. O., Czaijka, J. L., & Arber, S. (1976). Change in U.S. women's sex-role attitudes, 1964–1974. *American Sociological Review, 41,* 573–596.

Masovich, A., & Tallaferro, A. (1954). Studies on EEG and sex function orgasm. *Diseases of the Nervous System, 15,* 218–220.

Masters, F. W., & Greaves, D. C. (1967). The Quasimodo complex. *British Journal of Plastic Surgery, 22.*

Masters, R. D. (1983). Explaining "male chauvinism" and "feminism": Cultural differences in male and female reproductive strategies. In M. Watts (Ed.), *Biopolitics and gender,* (pp. 165–210). New York: Haworth Press.

Masters, W. H., & Johnson, V. (1966). *Human sexual response.* Boston: Little, Brown.

Masters, W. H., & Johnson, V. E. (1979). *Homosexuality in perspective.* Boston: Little, Brown.

Masters, W. H., Johnson, V. E., & Kolodny, R. C. (1982). *Human sexuality.* Boston: Little, Brown.

Matousek, M., & Peterson, I. (1973). Frequency analysis of the EEG in normal children and adolescents. In P. Kellaway & I. Petersen (Eds.) *Automation of clinical electroencephalography,* (pp. 240–251). New York: Raven Press.

Maugh, T. H. (1981). Is there a gene for depression? *Science, 214,* 1330–1331.

McCahill, T. W., Meyer, L. C., & Fischman, A. M. (1979). *The aftermath of rape.* Lexington, MA: D. C. Heath.

McCain, G. M., & Segal, E. M. (1982). *The game of science,* (4th ed.). Monterey, CA: Brooks/Cole.

McCleary, R. A., & Moore, R. Y. (1965). *Subcortical mechanisms of behavior.* New York: Basic Books.

McConville, B. J., Soudek, D., Sroka, H., Cote, J., Boag, L., & Berry, J. (1983). Length of the Y chromosome and chromosomal variants in inpatient children with psychiatric disorders: Two studies. *Canadian Journal of Psychiatry, 28,* 8–13.

McDermott, M. J. (1979). *Rape victimization in 26 American cities.* Washington, DC: U.S. Department of Justice, Law Enforcement Assistance Administration, National Criminal Justice Information Statistics Service.

McEwan, K. L., & Devins, G. M. (1983). Is increased arousal in social anxiety noticed by others? *Journal of Abnormal Psychology, 92,* 417–421.

McGinnis, P. R. (1979). Sexual behavior in free-living chimpanzees: Consort relationships. In D. A. Hamburg & E. R. McCown (Eds.), *The great apes,* (pp. 429–439). Menlo Park, CA: Benjamin/Cummings.

McGlone, J. (1980). Sex differences in human brain asymmetry: A critical survey. *Behavioral and Brain Sciences, 3,* 215–263.

McGrew, W. C. (1979). Evolutionary implications of sex differences in chimpanzees predation and tool use. In D. A. Hamburg & E. R. McCowen (Eds.), *The Great Apes* (pp. 440–462). Menlo Park, CA: Benjamin/Cummings.

McGuinness, D. (1972). Hearing: Individual differences in perceiving. *Perception, 1,* 465–473.

McGuinness, D. (1980). Strategies, demands and lateralized sex differences. *Behavioral and Brain Sciences, 3,* 244.

McKinney, F., Derrickson, S. R., & Mineau, P. (1983). Forced copulation in waterfowl. *Behavior, 86,* 250–294.

McShane, D., Risse, G. L., & Rubens, A. B. (1984). Cerebral asymmetries on CT scan in three ethnic groups. *International Journal of Neuroscience, 23,* 69–74.

Mechanic, D. (1975). Response factors in illness: The study of illness behavior. In T. Millon (Ed.), *Medical behavioral science,* (pp. 354–367). Philadelphia: Saunders.

Media, A., & Thompson, K. (1974). *Against rape.* New York: Farrar, Straus, and Giroux.

Mednick, S. A. (1977). Preface. In S. A. Mednick & K. O. Christiansen (Eds.), *Biosocial bases of criminal behavior,* (pp. ix–x). New York: Gardner.

Mednick, S. A. (1985, March). Crime in the family tree. *Psychology Today,* pp. 58–61.

Mednick, S. A., Gabrielli, W. F., & Hutchings, B. (1984). Genetic influences in criminal convictions: Evidence from an adoption cohort. *Science, 224,* 891–894.

Mednick, S. A., Gabrielli, W. F., & Hutchings, B. (1987). Genetic factors in the etiology of criminal behavior. In S. A. Mednick, T. E. Moffitt, & S. A. Stack (Eds.), *The causes of crime* (pp. 74–79). Cambridge MA: Cambridge University Press.

Mednick, S. A., & Hutchings, B. (1978). Genetic and psychophysiological factors in asocial behavior. In R. D. Hare & D. Schalling (Eds.), *Psychopathic behavior: Approaches to research,* (pp. 239–253). New York: Wiley.

Mednick, S. A. & Kandel, E. (1988). Genetic and perinatal factors in violence. In T. E. Moffitt & S. A. Mednick (Eds.), *Biological contributions to crime causation,* (pp. 121–131). Dordrecht: Martinus Nijhoff.

Mehrabian, A. (1976, August). The three dimensions of emotional reaction. *Psychology Today,* pp. 57–61.

Mehrhof, B., & Kearon, P. (1972). Rape: An act of terror. In *Notes from the third year.* New York: Women's Liberation Press.

Mellen, S. L. (1981). *The evolution of love.* San Francisco: Freeman.

Meo, R., Bilo, L., & Straiano, S. (1985). A unique case of masturbatory seizures in primary generalized epilepsy. *Acta Neurologica, 7,* 409–415.

Metzger, D. (1976). It is always the woman who is raped. *American Journal of Psychiatry, 133,* 405–408.

Meyer, T. (1972). The effects of sexually arousing and violent films on aggressive behavior. *Journal of Sex Research, 8,* 324–331.

Meyer, T. J. (1984, December 5). Date rape: A serious problem that few talk about. *Chronicle of Higher Education.*

Michalewski, H. J., Thompson, L. W., Patterson, J. V., Bowman, T. S., & Litzelman, D. (1980). Sex differences in the amplitudes and latencies of the human auditory brainstem potential. *Electroencephalography Clinical Neurophysiology, 48,* 351–356.

Michalowski, R. J. (1985). *Order, law and crime: An introduction to criminology.* New York: Random House.

Mills, J., & Mintz, P. M. (1972). Effect of unexplained arousal on affiliation. *Journal of Personality and Social Psychology, 24,* 11–13.

Milton, K. (1985). Urine washing behavior in the wooly spider monkey. *Zeitschrift fur Tierpsychologie, 67,* 154–160.

Mineau, P., & Cooke, P. (1979). Rape in the lesser snow goose *(Anser caerulescens caerulenscens). Behavior, 70,* 280–291.

Minton, C., Kagan, J., & Levine, J. A. (1971). Maternal control and obedience in the two-year-old. *Child Development, 42,* 1873–1894.

Minturn, L., Grosse, M., & Haider, S. (1969). Cultural patterning of sexual beliefs and behavior. *Ethology, 8,* 301–318.

Mitani, J. C. (1985). Mating behavior of male orangutans in Kutai Game Reserve, Indonesia. *Animal Behavior, 33,* 392–402.

Mochizuki, Y., Go, T., Ohkubo, H., Tatara, T., & Motomura, T. (1982). Developmental changes of BAEPs in normal human subjects from infants to young adults. *Brain Development, 4,* 127–136.

Moffitt, T. E. (1988). Neuropsychology and self-reported early delinquency in an unselected birth cohort: A preliminary report from New Zealand. In T. E. Moffitt & S. A. Mednick (Eds.), *Biological contributions to crime causation,* (pp. 93–117). Dordrecht: Martinus Nijhoff.

Monroe, R. R. (1986). Episodic behavioral disorders and limbic ictus. In B. K. Doane & K. E. Livingston (Eds.), *The limbic system.* New York: Raven.

Moore, C. L. (1985). Another psychobiological view of sexual differentiation. *Developmental Review, 5,* 18–55.

Morel, F. (1948). La massa intermedia ou commissure grise. *Acta Anatomica, 4,* 203–207.

Moreland, R. L., & Zajonc, R. B. (1976). A strong test of exposure effects. *Journal of Experimental Social Psychology, 12,* 170–179.

Morgan, E. (1980). *The descent of woman,* (2nd ed.). New York: Columbia University Press.

Morgan, R. (1980). Theory and practice: Pornography and rape. In L. Lwederer (Ed.), *Take back the night.* New York: Morrow.

Morris, D. (1970). *Patterns of reproductive behaviour: Collected papers by Desmond Morris.* London: Jonathan Cape Ltd.

Mosher, D. L. (1971). Psychological reactions to pornographic films. In *Technical report of the commission on Obscenity and Pornography, Vol. 8,* Washington, DC: U.S. Government Printing Office.

Mosher, D. L., & Anderson, R. D. (1986). Macho personality, sexual aggression, and reactions to guided imagery of realistic rape. *Journal of Research in Personality, 20,* 77–94.

Mourant, A. E., Kopec, A. C., & Domaniewska-Sobczak, K. (1978). *The genetics of the Jews.* New York: Oxford University Press.

Muehlenhard, C. L., & Cook, S. W. (1987). Men's self-reports of unwanted sexual activity. *Journal of Sex Research, 24,* 58–73.

Muehlenhard, C. L., Friedman, D. E., & Thomas, C. M. (1985). Is date rape justifiable?: The effects of dating activity, who initiated, who paid, and men's attitudes toward women. *Psychology of Women Quarterly, 9,* 297–310.

Muehlenhard, C. L., & Hollabaugh, L. C. (1988). Do women sometimes say no when they mean yes? The prevalence and correlates of women's token resistance to sex. *Journal of Personality and Social Psychology, 54,* 872–879.

Muehlenhard, C. L., & Linton, M. A. (1987). Date rape and sexual aggression in dating situations: Incidence and risk factors. *Journal of Counseling Psychology, 34,* 186–196.

Murphy, C. (1983, October). Men and women: How different are they? *Saturday Evening Post,* pp. 41–48, 101.

Murphy, R. F. (1959). Social structure and sex anagonism. *Southwestern Journal of Anthropology, 15,* 89–123.

Murphy, W. D., Coleman, E. M., & Haynes, M. R. (1986). Factors related to coercive sexual behavior in a nonclinical sample of males. *Violence and Victims, 1,* 255–278.

Murphy, W. D., Haynes, M. R., Coleman, E. M., & Flanagan, B. (1985). Sexual responding of nonrapists to aggressive sexual themes: Normative data. *Journal of Marriage and the Family, 32,* 465–481.

Myerowitz, R., & Hogikyan, N. D. (1986). Different mutations in Ashkenazi Jewish and non-Jewish French Canadians with Tay-Sachs disease. *Science, 232,* 1646–1648.

Myrianthopoulos, N. C., & Aronson, S. M. (1966). Population dynamics of Tay-Sachs disease. I. Reproductive fitness selection. *American Journal Human Genetics, 18,* 313–327.

Nachshon, I. (1988). Hemisphere function in violent offenders. In T. E. Moffitt & S. A. Mednick (Eds.), *Biological contributions to crime causation* (pp. 55–67). Dordrecht: Martinus Nijhoff.

Nachshon, I., Denno, D., & Aurand, S. (1983). Lateral preferences of hand, eye and foot: Relation to cerebral dominance. *International Journal of Neuroscience, 18,* 1–10.

Nadler, R. D. (1982). Laboratory research on sexual behavior and reproduction of gorillas and orangutans. *American Journal of Primatology Supplement 1,* 57–66.

Nadler, R. D. (1988). Sexual aggression in the great apes. *Annals of the New York Academy of Sciences, 528,* 154–162.

Nadler, R. D., Herndon, J. G., & Wallis, J. (1986). Adult sexual behavior: Hormones and reproduction. In J. Erwin (Ed.), *Comparative primate biology* (pp. 363–407). New York: Alan R. Liss.

Nadler, R. D., & Miller, L. C. (1982). Influence of male aggression on mating of gorillas in the laboratory. *Folia Primatologica, 38,* 233–239.

Nass, G. D., Libby, R. W., & Fisher, M. P. (1981). *Sexual choices.* North Scituate, MA: Wadsworth Health Sciences Division.

National Council on Crime and Delinquency. (1976–1977). 1974 female and male paroles—extrapolated analysis. *Newsletter—Uniform Parole Reports.* Davis, CA: NCCD Research Center.

National Institute of Mental Health. (1982). *Television and behavior: Ten years of scientific progress and implications for the eighties, Vol. 1: Summary report.* Rockville, MD: National Institute of Mental Health.

Nelson, E. (1982). Pornography and sexual aggression. In M. Yaffe & E. Nelson (Eds.), *The influence of pornography on behavior.* London: Academic Press.

Nelson, H., & Jurmain, R. (1982). *Introduction to physical anthropology,* (2nd ed.). St. Paul, MN: West.

Neufeld, W. J. (1978). Veridicality of cognitive mapping of stressor effects: Sex differences. *Journal of Personality, 46,* 623–633.

Neville, M. K. (1972). The population structure of red holer monkeys *(Alouatta seniculus)* in Trinidad and Venezuela. *Folia Primatologica, 17,* 56–86.

New South Wales Bureau of Crime Statistics. (1974). *Rape offenses.* (Statistical Report N. 21). Sydney, Australia.

New South Wales Bureau of Crime Statistics and Research. (1974). *A thousand prisoners,* (Statistical Report No. 16). Sydney, Australia.

Nishida, T. (1979). The social structure of chimpanzees of the Manhale Mountains. In D. A. Hamburg & E. R. McCown (Eds.), *The great apes*. (pp. 73–221. Menlo Park, CA: Benjamin/Cummings.

Noble, C. E. (1978). Age, race, and sex in the learning and performance of psychomotor skills. In R. T. Osborne, C. E. Noble, & N. Weyl (Eds.), *Human variations* (pp. 287–378). New York: Academic Press.

Nordeen, E. J., Nordeen, K. W., Sengelaub, D. R., & Arnold, A. P. (1985). Androgens prevent normally occuring cell death in a sexually dimorphic spinal nucleus. *Science, 229,* 671–673.

Nordeen, E. J., & Yahr, P. (1982). Hemispheric asymmetries in the behavioral and hormonal effects of sexually differentiating mammalian brain. *Science, 213,* 391–394.

Nurcombe, B. (1976). *Children of the dispossessed.* Honolulu: University Press of Hawaii.

Nylander, P. P. S. (1973). Serum levels of gonadotropins in relation to multiple pregnancy in Nigeria. *Journal of Obstetrics and Gynaecology of the British Commonwealth, 80,* 651–653.

O'Donald, P. (1980). *Genetic models of sexual selection.* New York: Cambridge University Press.

Ogburn, W. F., & Nimkoff, M. F. (1958). *Sociobiology,* (3rd ed.). Boston: Houghton Mifflin.

Orians, G. H. (1969). On the evolution of mating systems in birds and mammals. *American Naturalist, 103,* 589–603.

Osborne, R. H. (1971). The history and nature of race classification. In R. H. Osborne (Ed.), *The biological and social meaning of race* (pp. 159–170). San Francisco: Freeman.

Ottolenghi, S. (1896). La sensibilite de la femme. *Review in Science, 5,* 395–398.

Painter, S. L., & Dutton, D. (1985). Patterns of emotional bonding in battered women: Traumatic bonding. *International Journal of Women's Studies, 8,* 363–375.

Palays, T. S. (1986). Testing the common wisdom: The social content of vide pornography. *Canadian Psychologist, 27,* 22–35.

Pandey, R. (1986). Rape crimes and victimization of rape victims in free India. *Indian Journal Social Work, 47,* 169–186.

Panksepp, J. (1982). Toward a general psychobiological theory of emotions. *Behavioral and Brain Sciences, 5,* 407–467.

Panksepp, J., Siviy, S., & Normansell, L. (1985). Brain opioids and social emotions. In M. Reite & T. Fields (Eds.), *Biology of social attachments and separation* (pp. 3–49). New York: Academic Press.

Pare, W. P. (1969). Age, sex and strain differences in the aversive threshold to grid shock in the rat. *Journal of Comparative and Physiological Psychology, 69,* 214–218.

Park, J. Y., Huang, Y. H., Nagoshi, C. T., Yuen, S., Johnson, R. C., Ching, C. A., & Bowman, K. S. (1984). The flushing response to alcohol use among Koreans and Taiwanese. *Journal of Studies on Alcohol, 45,* 481–485.

Park, P. (1969). *Sociology tomorrow.* New York: Pegasus.

Paterson, E. J. (1979). How the legal system responds to battered women. In D. M. Moore (Ed.), *Battered women,* (pp. 79–99). Beverly Hills CA: Sage.

Pearson, D. E., Teicher, M. H., Shaywitz, B. A., Cohen, D. J., Young, J. G., & Anderson, G. M. (1980). Environmental influences on body weight and behavior in devloping rates after neonatal 6-hydroxydopamine. *Science, 209,* 715–717.

Persell, C. H. (1984). *Understanding society.* New York: Harper & Row.

Petter, J. J. (1965). The lemurs of Madagascar. In I. DeVore (Ed.), *Primate behavior.* New York: Holt, Rinehart & Winston.

Phillips, A. G., Cox, V. C., Kakolewski, J. W., & Valenstein, E. S. (1969). Object-carrying by rats: An approach to the behavior produced by brain stimulation. *Science, 166,* 903–905.

Phillips, J. H., & Burch, G. E. (1960). A review of cardiovascular diseases in the white and Negro races. *Medicine, 39,* 241–288.

Pitcairn, T. K. (1974). Aggression in natural groups of pongids. In R. L. Holloway (Ed.), *Primate aggression, territoriality, and enophobia,* (pp. 241–272). New York: Academic Press.

Pleszczynska, W. K. (1978). Microgeographic prediction of polygyny in the lark bunting. *Science, 201,* 935–938.

Ploog, D. W. (1967). The behavior of squirrel monkeys as revealed by sociometry, bioacoustics, and brain stimulation. In R. Altmann (Ed.), *Social communication among primates.* (pp.149–184). Chicago: University of Chicago Press.

Ploog, D. W. (1971). Neurological aspects of social behavior. *Social Science Information, 9,* 71–97.

Porter, R. (1986). Rape—Does it have a historical meaning? In S. Tomaselli & R. Porter (Eds.), *Rape,* (pp.216–236). New York: Basil Blackwell.

Pospisil, L. (1972). *the ethnology of law.* New York: Addison-Wesley.

President's Commission on Law Enforcement and Administration of Justice. (1967). *Task force report: Corrections.* Washington, DC: U.S. Government Printing Office.

Price, J. H., Allensworth, D. D., & Hillman, K. S. (1985). Comparison of sexual fantasies of homosexuals and of heterosexuals. *Psychological Reports, 57,* 871–877.

Price, J. H., & Miller, P. A. (1984). Sexual fantasies of black and of white college students. *Psychological Reports, 54,* 1007–1014.

Pumariega, A. J., Edwards, P., & Michell, C. B. (1984). Anorexia nervosa in black adolescents. *Journal of the American Academy of Child Psychiatry, 23,* 111–114.

Purins, J. E., & Langevin, R. (1985). Brain correlates of penile erection. In R. Langevin (Ed.), *Erotic preference, gender identity, and aggression in men: New research studies,* (pp. 113–126). Hillsdale, NJ: Lawrence Erlbaum Associates.

Queen's Bench Foundation. (1978). The rapist and his victim. In L. D. Savitz, & N. Johnston (Eds.), *Crime in society,* New York: Wiley.

Quinney, R. (1974). *Critique of legal order.* Boston: Little, Brown.

Quinsey, V. L. (1984). Sexual aggression: Studies of offenders against women. In D. Weisstub (Ed.), *Law and mental health: International perspectives, Vol. 1.* (pp. 84–121). New York: Pergamon.

Quinsey, V. L., & Chaplin, T. C. (1984). Stimulus control of rapists' and non-sex offenders sexual arousal. *Behavioral Assessment, 6,* 169–176.

Quinsey, V. L., Chaplin, T. C. & Upfold, D. (1984). Sexual arousal to nonsexual violence and sadomasochistic themes among rapists and non-sex-offenders. *Journal of Consulting and Clinical Psychology, 52,* 651–657.

Quinsey, V. L., Chaplin, T. C. & Varney, G. (1981). A comparison of rapists' and non-sex offenders' sexual preferences for mutually consenting sex, rape, and physical abuse of women. *Behavioral Assessment, 3,* 127–135.

Quitkin, F., & Klein, D. (1969). Two behavioral syndromes in young adults related to possible minimal brain dysfunction. *Journal of Psychiatric Research, 7,* 131–142.

Rabkin, J. G. (1979). The epidemiology of forcible rape. *American Journal of Orthopsychiatry, 49,* 634–647.

Rabl, R. (1958). Strukturstudien an der massa intermedia des thalamus opticus. *Journal Hirnforschung, 4,* 78–112.

Rada, R. T. (1978). Biological aspects and organic treatment of the rapist. In R. T. Rada (Ed.), *Clinical aspects of the rapist,* (pp. 133–161). New York: Grune & Stratton.

Rada, R. T., Laws, D. R., & Kellner, R. (1976). Plasma testosterone levels in the rapist. *Psychosomatic Medicine, 38,* 257–268.

Rada, R. T., Laws, D. R., Kellner, R., Stivastava, L., & Peake, G. (1983). Plasma androgens in violent and nonviolent sex offenders. *Bulletin of the American Academy of Psychiatry and the Law, 11,* 149–158.

Rafter, N. F., & Natalizia, E. M. (1981). Marxist feminism. *Crime and Delinquency, 28,* 81–87.

Raine, A. (1988). Evoked potentials and antisocial behavior. In T. E. Moffitt & S. A. Mednick (Eds.), *Biological contributions to crime causation,* (pp. 14–39). Dordrecht: Martinus Nijhoff.

Raisman, G., & Field, P. M. (1973). Sexual dimorphism in the neuropil of the preoptic area of the rat and its dependence on neonatal androgen. *Brain Research, 54,* 1–29.

Rajecki, P., Lamb, M., & Obmascher, P. (1978). Toward a general theory of infantile attachment: A comparative review of aspects of the social bond. *The Behavioral and Brain Sciences, 3,* 417–464.

Ramirez, J., Bryant, J., & Zillmann, D. (1982). Effects of erotica on retaliatory behavior as a function of level of provocation. *Journal of Personality and Social Psychology, 43,* 971–978.

Rapaport, K., & Burkhart, B. R. (1984). Personality and attitudinal characteristics of sexually coercive college males. *Journal of Abnormal Psychology, 93,* 216–221.

Rasmussen, D. R., & Rasmussen, K. L. (1979). Social ecology of adult males in a confined troop of Japanese macaques. *Animal Behavior, 27,* 434–445.

Razavi, L. (1975). Cytogenetic and dermotoglyphic studies in sexual offenders, violent criminals, and aggressively behaved temporal lobe epileptics. In R. R. Fieve, D. Rosenthal, & H. Brill (Eds.), *Genetic Research in Psychiatry* (pp.75–94). Baltimore and London: The John Hopkins University Press.

Redmond, D. E., Baulu, J., Murphy, D. L., Loriaux, D. L. & Zeigler, M. G. (1976). The effects of testosterone on plasma and platelet monoamine oxidase (MAO). *Psychosomatic Medicine, 38,* 315–326.

Rees, H. D., Bonsall, R. W., & Michael, R. P. (1986). Preoptic and hypothalamic neurons accumulate (3h) medroxprogesterone acetate in male cynomolgus monkeys. *Life Sciences, 39,* 1353–1359

Reinisch, J. M. (1974). Fetal hormones, the brain and human sex differences: A heuristic, integrative review of the recent literature. *Archives of Sexual Behavior, 3,* 51–89.

Reinisch, J. M., Gandelman, R., & Spiegel, F. S. (1979). Prenatal influences on cognitive abilities: DAta from experimental animals and human genetic and endocrine syndromes. In M. A. Wittig & A. C. Petersen (Eds.), *Sex-related differences in cognitive functioning* (p. 215–239). New York: Academic Press.

Reynolds, C. R., McBride, R. D., & Gibson, L. J. (1981). Black-white IQ discrepancies may be related to differences in hemisphericity. *Contemporary Educational Psychology, 6,* 180–184.

Reynolds, L. (1984). Rape: A social perspective. *Journal of Offender Counseling, Services, and Rehabilition, 9,* 149–156.

Rhodes, R. (1981, April). Why do men rape? *Playboy,* pp. 112–114, 172, and 224–230.

Richard, A. F., & Schulman, S. R. (1982). Sociobiology: primate field studies. *Annual Review in Anthropology, 11,* 231–255.

Richards, R. J. (1988). *Darwin and the emergence of evolutionary theories of mind and behavior.* Chicago Press.

Ridgeway, R., & Russell, J. A. (1980). Reliability and validity of the sensation-seeking scale: psychometric problems in form V. *Journal of Social Issues, 37,* 71–92.

Rijksen, H. D. (1975). Social structure in a wild orangutan population in Sumatra. In J. Kondo, M. Kawai, & A. Ehara (Eds.), *Contemporary Primatology,* (pp. 373–379). Basel: S. Karger.

Rijksen, H. D. (1978). A field study on Sumatran orangutans *(pPongo Pygmaeus Abelii, Lesson 1927) In* Ecology, Behavior and Conservation. Wageningsen, The Netherlands: H. Voeneman and Zonen BV.

Ripley, S. (1980). Infanticide in langurs and man: Adaptive advantage or social pathology? In M. N. Cohen, R. S. Malpass, & H. G. Klein (Eds.), *Biosocial Mechanisms of population regulation.* (pp. 349–390). New Haven, CT: Yale University Press.

Roberts, J., & Burch, T. A. (1966). Osteoarthritis prevalence in adults by age, sex, race, and geographic area. *Vital and Health Statistics,* (Series 11, Number 15).

Roberts, J., & Maurer, K. (1977). Blood pressure levels of persons 6–74 years. *Vital and Health Statistics,* (Series 11, Number 203).

Roberts, R. C. (1979). The evoluation of avian food-storing behavior, *American Naturalist, 114,* 418–438.

Robinson, D. S., Sourkes, T. L., Nies, A., Harris, L. S., Spector, S., Bartlett, D. L., & Kaye, I. S. (1977). Monoamine metabolism in human brain. *Archives of General psychiatry, 34:* 89–92.

Robinson, S. M., Fox, T. O., & Sidman, R. L. (1985). A genetic variant in the morphology of the medial preoptic area in mice. *Journal of Neurogenetics, 2,* 381–388.

Rodabaugh, B. J., & Austin, M. (1981). *Sexual assault—A guide for community action.* Washington, DC: American Institute for Research in the Behavioral Sciences.

Rose, R. J., Koskenvuo, M., Kaprio, J., Sarna, S., & Langinvainio, H. (1988). Shared genes, shared experiences, and similarity in personality: Data from 14,288 adult Finnish co-twins. *Journal of Personality and Social Psychology, 54,* 161–171.

Rose, V. M. (1977). Rape as a social problem: A by-product of the feminist movement. *Social Problems, 25,* 75–89.

Rosenblum, L. A. (1974). Sex differences in mother-infant attachment in monkeys. In R. C. Friendman, R. A. Richart, & R. L. Vande Wiele (Eds.), *Sex Differences in Behavior,* (pp. 123–141). New York: Wiley.

Rosenfeld, A. H., & Rosenfeld, S. A. (1976b). *The roots of individuality, brain waves, and perception.* (DHEW#77-352).Washington DC: U.S. Government Printing Office.

Ross, D. A., Glick, S. D., & Meibach, R. C. (1981). Sexually dimorphic brain and behavioral asymmetries in the neonatal rat. *Proceedings of the National Academy of Science, U.S.A., 78,* 1958–1961.

Rousseau, J. J. (1964). Discourse on the origin and foundations of the inequality among men. In R. D. Masters (Ed.), *The first and second discourses*. New York: St. Martin's Press.

Rowe, D. C. (1986). Genetic and environmental components of antisocial behavior: A study of 265 twin pairs. *Criminology, 24*, 513–532.

Rowe, D. C., & Herstand, S. E. (1986). Familial influences on television viewing and aggression: A sibling study. *Aggressive Behavior, 12*, 111–120.

Rowe, D. C. & Osgood, D. W. (1984). Heredity and sociological theories of delinquency: A reconsideration. *American Sociological Review, 49*, 526–540.

Rowell, T. E. (1973). Social organization of wild talapoin monkeys. *American Journal of Physical Anthropology, 38*, 593–597.

Rozin, P., & Fallon, A. E. (1987). A perspective on disgust. *Psychological Review, 94*, 23–41.

Rushton, J. P. (1984). Group differences, genetic similarity, and the importance of personality traits. In J. R. Royce & L. P. Mos (Eds.), *Annals of Theoretical Psychology*, (Vol. 2), New York: Plenum.

Rushton, J. P. (1985a) Differential K theory: The sociobiology of individual and group differences. *Personality and Individual Differences, 6*, 769–770.

Ruston, J. P. (1988). Epigenetic rules in moral development: Distal-proximal approaches to altruism and aggression. *Aggressive Behavior, 14*, 35–50.

Rushton, J. P. (in press-a). An evolutionary theory of human multiple birthing: Sociobiology and r/K reproductive strategies. *Acta Geneticae Medicae et Gemellologiae*.

Rushton, J. P. (in press-b). Race differences in behavior: A review and evolutionary analysis. *Personality and Individual Differences*.

Rushton, J. P., & Bogaert, A. F. (1987). Race differences in sexual behavior: Testing an evolutionary hypothesis. *Journal of Research in Personality, 21*, 529–551.

Rushton, J. P., Fulker, D. W., Neale, M. C., Nias, D. K. B., & Eysenck, H. J. (1986). Altruism and aggression: The heritability of individual differences. *Journal of Personality and Social Psychology, 50*, 1192–1198.

Russell, D. E. (1982). *Rape in marriage*. New York: Macmillan.

Russell, D. E. (1984). *Sexual exploitation*. Beverly Hills, CA: Sage.

Russell, D. E. H. (1988). Pornography and rape: A causal model. *Political Psychology, 9*, 41–73.

Russell, D. E. H., & Miller, D. L. (1979). *The prevalence of rape and sexual assault*. Final report to the National Institute of Mental Health (RO1-MH-28960).

Ryan, M. J. (1980). Female mate choice in a neotropical frog. *Science, 209*, 523–525.

Sabelli, H. C., Fawcett, S., Gusovsky, F., Javaid, J., Edwards, J., &

Jeffries, H. (1983). Urinary phenyl acetate: A diagnostic test for depression. *Science, 220,* 1187–1188.

Sachs, B. D. (1978). Conceptual and neural mechanisms of masculine copulatory behavior. In T. E. McGill, D. A. Dewsbury, & B. D. Sachs (Eds.), *Sex and behavior.* New York: Plenum.

Sachser, N., & Hendricks, H. (1982). *A longitudinal study on the social structure and its dynamics in a group of guinea pigs.* Munchen: BLV Verlagsgesellschaft mbH.

Sackett, G. P. (1968). Abnormal behavior in laboratory-reared rhesus monkeys. In M. W. Fox (Ed.), *Abnormal Behavior in Animals.* (pp. 293–331). Philadelphia: Saunders.

Sackett, G. (1974). Comment cited in discussion: Stress and early life experiences in nonhumans. In R. C. Friedman, R. M. Richart, & R. L. Vande Wiele (Eds.), *Sex differences in behavior,* (pp. 143–145). New York: Wiley.

Saint Louis Feminist Research Project. (1976). *The rape bibliography.* St. Louis, MO: Edy Netter.

Sakaluk, S. K. (1986). Is courtship feeding by male insects parental investment? *Ethology, 73,* 161–166.

Sanday, P. R. (1981). The socio-cultural context of rape: A cross-cultural study. *The Journal of Social Issues, 37,* 5–27.

Sanday, P. R. (1986). Rape and the silencing of the feminine. In S. Tomaselli & R. Porter (Eds.), *Rape,* (pp. 84–101). New York: Basel Blackwell.

Sapolsky, B. S. (1977). *The effect of erotica on annoyance and hostile behavior in provoked and unprovoked males.* Unpublished doctoral dissertation, Indiana University, Bloomington.

Sapolsky, B. S. (1984). Arousal, affect, and the aggression-moderating effect of erotica. In N. M. Malamuth & E. Donnerstein (Eds.), *Pornography and sexual aggression,* (pp. 85–113). New York: Academic Press.

Sapolsky, B. S., & Zillmann, D. (1981). The effect of soft-core and hard-core erotica on provoked and unprovoked hostile behavior. *Journal of Sex Research, 17,* 319–343.

Sarrel, P. M., & Masters, W. H. (1982). Sexual molestation of men by women. *Archives of Sexual Behavior, 11,* 117–131.

Sayers, J. (1982). *Biological politics.* London: Tavistock.

Scarpitti, F., & Scarpitti, E. (1977). Victims of rape. *Transaction, 14,* 29–32.

Scarr, S., Webber, P. L., Weinberg, R. A., & Wittig, M. A. (1981). Personality resemblance among adolescents and their parents in biologically related and adoptive families. *Journal of Personality and Social Psychology, 40,* 885–898.

Schiff, A. F. (1971). Rape in other countries. *Medicine, Science and the Law, 11,* 139–143.

Schiff, A. F. (1972). Rape. *Medical Aspects of Human Sex, 6,* 76–84.

Schmidt, G. (1974). Male-female differences in sexual arousal and behavior. *Archives of Sexual Behavior, 4,* 353–364.

Schmidt, G., & Sigusch, V. (1970). Sex differences in responses to psychosexual stimulation by films and slides. *Journal of Sex Research, 6,* 268–283.

Schmidt, G., Sigusch, V., & Schafer, S. (1973). Responses to reading erotic stories: Male-female differences. *Archives of Sexual Behavior, 2,* 181–199.

Schurmann, C. L., & Van Hooff, J. A. R. (1986). Reproductive strategies of the orangutan: New data and a reconsideration of existing socio-sexual models. *International Journal of Primatology, 7,* 265–287.

Schwendinger, J., & Schwendinger, H. (1983). *Rape and inequality.* Beverly Hills, CA: Sage.

Schwendinger, J., & Schwendinger, H. (1982). Rape, the law, and private property. *Crime and Delinquency, 15,* 270–291.

Schwendinger, J., & Schwendinger, H. (1985). Homo economicus as the rapist in sociobiology. In S. R. Sunday & E. Tobach (Eds.), *Violence against women,* (pp. 85–114). New York: Gordian Press.

Schwitters, S. Y., Johnson, R. C., McClearn, G. E., & Wilson, J. R. (1982). Alcohol use and the flushing response in different racial-ethnic groups. *Journal of Studies on Alcohol, 43,* 1259–1262.

Scott, J. E., & Cuvelier, S. J. (1987). Sexual violence in *Playboy* magazine: A longitudinal content analysis. *Journal Sex Research, 23,* 534–540.

Scott, J. E., & Schwalm, L. A. (1988a). Rape rates and the circulation rates of adult magazines. *Journal of Sex Research, 24,* 241–250.

Scott, J. E., & Schwalm, L. A. (1988b). Pornography and rape: An examination of adult theater rates and rape rates by state. In J. E. Scott & T. Hirschi (Eds.), *Controversial issues in crime and justice.* Beverly Hills, CA: Sage.

Scott, J. P. (1963). The process of primary socialization in canine and human infants. *Monographs of the Society for Research in Child Development, 28,* 1–47.

Scriver, C. R., Laberge, C., Clow, C. L., & Fraser, O. F. C. (1978). Genetics and medicine: An evolving relationship. *Science, 200,* 946–952.

Scully, D. & Marolla, J. (1984). Convicted rapists' vocabulary of motives: Excuses and justifications. *Social Problems, 31,* 530–544.

Scully, D., & Marolla, J. (1985). "Riding the bull at Gilley's": Convicted rapists describe the rewards of rape. *Social Problems, 32,* 251–262.

Segal, Z. V., & Marshall, W. L. (1985). Heterosexual skills in a population of rapists and child molesters. *Journal of Consulting and Clinical Psychology, 53,* 55–63.

Seligman, C., Brockman, J., & Kouback, E. (1977). Rape and physical attractiveness: Assigning responsibility to victims. *Journal of Personality, 45,* 554–563.

Seligmann, J., Huck, J., Joseph, N., Namuth, T., Prout, L. R., Robinson,

T. L., McDaniel, A. L. (1984, April 9). The date who rapes. *Newsweek,* pp. 91–92.

Seto, A., Tricomi, S., Goodwin, D. W., Kolodny, R., & Sullivan, T. (1978). Biochemical correlates of ethanol induced flushing in Orientals. *Journal of Studies on Alcoholism, 39,* 1–11.

Shallan, M., El-Akabaoui, A. S., & El-Kott, S. (1983). Rape victimology in Egypt. *Victimology, 8,* 277–290.

Shagass, C., & Schwartz, M. (1965). Visual cerebral evoked response characteristics in a psychiatric population. *American Journal Psychiatry, 121,* 979–987.

Shainess, N. (1976). Psychological significance of rape. *New York State Journal of Medicine, 76,* 2044–2048.

Shaver, P., & Freedman, J. (1976, August). Your pursuit of happiness. *Psychology Today,* pp. 29–32, 75.

Shaw, R. F., & Smith, A. P. (1969). Is Tay-Sachs disease increasing? *Nature, 224,* 1214–1215.

Shaw, S., Stimmel, B., & Lilber, C. S. (1976). Plasma alpha amino-n-butyric acid to leucine ratio: An empirical biochemical marker of alcoholism. *Science, 194,* 1057–1058.

Shepher, J., & Reisman, J. (1985). Pornography: A sociobiological attempt at understanding. *Ethology and Sociobiology, 6,* 103–114.

Shepherd-Look, D. L. (1982). Sex differentiation and the development of sex roles. In B. B. Walman (Ed.), *Handbook of Developmental Psychology,* (pp. 403–433). Englewood Cliffs, NJ: Prentice-Hall.

Shields, S. A. (1975). Functionalism, Darwinism, and the psychology of women. *American Psychologist, 30,* 739–754.

Shields, W. M., & Shields, L. M. (1983). Forcible rape: An evolutionary perspective. *Ethology and Sociobiology, 4,* 115–136.

Sigelman, C. K., Berry, C. J., & Wiles, K. A. (1984). Violence in college students' dating relationships. *Journal of Applied Social Psychology, 14,* 530–548.

Sigg, H., & Falett, J. (1985). Experiments on respect of possession and property in hamadryas baboons (*Papio hamadryas*). *Animal Behavior, 33,* 978–984.

Sigvardsson, S., Cloninger, C. R., Gohman, M., & von Knorring, A. (1982). Predisposition to petty criminality in Swedish adoptees: III. Sex differences and validation of male typology. *Archives of General Psychiatry, 39,* 1248–1253.

Simon, N. G., Gandelman, R., & Gray, J. L. (1984). Endocrine induction of intermale aggression in mice: A comparison of hormonal regimens and their relationship to naturally occurring behavior. *Physiology and Behavior, 33,* 379–383.

Singleton, G. R., & Day, D. A. (1982). A genetic study of male social aggression in wild and laboratory mice. *Behavioral Genetics, 12,* 435–448.

Skinner, B. F. (1953). *Science and human behavior.* New York: Free Press.

Smith, C. C., & Reichmann, O. J. (1984). The evolution of food caching by birds and mammals. *Annual Review of Ecological Systems, 15,* 329–351.

Smith, C. J. (1974). History of rape and rape laws. *Women's Law Journal, 60,* 188–190.

Smith, D. D. (1976). The social content of pornography. *Journal of Communication, 26,* 16–33.

Smith, J. M. (1978). *The evolution of sex.* New York: Cambridge University Press.

Smith, J. M. (1978, September). The evolution of behavior. *Scientific American,* pp. 176–192.

Smith, J. M. (1978). Evolution and the theory of games. In H. Clutton-Brock & P. H. Harvey (Eds.), *Readings in sociobiology,* (pp. 258–270). San Francisco: Freeman.

Smith, M. D., & Bennett, N. (1985). Poverty, inequality, and theories of forcible rape. *Crime and Delinquency, 31,* 295–305.

Smith, S. D., Kimberling, W. J., Pennington, B. F., & Lubs, R. (1983). Specific reading disability: Identification of an inherited form through linkage analysis. *Science, 219,* 1345–1347.

Smithyman, S. D. (1978). The undetected rapists. Unpublished doctoral dissertation, Claremont Graduate School, Claremont, Calif.

Smuts, B. B. (1987). Sexual competition and male choice. In B. Smuts, D. Cheney, R. Seyforth, R. Wranghon, & T. Struhsaker (Eds.), *Primate Societies* (pp. 385–399). Chicago: Univ. of Chicago Press.

Snowdon, C. T. (1983). Ethology, comparative psychology, and animal behavior. *Annual Review in Psychology, 34,* 63–94.

Soma, H., Takayama, M., Kiyokawa, T., Akaeda, T., & Tokoro, K. (1975). Serum gonadotropin levels in Japanese women. *Obstetrics and Gynecology, 46,* 311–312.

Sorenson, M. W. (1974). A review of aggressive behavior in the three shrews. In R. L. Holloway (Ed.), *Primate aggression, territoriality, and xenophobia,* (pp. 13–20). New York: Academic Press.

Spence, K. W. (1966). Cognitive and drive factors in the extinction of the conditioned eye blink in human subjects. *Psychological Review, 73,* 445–458.

Spence, K. W., & Spence, J. T. (1966). Sex and anxiety differences in eyelid conditioning. *Psychological Bulletin, 65,* 137–142.

Spiro, M. E. (1977). *Kinship and marriage in Burma.* Berkeley: University of California Press.

Spock, B. (1964). Are we minimizing differences between the sexes? *Redbook, 122,* 20–30.

Spodak, M. K., Falck, Z. A., & Rappeport, J. R. (1978). The hormonal treatment of paraphiliacs with Depo-provera. *Criminal Justice and Behavior, 5,* 304–314.

Stein, A. H., & Bailey, M. M. (1973). Socialization of achievement orientation in females. *Psychological Bulletin, 89,* 345–366.

Steinem, G. (1980). Erotica and pornography: A clear and present difference. In L. Lederer (Ed.), *Take back the night: Women on pornography,* (pp. 35–39). New York: William Morrow.

Stern, D. N., & Bender, E. P. (1974). An ethological study of children approaching a strange adult: Sex differences. In R. C. Friedman, R. M. Richart, & R. L. Van de Wiele (Eds.), *Sex differences in behavior,* (pp. 233–258). New York: Wiley.

Stets, J. E., & Pirog-Good, M. A. (1987). Violence in dating relationships. *Social Psychology Quarterly, 50,* 237–246.

Stokard, J. J., Stokard, J. E., & Sharbrough, F. W. (1978). Nonpathologic factors influencing brainstem auditory evoked potentials. *American Journal of EEG Technology, 18,* 177–209.

Stoller, R. J. (1976). Sexual excitement. *Archives of General Psychiatry, 33,* 899–909.

Story, M. D. (1982). A comparison of university students experience with various sexual outlets in 1974 & 1980. *Adolescence, 17,* 737–747.

Straus, M. A., Gelles, R. J., & Steinmetz, Susan K. (1980). *Behind closed doors: Violence in the American family.* New York: Doubleday.

Struckman-Johnson, C. (1986, May). Forced sex on dates: It happens to men, too. Paper presented at the annual meeting of the Midwestern Psychological Association, Chicago.

Struhsaker, T. T. (1967). Auditory communication among vervet monkeys. In S. A. Altmann (Ed.), *Social communication among primates,* (pp. 281–324). Chicago: University of Chicago Press.

Subramoniam, T. (1979). Heterosexual raping in the mole crab, *Emerita asiatica. International Journal of Invertebrate Reproduction, 1,* 197–199.

Sue, D. (1987). Use and abuse of alcohol by Asian Americans. *Journal of Psychoactive Drugs, 19,* 64.

Svalastoga, K. (1962). Rape and social structure. *Pacific Sociological Review, 5,* 48–53.

Swaab, D. F., & Fliers, E. (1985). A sexually dimorphic nucleus in the human brain. *Science, 228,* 1112–1115.

Symons, D. (1979). *The evolution of human sexuality.* New York: Oxford University Press.

Takahata, Y., Hasegawa, T., & Nishida, T. (1984). Chimpanzee predation in the Mahale mountains from August 1979 to May 1982. *International Journal of Primatology, 5,* 213–233.

Talmage-Riggs, G., & Anschel, S. (1973). Homosexual behavior and dominance hierarchy in a group of captive female squirrel monkeys *(Saimiri sciureus)*. *Folia Primatologica, 19,* 61–72.

Tannenbaum, P. H. (1971). Emotional arousal as a mediator of erotic communication effects. In *Technical report of the Commission on Obscenity and Pornography, Vol. I.* Washington, DC: U.S. Government Printing Office.

Tarter, R. E., Alterman, A. I., & Edwards, K. L. (1984). Alcoholic denial: A biophysiological interpretation. *Journal of Studies on Alcohol, 46,* 329–256.

Taylor, G. T., Griffin, M., & Rupich, R. (1988). Conspecific urine marking in male rats *(Rattus norvegicus)* selected for relative aggressiveness. *Journal of Comparative Psychology, 102,* 72–77.

Taylor, G. T., Haller, J., & Bartko, G. (1983). Conspecific urine marking in male-female pairs of laboratory rats. *Physiology and Behavior, 32,* 541–546.

Taylor, L. (1984). *Born to crime.* Westport, CT: Greenwood Press.

Taylor, S. P., & Smith, I. (1974). Aggression as a function of sex of victim and male subject's attitude toward women. *Psychological Reports, 35,* 1095–1098.

TenHouten, W. D. (1980). Social dominance and cerebral hemisphericity: Discriminating race, socioeconomic status, and sex groups by performance on two lateralized tests. *International Journal of Neuroscience, 10,* 223–232.

Theilgaard, A. (1984). A psychological study of the personalities of XYY- and XXY-men. *Acta Psychiatrica Scandinavica, 69* (SUpplimentum N. 315), 5–133.

Thiessen, D. D. (1986). The unseen roots of rape: The Theoretical untouchable. *Revue Europeanne des Sciences Sociales, 24,* 9–40.

Thiessen, D. D. (in press). Biobehavioral influences on human rape. In L. Ellis & H. Hoffman (Eds.), *Evolution, the brain and criminal behavior: Explorations in biosocial criminology.* New York: Praeger.

Thiessen, D. D., Owen, K., & Lindzey, G. (1971). Mechanisms of territorial marking in the male and female Mongolian gerbil. *Journal of Comparative and Physicological Psychology, 77,* 38–47.

Thio, A. (1983). *Deviant behavior.* Boston: Houghton-Mifflin.

Thomann, D. A., & Wiencer, R. L. (1987). Physical and psychological causality as determinants of culpability in sexual harassment. *Sex Roles, 17,* 573–591.

Thomas, J. A. (1984). Race, color and essential hypertension: A proposal for an international symposium. *Journal of the National Medical Association, 76,* 393–399.

Thompson, A. L., Bogen, J. E., & March, J. F., Jr. (1979). Cultural hemisphericity: Evidence from cognitive tests. *International Journal of Neuroscience, 9,* 37–43.

Thompson, W. E., & Buttell, A. J. (1984). Sexual deviance in America. *Emporia State Research Studies, 33,* 6–47.

Thornhill, R. (1976). Sexual selection and paternal investment in insects. *American Naturalist, 110,* 153–163.

Thornhill, R. (1979). Male and female sexual selection and the evolution of mating systems in insects. In M. S. Blum & N. A. Blum (Eds.), *Sexual selection and reproductive competition in insects.* New York: Academic Press.

Thornhill, R. (1980). Rape in Panorpa Scorpionflies and a general rape hypothesis. *Animal Behavior, 28,* 52–59.

Thornhill, R. (1981). Panorpa *(Mesocoptera: Panorpidae)* scorpionflies: Systems for understanding resource-defense polygyny and alternative male reproductive efforts. *Annual Review of Ecological System, 12,* 355–386.

Thornhill, R. (1983). Cryptic female choice and its implications in the scorpionfly Harpobittacus Nigriceps. *American Naturalist, 122,* 765–788.

Thornhill, R., & Thornhill, N. W. (1983). Human rape: An evolutionary analysis. *Ethology and Sociobiology, 4,* 137–173.

Thornhill, R., & Thornhill, N. W. (1987). Human rape: The stengths of the evolutionary perspective. In C. Crawford, M. Smith, & D. Krebs (Eds.), *Sociobiology and psychology: Ideas, issues, and applications.* (pp. 269–292). Hillsdale, NJ: Lawrence Erlbaum Associates.

Thornhill, R., Thornhill, N. W., & Dizinno, G. A. (1986). The biology of rape. In S. Tomasselli & R. Porter (Eds.), *Rape.* New York: Basil Blackwell.

Thornton, A., Alwin, D. F., & Camburn, D. (1983). Causes and consequences of sex-role attitudes and attitude change. *American Sociological Review, 48,* 211–227.

Thornton, A., & Freedman, D. (1979). Changes in the sex-role attitudes of women, 1962-1977: Evidence from a panel study. *American Sociological Review, 44,* 832–842.

Tieger, T. (1981). Self-rated likelihood of raping and the social perception of rape. *Journal of Research in Personality, 15,* 147–158.

Tinbergen, N. (1965). Some recent studies of the evolution of sexual behavior. In F. A. Beach (Ed.), *Sex and behavior* (pp. 1–33). New York: John Wiley & Sons.

Titman, R. D., & Lowther, J. K. (1975). The breeding behavior of a crowded population of mallards. *Canadian Journal of Zoology, 53,* 1270–1283.

Tobach, E., & Sunday, S. R. (1985). Epilogue. In S. R. Sunday & E. Tobach (Eds.), *Violence against women.* (pp. 129–158). New York: Gordian Press.

Trivers, R. (1972). Parental investment and sexual selection. In B. Campbell (Ed.), *Sexual selection and the descent of man,* (pp. 136–179). Chicago: Aldine.

Truscott, D., & Fehr, R. C. (1986). Perceptual reactance and criminal risk-taking. *Personality and Individual Differences, 7*, 373–377.

Turnbull, C. M. (1972). *The mountain people.* New York: Simon and Schuster.

Tutin, C. E. G. (1979). Mating patterns and reproductive strategies in a community of wild chimpanzees *(Pan troglodytes schweinfurthii). Behavioral Ecology and Sociobiology, 6,* 29–38.

Tutin, C. E. G., & McGinnis, R. P. (1981). Sexuality of the chimpanzee in the wild. In C. E. Graham (Ed.), *Reproductive biology of the great apes: Comparative and biomedical perspectives,* (pp. 239–264). New York: Academic Press.

Tyroler, H. A. (1977). The Detroit Project studies of blood pressure. A prologue and review of related studies and epidemiological issues. *Journal Chronic Diseases, 30,* 613–624.

Tyroler, H. A. (1980). Hypertension. In J. M. Lasp (Ed.), *Public health and preventive medicine,* (11th ed.), (pp. 1202–1227). New York: Appleton-Century-Crofts.

U.S. Bureau of Justice, Statistics. (1982). *Criminal Victimization in the United States. 1980.* Washington, DC: U.S. Government Printing Office.

U.S. Bureau of Justice, Statistics. (1985). *Sourcebooks of crime and justice, statistics, 1984.* Washington, DC: U.S. Government Printing Office.

U.S. Bureau of Justice, Statistics. (1986). *Criminal Victimization, 1985.* Washington, DC: U.S. Government Printing Office.

U.S. Department of Justice. (1985, March), The crime of rape. *Bureau of Justice Statistics Bulletin* (NCJ-96777).

U.S. Public Health Service. (1970). Persons injured and disability days due to injury. *Vital and Health Statistics* (Series 10, Number 58).

Vaccari, A. (1980). Sexual differentiation of monoamine neurotransmitters. In H. Parvey & S. Parvey, (Eds.), *Biogenic amines in development.* Amsterdam: Elsevier/North Holland.

Van der Zanden, J. W. (1978). *Human development.* New York: Knopf.

Verner, J., & Willson, M. F. (1966). The influence of habitats on mating systems of North American passerine birds. *Ecology, 47,* 143–147.

Virkkunen, M. (1988). Cerebrospinal fluid: Monoamine metabolites among habitually violent and impulsive offenders. In T. E. Moffitt & S. A. Mednick (Eds.), *Biological contributions to crime causation,* (pp. 147–157). Dordrecht: Martinus Nijhoff.

Von Berswordt-Wallrabe, R. (1983). Antiandrogenic actions of progestins. In C. Wayne (Ed.), *Progesterone and progestins,* (pp. 109–119). New York: Raven Press.

von Hentig, H. (1951). The sex ratio. *Social Forces, 30,* 443–449.

Voors, A. W., Berenson, G. S., Dalferes, E. R., Webber, L. S., & Shuler, S. E. (1979). Racial differences in blood pressure control. *Science, 204,* 1091–1094.

Waddlington, C. H. (1961). *The ethical animal.* New York: Atheneum.

Walker, P. A., & Meyer, W. J. (1981). Medroxyprogesterone acetate treatment for paraphiliac sex offenders. In J. R. Hays, et al. (Eds.), *Violence and the violent individual.* New York: Spectrum.

Walker, P. A., Meyer, W. J., Emory, L. E., & Rubin, A. L. (1984). In H. C. Stancer, et. al. (Eds), *Guidelines for the use of psychotropic drugs,* (pp. 427–442). New York: Spectrum.

Wallace, D. C., Garrison, K., & Knowler, W. C. (1985). Dramatic founder effects in Amerindian mitochondria DNA's. *American Journal of Physical Anthropology, 68,* 149–155.

Walster, E., & Bersheid, E. (1971, June). Adrenaline makes the heart grow fonder. *Psychology Today,* pp. 46–50, 62.

Watson, A., & Moss, R. (1972). A current model of population dynamics in red grouse. *Proceedings of the 15th International Ornithology Conference,* (pp. 134–149). Netherlands: E. J. Brill.

Weisfeld, G. E. (1982). The nature-nurture issue and the integrating concept of function. In B. Wolman (Ed.), *Handbook of developmental psychology,* (pp. 208–229). Engelwood Cliffs, NJ: Prentice-Hall.

Weisz, J., & Ward, I. L. (1980). Plasma testosterone and progesterone titers of pregnant rats, their male and female fetuses and neonatal offspring. *Endocrinology, 106,* 306–316.

Wells, B. (1980). *Personality and heredity.* London: Longman.

West, D. H., Roy, C., & Nichols, F. L. (1978). *Understanding sexual attacks.* London: Heinemann Educational Books.

Wheeler, Hollis. (1985). Pornography and rape: A feminist perspective. In A. W. Burgess (Ed.), *Rape and sexual assault.* (pp. 374–412). New York: Garland.

White, L. A. (1979). Erotica and aggression: The influence of sexual arousal, positive affect, and negative affect on aggressive behavior. *Journal of Personality and Social Psychology, 37,* 591–601.

Whitman, W. P., & Quinsey, V. L. (1981). Heterosocial skill training for institutionalized rapists and child molesters. *Canadian Journal of Behavioral Science, 13,* 105–114.

Whitney, G. (in press). On possible genetic bases of race differences in criminality. In L. Ellis & H. Hoffman (Eds.), *Crime, Evolution, and the Brain: Pro/Antisociality from a Biosocial Perspective.* New York: Praeger.

Wickler, W. (1969). Socio-sexual signals and their intraspecific imitation among primates. In D. Morris (Ed.), *Primate ethology,* (pp. 89–189). Garden City, NJ: Anchor.

Wilder, R. (1982, July). Are sexual standards inherited? *Science Digest,* p. 69.

Willerman, L. (1979). *The psychology of individual differences.* San Francisco: Freeman.

Willhoite, F. H. (1981). Rand and reciprocity: Speculations on human emotions and political life. In E. White (Ed.), *Sociobiology and human politics,* (pp. 239–258). Lexington KY: Heath.

Williams, G. C. (1975). *Sex and evolution.* Princeton, NJ: Princeton University Press.

Williams K. R. (1984). Economic sources of homicide: Reestimating the effects of poverty and inequality. *American Sociological Review, 49,* 283–289.

Wilson, C. A., Pearson, J. R., Hunter, A. J., Tuohy, P. A., & Payne, A. P. (1986). The effect of neonatal manipuation of hypothalamic serotonin levels of sexual activity in the adult rat. *Pharmacology, Biochemistry & Behavior, 24,* 1175–1183.

Wilson, E. O. (1975). *Sociobiology: The new synthesis.* Cambridge, MA: Harvard University Press.

Wilson, G. D. (1987). Male-female differences in sexual activity, enjoyment, and fantasies. *Personality and Individual Differences, 8,* 125–127.

Wilson, J. Q. (1976, April 26). Crime and punishment, 1176–1976. *Time,* pp. 82–84.

Wilson, J. Q., & Herrnstein, R. J. (1985). *Crime and human nature.* New York: Simon and Schuster.

Wilson, M. I., & Daly, M. (1985). Competitiveness, risk taking, and violence: The young male syndrome. *Ethology and Sociobiology, 6,* 59–73.

Wilson, W., & Durenberger, R. (1982). Comparison of rape and attempted rape victims. *Psychological Reports, 50,* 198–199.

Wilson, W., & Nakajo, H. (1965). Preference for photographs as a function of frequency of presentation. *Psychonomic Science, 3,* 577–578.

Wimer, R. E., & Wimer, C. C. (1985). Animal behavior genetics: A search for the biological foundations of behavior. *Annual Review of Psychology, 36,* 171–218.

Witelson, S. F. (1985). The brain connection: The corpus callosum is larger in left handers. *Science, 229,* 665–668.

Wolff, P. H. (1972). Ethnic differences in alcohol sensitivity. *Science, 175,* 449–450.

Wolfgang, M. E. (1975). Delinquency and violence from the viewpoint of criminology. In W. S. Field & W. A. Sweet (Eds.), *Neurological bases of violence and aggression* (pp. 456–489). St Louis: Green.

Workman, P. L. (1973). Genetic analyses of hybrid populations. In M. H. Crawford & P. L. Workman (Eds.), *Methods and theories of anthropological genetics* (pp. 117–157). Albuquerque: University of New Mexico Press.

Yahr, P. (1983). Hormonal influences on territorial marking behavior. In B. B. Svare (Ed.), *Hormones and aggressive behavior.* New York: Plenum.

Yamamoto, J., Fung, D., Lo, S., & Reece, S. (1979). Psychophaarmacology for Asian Americans and Pacific Islanders. *Psychopharmacology Bulletin, 15,* 29–34.

Yegidis, B. L. (1986). Date rape and other forced sexual encounters among college students. *Journal of Sex Education and Therapy, 12,* 51–54.

Young, D. M., Beier, E. G., Beier, P., & Barton, C. (1975). Is chivalry dead? *Journal of Communication, 25,* 57–64.

Zajonc, R. B. (1968). Attitudinal effects of mere exposure. *Journal of Personality and Social Psychology Monograph Supplement, 9,* 1–27.

Zajonc, R. B., & Rajecki, D. W. (1969). Exposure and affect: A field experiment. *Psychonomic Science, 17,* 216–217.

Zeltall, S. S., Gohs, D. E. & Culatta, B. (1983). Language and activity of hyperactive and comparison children during listening tasks. *Exceptional Children, 50,* 255.

Zetterberg, H. L. (1965). *On theory and verification in sociology* (3rd ed.). New York: Bedminster Press.

Zillman, D. (1971). Excitation transfer in communication-mediated aggressive behavior. *Journal of Experimental Social Psychology, 7,* 419–433.

Zillmann, D. (1979). *Hostility and aggression.* Hillsdale, NJ: Lawrence Erlbaum Associates.

Zillmann, D. (1984). *Connections between sex and aggression.* Hillsdale, NJ: Lawrence Erlbaum Associates.

Zillmann, D. (1986). Effects of prolonged consumption of pornography. In E. P. Mulvey & J. L. Haugaard (Preparers), *Report of the Surgeon General's workshop on pornography and public health.* Washington, DC: U.S. Public Health Service.

Zillmann, D., & Bryant, J. (1982). Pornography, sexual callousness, and the trivialization of rape. *Journal of Communication, 32,* 10–21.

Zillmann, D., & Bryant, J. (1984). Effects of massive exposure to pornography. In N. M. Malamuth and E. Donnerstein (Eds.), *Pornography and sexual aggression* (pp. 115–148). New York: Academic Press.

Zillmann, D., & Bryant, J. (1986). Shifting preferences in pornography consumption. *Communication Research, 13,* 560–578.

Zillman, D., Bryant, J., & Carveth, R. A. (1981). The effect of erotica featuring sadomasochism and bestiality on motivated intermale aggression. *Personality and Social Psychology Bulletin, 7,* 153–159.

Zillmann, D., Hoyt, J. L., & Day, K. D. (1974). Strength and duration of the effect of aggressive, violent, and erotic communications on subsequent aggressive behavior. *Communication Research, 1,* 286–306.

Zillmann, M., & Sapolsky, B. S. (1977). What mediates the effect of mild erotica on annoyance and hostile behavior in males? *Journal of Personality and Social Psychology, 35,* 587–596.

Zuckerman, M. (1974). The sensation seeking motive. *Progress in Experimental Personality Research, 7,* 79–148.

Zuckerman, M. (1979). *Sensation seeking: Beyond the optimal level of arousal.* Hillsdale, NJ: Lawrence Erlbaum Associates.

Zuckerman, M. (1983). A biological theory of sensation seeking. In M. Zuckerman (Ed.), *Biological bases of sensation seeking, impulsivity and anxiety* (pp. 37–76). Hillsdale, NJ: Lawrence Erlbaum Associates.

Zuckerman, M. (1984). Sensation seeking: A comparative approach to a human trait. *Behavioral and Brain Sciences, 7,* 413–471.

Zuckerman, M., Buchsbaum, M. S., Monte, S., & Murphy, D. L. (1980). Sensation seeking and its biological correlates. *Psychological Bulletin, 88,* 187–214.

Zuckerman, M., & Litle, P. (1986). Personality and curiosity about morbid and sexual events. *Personality and Individual Differences, 7,* 49–56.

Zuckerman, M., & Neeb, M. (1980). Demographic influences in sensation seeking and expressions of sensation seeking in religion, smoking and driving habits. *Personality and Individual Differences, 1,* 197–206.

Zuckerman, S. (1981). *The social life of monkeys and apes.* London: Routledge & Kegan Paul.

NAME INDEX

SUBJECT INDEX